Genre, Gender and the Effects of Neoliberalism

D1239218

The romantic comedy has long been regarded as an inferior film genre by critics and scholars alike, accused of maintaining a strict narrative formula which is considered superficial and highly predictable. However, the genre has resisted the negative scholarly and critical comments and for the last three decades the steady increase in the numbers of romantic comedies position the genre among the most popular ones in the globally dominant Hollywood film industry. The enduring power of the new millennium romantic comedy proves that therein lies something deeper and worth investigating.

This new work draws together a discussion of the full range of romantic comedies in the new millennium, exploring the cycles of films that tackle areas including teen romance, the new career woman, women as action heroes, motherhood and pregnancy and the mature millennium woman. The work evaluates the structure of these different types of films and examines in detail the ways in which they choose to frame key contemporary issues which influence how we analyse global politics, including gender, class, race and society.

Providing a rich understanding of the complexities and potential of the genre for understanding contemporary society, this work will be of interest to students and scholars of cultural and film studies, gender and politics and world politics in general.

Betty Kaklamanidou is lecturer in Film History and Theory at the Film Studies Department at the Aristotle University of Thessaloniki, Greece.

Popular Culture and World Politics

Edited by **Matt Davies**, *Newcastle University*, **Kyle Grayson**, *Newcastle University*, **Simon Philpott**, *Newcastle University*, **Christina Rowley**, *University of Bristol*, and **Jutta Weldes**, *University of Bristol.*

The Popular Culture World Politics (PCWP) book series is the forum for leading interdisciplinary research that explores the profound and diverse interconnections between popular culture and world politics. It aims to bring further innovation, rigor, and recognition to this emerging sub-field of international relations.

To these ends, the PCWP series is interested in various themes, from the juxtaposition of cultural artefacts that are increasingly global in scope and regional, local and domestic forms of production, distribution and consumption; to the confrontations between cultural life and global political, social and economic forces; to the new or emergent forms of politics that result from the rescaling or internationalization of popular culture.

Similarly, the series provides a venue for work that explores the effects of new technologies and new media on established practices of representation and the making of political meaning. It encourages engagement with popular culture as a means for contesting powerful narratives of particular events and political settlements as well as explorations of the ways that popular culture informs mainstream political discourse. The series promotes investigation into how popular culture contributes to changing perceptions of time, space, scale, identity and participation while establishing the outer limits of what is popularly understood as 'political' or 'cultural'.

In addition to film, television, literature and art, the series actively encourages research into diverse artefacts including sound, music, food cultures, gaming, design, architecture, programming, leisure, sport, fandom and celebrity. The series is fiercely pluralist in its approaches to the study of popular culture and world politics and is interested in the past, present and future cultural dimensions of hegemony, resistance and power.

Gender, Violence and Popular Culture
Telling stories
Laura J. Shepherd

Aesthetic Modernism and Masculinity in Fascist Italy
John Champagne

Genre, Gender and the Effects of Neoliberalism
The new millennium Hollywood rom com
Betty Kaklamanidou

Battlestar Galactica and International Relations
Edited by Iver B. Neumann and Nicholas J. Kiersey

First published 2013
by Routledge
2 Park Square, Milton Park, Abingdon, Oxfordshire OX14 4RN

Simultaneously published in the USA and Canada
by Routledge
711 Third Avenue, New York, NY 10017

First issued in paperback 2014

Routledge is an imprint of the Taylor and Francis Group, an informa business

British Library Cataloguing in Publication Data
A catalogue record for this book is available from the British Library

Library of Congress Cataloging in Publication Data
Kaklamanidou, Betty, 1972-
Genre, gender and the effects of neoliberalism : the new millennium
Hollywood rom com / Betty Kaklamanidou.
p. cm. – (Popular culture and world politics)
Includes bibliographical references and index.
1. Romantic comedy films–United States–History and criticism.
2. Motion pictures–United States–History–21st century. 3. Love in motion
pictures. 4. Sex role in motion pictures. I. Title.
PN1995.9.C55K35 2013
791.43'6543–dc23
2012029648

ISBN 978-0-415-63274-4 (hbk)
ISBN 978-1-138-90932-8 (pbk)
ISBN 978-0-203-07010-9 (ebk)

Typeset in Times New Roman
by Taylor & Francis Books

Genre, Gender and the Effects of Neoliberalism

The new millennium Hollywood rom com

Betty Kaklamanidou

LONDON AND NEW YORK

To my mom, the strongest, bravest and most beautiful woman in the world. Thank you for showing me what unconditional love truly means. I love you.

Contents

Foreword

When I first met Dr Kaklamanidou in 2010, we were both on the same panel at the Second International Conference on Popular Romance, in Brussels. In a relatively new field, Dr Kaklamanidou or 'Betty', as I would come to know her, was already able to make fascinating historical, literary and popular references and exciting contributions to this burgeoning field of academic studies. One of the key tensions that she discussed was the way in which the field of popular romance studies needed to somehow transcend the stereotypes of popular romance as 'only' Harlequin Romances with Fabio on the cover. As the conference unfolded, and as I was later to learn about Betty's work, there was neither anything simple or unproblematic about how these seemingly benign and frothy confections of popular culture were produced, received or ultimately analyzed. Whereas other genres of film have been theorized and dissected not only historically, but also in terms of contemporary films, the romantic comedies of the past decade have had relatively few commentaries or attempts to understand how they function within the larger culture.

Dr Kaklamanidou has responded to this gap in the literature by producing a scholarly work that is both accessible and timely. This focus on popular romantic comedies of the new millennium arises both as a response to the lacunae in the literature, as well as a kind of invitation to take seriously what some would deride as simply a hackneyed and formulaic Hollywood product that deserves no special scholarly attention. Dr Kaklamanidou offers us a rich analysis based not only on a careful and scholarly reading of the mainstream 'rom com' films Hollywood produced during the last decade, but also ties them to larger developments happening in North American culture and society. Much like their forebears of the 1930s and 1940s, contemporary romantic comedies speak directly to the hopes and desires of an entire generation. And, just as those films offered both a release valve, or 'escape', from the dire economic situation audiences found themselves in, contemporary romantic comedies similarly reflect on and question the neoliberal political climate that viewers are inhabiting. If we have just lived, and are arguably still living through, what has been referred to as the worst economic turn since the Great Depression, then we can begin to understand the ways in which the films of this decade represent an attempt both to take flight from, and express, the extraordinary stresses and strains that viewers find themselves in.

Coupled with this economic crisis is the profound, and perhaps still relatively little understood, impact of 9/11 and the huge bow wave this caused in the psyches of millions of people. The supposedly light-hearted romantic comedies of this past decade offer a window onto how the romantic and life possibilities of their characters are reflected in a world that lived 'after' such a profound political event. Not only is the impact of 9/11 felt in terms of the possibilities and ways in which America is reflected in Hollywood films, including the romantic comedy genre, but social roles, and in particular, gender roles, are questioned anew. How are men and women to relate to one another in this new world order? What do traditional understandings of femininity and masculinity mean in a society where contingency, both in the workplace and family, is the new 'normal'? Finally, what does it mean for the conventional 'happy ending' that characterizes this genre when the world within its celluloid (transparent) frames is so unstable and open to change at any moment?

These questions are confronted directly in Dr Kaklamanidou's research and are presented to us here in all their complexity and dynamism. And, for those who are still struggling with the meaning and desire to live through some of these contradictions, Dr Kaklamanidou's journey through these 'rom coms' offers not only insights, but perhaps even more important, some significant truths about who we are and how we understand ourselves at this precise moment of history.

Margaret J. Tally
Chair, Policy Studies
School for Graduate Studies
Empire State College
State University of New York

Series editor's preface

When approached to consider a manuscript on 21st century Hollywood romantic comedies for this series, I confess that my first response was to ponder what romantic comedy could possibly contribute to a deeper understanding of world politics. As Betty Kaklamanidou says in the opening lines of this book, romantic comedies are widely understood to be 'plotless, pointless and a comedy of exhaustion.' While my own view was not quite that bleak, I did struggle to see how the proposed book would speak to the themes of the series.

However, it quickly became clear to me that Kaklamanidou had a compelling story to tell about the ways that romantic comedies have charted significant changes in social relations. Screwball comedies of the 1930s and 1940s couched criticism of the wealthy and powerful in seemingly light-hearted dialogues which nevertheless also featured strong and articulate female characters. From the 1950s onwards, romantic comedies went even further in addressing changing relations between men and women as the era of so-called sexual liberation unfolded across the west. For example, the temptations of extra-marital sex are explored in *The Seven Year Itch* (1955) while *Some Like it Hot* (1959) takes a humorous look at gender bending practices. This well-loved film is in part memorable for its close when Jack Lemmon finally reveals to the determinedly amorous Joe E. Brown that he is a man. 'Well, nobody's perfect' says Brown, indicating Lemmon's masquerading as a woman has not fooled Brown but won his heart anyway. Perhaps it is only in a Billy Wilder comedy that open acknowledgement of homosexuality could be made as early as the late 1950s. Comedies like *Bob and Carol and Ted and Alice* (1969) explored, even if rather timidly, what the sexual revolution meant for mature, married couples but also the emergence of individual, couples and group therapy as simultaneously new ways of self-realisation and a new form of consumption. From this time on, as Kaklamanidou so ably demonstrates, the issues explored in romantic comedy have expanded dramatically.

This is one notable feature of the genre: its enduring capacity to adapt to and explore social change. Compare this record to another of the mainstays of Hollywood output over a number of decades, the western. Westerns struggled to maintain their popularity in the great upheavals of the 1960s and particularly in the context of changes in attitudes towards ethnic others. The staple of many westerns, profound negativity about the supposed character and morals of native Americans and an account of the frontier as a wild and barbaric space in need of the rough civilising values of white, Anglo-Saxon males, became uncomfortable fare when US dominant culture was challenged by the civil rights movement, the rise of feminism and, importantly, domestic opposition to the US war in Vietnam. While the genre never quite disappeared and, indeed, responded with a number of more nuanced products, it is films such as Clint Eastwood's *Unforgiven* (1992) and Ang Lee's *Brokeback Mountain* (2005) dealing with complex issues of gender and sexuality that breathed new life back into the genre.

Romantic comedies, however, have never faded from the screen but have arguably become more diverse in their plot lines and appeal. One common criticism of romantic comedies has been their lack of engagement with political economy. In many romantic comedies, the protagonists live lives seemingly unencumbered by economic struggle, inhabit delightful apartments or houses, engage in fine dining and extensive travel and all without any visible means of support. Yet in this volume, Kaklamanidou offers rich insights into how some romantic comedies of the 21st century provide a critical account of the effects of neoliberalism on the lives of ordinary people. Kaklamanidou does this with a thoughtful categorisation of romantic comedy's 21st century sub-genres. Here we begin to see the profound social changes of the last three or four decades being made clear in what are, seemingly, among Hollywood's least serious offerings. In her chapter 'The "New" Career Woman', Kaklamanidou demonstrates that women have become political subjects quite capable of fulfilling their career ambitions and able to do so without the patronage of men. But having succeeded in negotiating their way into the workplace (if still not yet anything like equal representation in senior executive positions) Kaklamanidou also observes how the American search for security in the wake of September 2001 has seen pressures for women to return to 'hearth and home' in romantic comedy as well as the US workplace. In her chapter on the 'baby-crazed cycle' Kaklamanidou charts the almost impossible contradictions faced by women pursuing corporate careers and desiring to establish families. Surrogacy is the focus of this chapter which entails a nuanced examination of class relations, the commodification of the female body, and an analysis of ethnic relations within and beyond the borders of the US. As Sigourney Weaver says to Tina Fey (in *Baby Mama* (2008)) as the latter investigates options for outsourcing her pregnancy, 'don't worry, your baby will not be carried by some poor, underpaid woman in the Third World.' One cannot help but wonder at what this remark implies about the politics of the white body given so many consumer goods are manufactured precisely under these conditions. Is it only when one's own genes are fed into complex international economic processes that the plight of unprotected labour beyond the borders of the west becomes of concern to privileged citizens of the US and other western countries?

Similarly, Kaklamanidou's analysis of the various themes of the man-com and the mature cycle examines the manifold forces that have made and remade masculinity in post-Vietnam US culture. Of great interest is her focus on the hollowing out of traditional ideas of masculinity by contemporary neoliberalism. In these chapters Kaklamanidou introduces us to men whose success in business provides little by way of emotional comfort suggesting the shallow and single dimensional pleasures of a life based on consumption of goods and women. We meet the typically troubled, neurotic older man of Woody Allen's cinema and his struggles to find either acceptance or employment in a society increasingly geared to youth and the young. Other men find themselves thrust into the role of primary carer for children while their successful wives enjoy high profile careers in the public domain. And in *It's Complicated* (2009), an ageing Alec Baldwin comes to realise how much he values the woman and family he earlier abandoned for a younger woman and despite a torrid affair with his former wife, must finally concede that she is lost to him for good. In these and other examples in Kaklamanidou's work we see how the curiously contradictory imperatives of economic and social neoliberalism, at once effacing of gender norms, institutions, and a welter of social traditions, simultaneously attempts to valorise institutions such as marriage and the nuclear family. What Kaklamanidou's analysis demonstrates is that the conflicting impulses of neoliberalism produce opportunity and insecurity (though not necessarily in equal measure) leading to significant debates about the contemporary nature of class, gender, and ethnic relations.

It is through her reading of a great many films made in the wake of 2001 that Kaklamanidou successfully demonstrates that many of the key issues that animate the lives of individuals and broader communities are explored with wit and insight in romantic comedies. But more than that, it is impossible to read this book without realising that the great changes charted in romantic comedies are those in part produced by the sweeping away of many of the conventions and norms that underpinned US society up until the middle decades of the 20th century. In the films and characters under Kaklamanidou's analysis we see repeated attempts to answer the question of what it means to be an American or resident of the United States in a world made ever more uncertain, insecure and open by the relentless spread and entrenchment of neoliberalism. Far from being a plotless, pointless and exhausted comic genre what emerges from Kaklamanidou's book is evidence of a world being remade in neoliberalism's image. It may be there that we need to look for pointlessness and exhaustion.

Acknowledgements

They say that writing a book, whether it's fiction or an academic study is a solitary task. It is true that from the moment you begin your research to that magnificent instance you finally submit your complete manuscript, you are alone with your thoughts, your notes, your photocopies, your references, your writing. Or aren't you? There are usually many people who in their own special way make your writing 'journey' feel less like a lonely trek on the Himalayas, and more like a leisurely walk on a lovely Greek beach.

That's why I would like to now acknowledge all the wonderful individuals who helped me directly and/or indirectly in completing the book you are holding in your hands or reading on your PC, laptop, tablet, phone or whatever device may have been invented until its publication.

First and foremost, I want to publicly thank Professor Emeritus Alexandros-Phaidon Lagopoulos, who introduced me to semiotics and structuralism during my MA years back in the 1990s and who supervised my Ph.D. thesis. Alexandros is the kind of academic I could only aspire to become, the kind of teacher I wish all my students could be lucky enough to meet in their life and the kind of individual whose integrity, fairness, politeness and encouragement are a paradigm I often fail to follow but always try to remember. Second, I want to thank Professor Karin Boklund-Lagopoulos for her constant reassurance during my Ph.D. years, her knowledge and the pages of handwritten notes she selflessly wrote to help me improve my work. These two people are the main reason I have become the scholar I am today, and I would like to express my deep appreciation for the instrumental role they have played in my academic career.

This book was born out of a happy coincidence. While my proposal was being reviewed, I found out that I was awarded with a Fulbright Scholarship to conduct research at Empire State College, in New York. I would like, therefore, to thank the Fulbright Foundation in Greece for its invaluable support. Special thanks go to Tatiana Hadjiemmanuel, the Greek program coordinator, and Artemis Zenetou, director of the Foundation, for all the help they provided me with.

I would also like to thank the following: Dan Georgakas, who introduced me to Martha Nochimson with whom I had a stimulating discussion on film and my work over frozen yoghurts in New York, Professor Stratos Konstantinidis, who via e-mail introduced me to Sheril Antonio, Associate Dean at Tisch School of the Art, New York University. Sheril generously gave me permission to do the greater part of my research at the Bobst Library in New York, for which I will always be grateful.

Special thanks to all the colleagues, administrative personnel and students I've met and had wonderful discussions with at Empire State; in particular, I'd like to acknowledge Provost Meg Menke, who graciously invited me to Empire, Dean Bob Clougherty, whom I can now proudly call a Fulbright alumnus, Cynthia Ward, who arranged for my office space, Dianne Ramdeholl, who helped me avoid 'homelessness', Bidhan Chandra, who arranged my presentation in Albany, Mark Soderstrom, who shared his film evening with me, Eric Ball, who generously put me up with his wife, Aliki, Ruth Goldberg for our film talks and much more, and the wonderful Alan Mandell for always coming up with new ways to keep me intellectually occupied. Finally, a very special thank you to the woman without whom this book may have not been written: Professor Margaret J. Tally. Peggy was the one who encouraged me to put the proposal forward, helped me with my Fulbright application process, not to mention her help during my two-month stay in New York and the insightful comments she made during the writing process. I am deeply honored and moved that this book starts with her foreword.

I also want to thank my friend and colleague Tony Spanakos, who introduced me electronically to Simon Philpott so that I could 'pitch' him my idea. Not only did Tony unknowingly secure the first step towards this publication but he was one of the few people I could count on for guidance and academic 'assistance' at all times.

Many thanks to my New York friends, Lynne Sherman and Josefa Vincent, without whom I am certain my Fulbright experience would be much poorer. In their own, unique way, they both played a much greater role than they could ever imagine in providing a stable environment for me to work in. I can only cherish the moments I spent with each of them and hope our paths cross again soon.

What can I say about my editor, Simon Philpott? His comments, suggestions, as well as our discussions have not only improved the content of this book but have broadened my academic horizons. I would also like to thank Nicola Parkin, Emma Hart, Ira Brodsky and all the people at Routledge who have contributed to the publication of this volume.

Finally, I would like to thank my Athenian friend Maria Katsaridou for her patience, the two-o'clock-in-the-morning phonecalls, her constant encouragement, and her always believing in me – and showing it.

They say that the 'institution' of family is changing, and I agree. However, I am what I am thanks to and/or because of my family. So, I could not but express my eternal thanks and love to my mom, Eleni, for always being there, even though she shouldn't have to and my little sister, Lia, for always telling me the truth.

This is a book about romantic comedy and politics. Although I am not a romantic and I don't believe in the fairy-tale concept of 'the one', I do believe in partnerships and marriages based on friendship, trust and sex. I have been incredibly fortunate to meet and marry Petros, a selfless individual who understood the hours of concentration and the months of physical and mental absence he had to endure during my 'journey'. Petros proves everyday what love is all about and for that I consider myself one of the luckiest people in the world.

1 Introduction

'Plotless and pointless', 'soft and sweet as a marshmallow and about as interesting', 'scatterbrained', 'a comedy of exhaustion'.[1] These are a few examples of how film reviewers in major American publications characterized the millennial romantic comedies *Sex and the City* (2008), *Hitch* (2005), *The Switch* (2010) and *Couples Retreat* (2009) respectively. The above negative adjectives and phrases are no 'strangers' to the genre of the romantic comedy, which 'has been so degraded in the past twenty years that saying you like romantic comedies is essentially an admission of mild stupidity' (Mindy Kaling 2011). Similarly, contemporary scholars tend to also treat recent productions quite sceptically. For instance, Diane Negra (2009, p. 8) supports that 'the 1990s and 2000s chick flicks [speak] from and to a neoconservative cultural context' while Hilary Radner (2011, p. 4) argues that these films 'have [...] a limited scope and perspective'. However, despite the doubts that surround the genre, romantic comedy has started to become the subject of systematic scholarly work in the last two decades. Examination of the genre can be divided into two broad categories: The first mainly focuses on analysis of cycles of the past, such as the screwball comedies of the 1930s and 1940s and the sex comedies of the late 1950s and 1960s (see Ed Sikov, 1989, James Harvey, 1998, Christopher Beach, 2002, Wes D. Gehring, 2002, and Kathrina Glitre, 2006, among others), which are today considered paradigmatic cinematic instances of gender and/or class articulation. The second category focuses on the romantic comedies of the last three decades (Peter Williams Evans and Celestino Deleyto, 1998, Tamar Jeffers McDonald, 2007, Celestino Deleyto, 2009, Stacey Abbott and Deborah Jermyn, 2009, and Claire Mortimer, 2010). The books in the second category are part of an important scholarly effort to extort the stigma of superficiality that continues to accompany the genre by providing methodical historical information, but also insisting on the importance of the examination of the genre's significant contribution to gender politics in recent years, considering its enduring popularity in the twenty-first century.

Citing information from the InHollywood website Frank Krutnik (2002, p. 131) underscored the fact that

[i]f even half the projects picked up this year actually get the greenlight, the first decade of the next millennium may be known as 'the Romantic Comedy Decade'. Sales totals for the genre surged ahead of former rivals Action-Adventure and Science fiction, landing squarely in the coveted fourth spot [below Comedy, Drama and Thriller].

The above hypothesis was confirmed as rom coms have been steadily produced and enjoyed considerable box-office success worldwide from 2000 to 2010, while the second decade of this millennium does not seem to decelerate the genre's momentum. The number of romantic comedies during the first decade of the new millennium, their global appeal, the emergence of new and interesting cycles, along with the continuance in the production of old formulae with a modern twist led to this book, whose exclusive focus is the Hollywood romantic comedy of last decade.

Genre and Hollywood are two concepts that have gone together ever since the very first decades of the invention of the cinema. However, this is not just a book about genre theory or a specific genre history in the twenty-first century – although genre theory and history will assist in the analysis of the film narratives included in the ensuing chapters. This is mainly a book which will endeavour to look into how the neoliberal climate of the decade influences the politics and ideology produced by the films themselves and help shape 'our own personal narratives' (Lincoln Geraghty, 2011, p. 8). This is a book which will offer a comprehensive description of the genre in the last decade by grouping romantic comedies in thematic cycles. This is finally a book which will explore what Hollywood romantic narratives have to 'say' about gender politics and identities, and how they use and/or alter the genre conventions to echo, support, promote and/or subvert the American social climate regarding romantic relationships, and more specifically, working women, the institution of marriage, the wedding industry, male and female friendships, children and sexuality in maturity.

One of the main theoretical premises of the book is that the new millennium Hollywood produces film texts which are part of the global popular culture and as such have an even more pervasive influence on the world than in past decades. I contend that just as 'culture is always in a process of negotiation, with positions and identities shifting, with official voices being parodied and satirized, with power being contested' (Neil Campbell and Alasdair Kean, 2000, p. 15), new millennium romantic comedies are part of an ongoing dialogue regarding romantic and/or sexual relationships, adding therefore significant insight into the world of gender politics. Films have always been a popular form of entertainment. Louis Giannetti and Scott Eyman (2001, p. 112) underline that

[t]he American cinema was the most democratic art form in history, reflecting most of the strengths and failings of the society that nurtured it. To guarantee their continued employment in this expensive medium, fiction filmmakers had to be sensitive to the demands of the box office.

Giannetti and Eyman's remark remains true in the twenty-first century. Even though the film industry has undergone many changes from the establishment of the powerful studio system in the 1930s and the 1940s to today, the fact remains that the business of making films is primarily exactly that – a business. And as such it has to be profitable in order to survive. The paradox, however, lies in the fact that the film business produces works of mostly popular art and has always been influenced by and also influences politics worldwide. As Alan Parker astutely observes: 'All of our European influences have been American films because American society has been sold to the rest of the world with the greatest propaganda machine any nation ever invented – the Hollywood movie' (cited in William J. Palmer, 1993, p. 9). The history of the Hollywood industry proves not only the American worldwide domination but its intricate mechanisms which combine a ruthless profit-making politics with the production of a vast number of film narratives which reflect, promote, support and/or criticize, subvert the sociopolitical climate in which they were produced. In other words, there is a definite affinity between each film narrative with the era that gave birth to it. For instance, the screwball comedy emerged in the 1930s, in the context of the powerful studio system, as a means of escapism from the harsh reality but was also a way for the filmmakers to cleverly avoid the Production Code regulations and use those seemingly light films to criticize the wealthy and also empower women.

Another basic premise of this book is that all films are political in the sense that 'they offer competing ideological significations of the way the world is or should be' (John Storey, 2008, p. 4). Even though Hollywood has always been accused of superficiality and light treatment of serious sociopolitical issues in favour of the greatest profit margin, I agree with both Palmer (1993, p. 9) and Bruce Babington and Peter Williams Evans (1989, p. vi) who respectively observe that 'American movies are always made in terms of those modes of discourse that will attract the widest possible audience yet those films still are able to subtextualize those surface modes of discourse with potent socio-historical messages' and that 'Hollywood cinema is not [...] a simply monolithic, oppressive and conservative force, but [...] a multi-levelled and contradictory phenomenon capable of producing from within its contradictions works of art that are worth our constructive as well as deconstructive meditation'. I will therefore determine and examine the various cycles and specific texts of the romantic comedy genre of the last decade, as individual instances of specific meanings about love, intimacy and romance that result from their specific sociocultural production and/or promotional context and that may reach and/or be understood by the global audience. The romantic comedy is one of the most durable film genres in history. However, the Hollywood that produced the screwball comedies of the 1930s and 1940s is not the same as the Hollywood that welcomed the new millennium. Drawing from the work of Russian formalists Mikhail Bakhtin and Pavel Nikolaevich Medvedev, Robert Stam (1989) argues that just like literature, film too can be read within the ideological and sociopolitical environment it is born. It will therefore be necessary to place the romantic comedies in their context of production and discuss what Thomas Schatz (2009, p. 19) calls 'Conglomerate Hollywood'.

Hollywood in the new millennium and the popularity of the romantic comedy

Thomas Schatz considers the first decade of the new millennium as the era of conglomerate or millennial Hollywood. He outlines seven major 'key advances over or distinct departures from the New Hollywood of the 1990s' (2009, p. 20) which include

> the culmination of an epochal merger-and-acquisition wave and the consolidation of U.S. media industry control in the hands of half-dozen global media superpowers; the related integration of the U.S. film, TV, and home entertainment industries, a far more coherent system [...] the enormous success of DVD [...], the surging global film and TV markets, [...] the emergence of a new breed of blockbuster-driven franchises specifically geared to the global, digital, conglomerate-controlled marketplace, which spawn billion-dollar film series installments [...] the annexation of the 'indie film movement' by the media conglomerates, [...] and the rapid development of three distinct film industry sectors [...] – traditional major studios, the conglomerate-owned indie divisions, and the genuine independents – which generate three very different classes of movie product (ibid.).

Although the franchises Schatz mentions are primarily male-centred – from the *Harry Potter* series to the *Pirates of the Caribbean* franchise – romantic comedies generated impressive revenue (eighteen new millennium romantic comedies surpassed $200 million in admissions worldwide and combined brought more than $4.7 billion)[2] and proved why the genre remains among the most popular choices of the Hollywood industry. The genre's popularity is also confirmed by the fact that the top ten most commercially successful worldwide romantic comedies of all time comprise six new-millennium romantic comedies (*Mr. & Mrs. Smith*, 2005, *Sex and the City*, *What Women Want*, 2000, *My Big Fat Greek Wedding*, 2002, *Hitch* and *Enchanted*, 2007).

In the context of millennial Hollywood and the new globalized marketing strategies and synergies Ashley Elaine York (2010, p. 4), observed that two female-centred films, *Mamma Mia!* and *Sex and the City* (both, 2008) constitute a landmark point as they had a great impact on 'the types of women's films that are produced in the future'. These 'women's blockbusters', to use York's definition, 'present a focused package of image, advertising, and text beyond the chick flick audience of 18–34-year-old heterosexual women.' *Mamma Mia!* and *Sex and the City* appealed to a wider demographic 'that brought older and younger heterosexual women, lesbians and gays, heterosexual men, and transnational viewers together to transform what was once a small domestic following into a large, sutured, global audience' (ibid. 5). What is more, these two films, along with many romantic comedies that preceded or followed also confirmed that it is not just teenage boys that go to the movies. As Melissa Silverstein (2011) notes, 'Hollywood lives and breathes on the narrative that young men drive the box office. That is just not true. There were 4.2 million 18–24 year old female frequent filmgoers compared to 3.3 million male frequent filmgoers' in 2010. Although women bought more tickets in 2009 than in 2010, both sexes bought 'tickets in equal amount [in 2010] and women made up 51% of the moviegoers in 2010 compared to 49% of men' (Silverstein, 2011).

What is more, conglomerate Hollywood is not so much dependent on the domestic market anymore as it is on the international audience. This is a trend that began in the 1980s resulting 'from the upgrading of motion picture cinemas, the emancipation of state-controlled broadcasting, the spread of cable and satellite services, and pent-up demand for entertainment of all types' (Tino Balio, 1998, p. 59). As evidenced by the Motion Picture Association theatrical market statistics for 2010, the US box office was $10.6 billion while the international box office was $21.2 billion making up for 67 per cent of the total revenue.[3] What these numbers show is that not only the biggest slice of the profits comes from foreign markets – even hits such as *What Women Want*, *Along Came Polly* (2001), *Two Weeks Notice* (2002), and *Sex and the City* earned more money overseas than domestically – but films that are considered failures in the USA can recuperate if they are successful internationally. *About a Boy* (2002), *40 Days and 40 Nights* (2002), *The Sweetest Thing* (2002), *Intolerable Cruelty* (2003), *Eternal Sunshine of the Spotless Mind* (2004), *The Heartbreak Kid* (2007), *Made of Honor* (2008), *Vicky Christina Barcelona* (2009), *The Bounty Hunter* (2010) and *Sex and the City 2* (2010), are among some of the romantic comedies whose profits came mostly from the international market, confirming not only its power and its influence on the Hollywood film industry but also the global popularity of the genre in the first decade of the new millennium, a decade with particular sociopolitical parameters which affect the genre and will be now discussed.

Twenty-first century neoliberalism: Masculinities and femininities

The first decade of the new millennium in the USA will be forever associated with the attack on the World Trade Center, George W. Bush's eight-year presidency, the proliferation and increasing importance of social networks which changed our communication habits, the 2008 stock exchange crash and the subsequent global recession and the first African-American president in the White House. This time period will also be associated with the consolidation of neoliberalism and its 'extension of market-based economic integration across all local, regional and national borders' (George DeMartino, 2000,

p. 1) which was championed in the 1980s by Margaret Thatcher in the UK and Ronald Reagan in the USA. These two countries, 'by embracing neoliberal ideas, both as a critique of existing institutions and as a guide for their replacement, reorganized their economies in such a way as to redistribute from bottom to top, weaken the power of labor, and delegitimate state interventionism' (Mark Blyth, 2008, p. 122). According to Rosalind Gill and Christina Scharff (2007, p. 5), after its rise to prominence in the 1980s, neoliberalism

> expanded its economic reach globally through international organizations such as the IMF, the World Trade Organization and the World Bank. Equally significant as its geographical reach, however, was its expansion across different spheres of life to constitute a novel form of governance.

Gill and Scharff (2007, p. 5) note that '[n]eoliberalism is a mobile, calculated technology for governing subjects who are constituted as self-managing, autonomous and enterprising', and that it can no longer be associated 'with Republicans in the US or Conservatives in the UK but was as central to the Clinton administration as it was to New Labour's period in office in the UK until mid-2010' (ibid. 6). Although neoliberalism is a system which sees the individual as its driving force, it is also a system which brought great inequality in the USA since it led to 'an upward redistribution of wealth, increased labor market "flexibility" (growth in low-paid jobs without benefits and with rapid turnover), and longer hours' (Blyth, 2008, p. 126). This social inequality and its dramatic consequences (increase in unemployment, decrease in paid employment, deterioration of health care and loss of benefits), along with a post-9/11 climate, which augmented sentiments of insecurity and fear, and a president who for the better part of the decade promoted the image of 'old masculinity', could not help but bring about changes in both gender politics as well as imbue the film narratives Hollywood produces.

According to Michael Kimmell (2010, p. 7), the Bush–Cheney years promoted a 'militarized masculinity', in a way emulating and reworking the 'traditional masculinity' promoted by Reagan in the 1980s, 'that proudly proclaims the United States not only as the world's only true superpower, but the axis of an emerging global empire, beholden and accountable to no one'. Hollywood responded to the re-emergence of the 'real man' with the production of an impressive number of superhero films, and by becoming 'more of a dream factory than ever, embracing fantastic escapism at a time when audiences needed it most' (David Germain, 2009). At the same time, the continuing release of romantic comedies and their commercial success added to the audience's escapist need while also exploring various models of masculinity. From the playboy, funny millionaire Hugh Grant in *Two Weeks Notice* (2002), the older rich womanizer Jack Nicholson in *Something's Gotta Give* (2003), the unscrupulous top lawyer George Clooney in *Intolerable Cruelty*, the spoilt film star Josh Duhamel in *Win a Date with Tad Hamilton* (2004) and the renowned photographer Matthew McConaughey in *Ghosts of Girlfriends Past* (2009), to the middle-class law student Mark Ruffalo in *View from the Top* (2003), the lonely widower Steve Carell in *Dan in Real Life* (2007), the ambitious assistant Ryan Reynolds in *The Proposal* (2009) and the hesitant best friend Jason Bateman in *The Switch* (2010), romantic comedies included both 'traditional' and 'softer' male representations corresponding to recent theoretical work (Christian Haywood, and Máirtín Mac an Ghaill, 2003, R. W. Connell, 2005, and Donna Peberdy, 2011), which views masculinity as a complex concept with many facets and strives to avoid reduction 'to mono-lithic and universal categories' (Raya Morag, 2009, p. 25). At the same time, the new millennium romantic films negotiate different femininities, a notion which 'seeks to open up questions about the ways in which gender is lived, experienced and represented', and 'is a way of highlighting the *social produc-tion and construction of gender* and avoiding essentialism' (Gill and Scharff, 2007, p. 2). Although most romantic comedy heroines are presented as inde-pendent, hard-working, and resourceful, there are considerable differences in the way they fictionally perform their gender. From the ambitious Kate Hudson in *How to Lose a Guy in 10 Days* (2003), the amnesiac Drew Barry-more in *50 First Dates* (2004), the free-spirited Kirsten Dunst in *Elizabeth-town* (2005), to the career-driven Sarah Jessica Parker in *Failure to Launch* (2006) and the bossy Eva Longoria in *Over Her Dead Body* (2008), one can observe how femininities are performed and take different paths according to each film's plot but also responding to specific societal circumstances.

The romantic comedy

Despite being regarded as the 'underdog' of film genre theory and history, the romantic comedy has recently witnessed an increasing number of academic books (Jeffers McDonald, 2007, Mortimer, 2007, Deleyto, 2009, Grindon 2011), which examine its history, its generic building blocks, as well as the subtle nuances of gender, class and race articulation and negotiation that are a significant part of the romantic narratives. Most of these genre studies begin by attempting to delineate it. According to the latest contributions to the bibliography of the genre, Mortimer (2007, p. 5) defines romantic comedy as 'a hybrid of the romance and comedy genres, featuring a narrative that cen-tres on the progress of a relationship, and, being a comedy, resulting in a happy ending'. Similarly, Jeffers McDonald (2007, p. 9) argues that 'a romantic comedy is a film which has as its central narrative motor a quest for love, which portrays this quest in a light-hearted way and almost always to a successful resolution'. Finally, Deleyto (2009, p. 30) defines the romantic comedy 'as the genre which uses humour, laughter and the comic to tell stories about interpersonal affective and erotic relationships'. Although Mortimer's and Jeffers McDonald's definitions echo Geoff King's (2002, p. 51) earlier attempt to define the genre as 'a format in which romance is the main and foregrounded element of the narrative, rather than occupying a secondary position', where 'the romance is generally treated lightly, as a matter of comedy rather than of more "seriously" dramatic or melodramatic relationships', it is evident that the three authors agree on the genre's dominant features: the pursuit of love and the importance of humour and the comic which provide the context in which this pursuit is deployed. Interestingly, none of these definitions constrains the genre in a heteronormative context, even though the heterosexual couple still constitutes the main paradigm of mainstream Hollywood romantic comedies. Mortimer, Jeffers McDonald and Deleyto, notwithstanding, do not limit the genre in gender and/or race boundaries since the production of mostly independent romantic narratives focused on gay, bisexual, ethnic and/or interracial relationships in the last two decades has destabilized the genre's insistence on heterosexual romance.[4]

Mortimer's, Jeffers McDonald's and Deleyto's definitions of the genre, which encompass its main structural features, focus on the romantic 'adventures' of two people who strive to get together and/or stay together in a sociopolitical environment which does not seem to cause any serious problems to their evolving and/or already formed relationship. Furthermore, the course of the relationship is filled with comic instances and despite the existence of dramatic moments and/or even tears, the vast majority of cinematic texts culminate in the celebration of erotic love through the couple's union. However, despite the fact that the structure of the genre has not undergone significant changes in its long history, not much scholarly attention has been paid to the socio-economic circumstances that produce these films nor the backdrop of the narratives. Although, it is true that the genre by definition explores romantic relationships in a bourgeois milieu where money is almost never an issue, contemporary romantic comedies are undervalued exactly because it is mistakenly inferred that they do not provide social commentary. However, this dismissal does not accompany, for instance, the today celebrated screwball comedies of the 1930s and 1940s whose protagonists were mostly wealthy, whose settings were mansions and whose costumes were lavish. *The Philadelphia Story* (1940) centred around one of the richest families in the title city and its setting was a mansion against which most of the contemporary trendy New York apartments featured in rom coms would pale in comparison. Similarly, *My Man Godfrey* (1936) narrated the story of a Fifth Avenue socialite who changed gowns in every scene. Nevertheless, these films are today considered as paradigmatic instances of not only the genre but also of class articulation and astute social observation.

I would contend that just like its predecessors, the Hollywood new millennium romantic comedies are not as one-dimensional as most critics and some scholars believe. First, they explore issues of intimate relationships, male and female friendships, marriage and work, and as such they may serve as conveyors of helpful paradigms or food for thought for the global audience as they allow reflection 'upon romance as a personal experience and a social phenomenon' (Grindon, 2011, p. 2). Despite the fact that most romantic comedies complete their narrative circle with the union of the heterosexual couple, it can be more fruitful 'to move away from the Althusserian determinism that still pervades much contemporary generic criticism and towards a view of genre as culturally and historically mediated' (Deleyto, 2009, p. 18). Deleyto acknowledges that once we approach the romantic comedy as a narrative which culminates with the validation of the heterosexual union, 'then it follows that the genre as a whole is conservative' (ibid. 25). This approach has led to 'the relegation ... of the rest of the comic narrative, especially of the middle section' whose examination can 'allow us to explore the flexibility of the genre' (ibid. 24). After all, there are new millennium rom-coms which prefer to end with two single people (*Prime*, 2005, *The Break-Up,* 2006, *(500) Days of Summer*, 2009), a fact which 'suggest[s] that the final separation of the lovers is becoming more and more usual as part of the happy ending' (ibid. 25).

Second, I would argue that the avoidance of explicit social critique does not imply its absence. Every film, regardless of generic category, addresses issues about the time of its production. Barry Keith Grant observes (2007, p. 33) that '[p]opular culture does tend to adhere to dominant ideology, although this is not always the case. Many horror films, melodramas and film noirs, among others, have been shown to question if not subvert accepted values'. Consequently, the millennial romantic comedies should not be discarded as a product of a neoliberal society which seeks profit irrespective of content. On the one hand, contemporary romantic comedies reflect this socio-economic climate but there are many examples of texts which critique, evaluate and/or offer alternatives to the dominance of neoliberalism. Furthermore, the abundance and variety of the genre's production cannot easily lead to a single conclusion since even films that were shot and/or released in the same year present contradicting views on social issues as will be discussed in the ensuing chapters.

Third, the genre has also been accused of being formulaic and predictable. However, the intertextual layers found in a given romantic narrative should be seen as enriching and not undermining the evolution of the genre. Gérard Genette (1982, p. 7) uses the term 'transtextuality', influenced by Mikhail Bakhtin's concept of 'dialogism', and Julia Kristeva's 'intertextuality', to refer to anything that 'puts a text in an overt or covert relation with other texts'. For example, when Sarah (Eva Mendes) breaks up with Alex (Will Smith) in *Hitch*, she cries on her sofa watching *Jerry Maguire* (1996). The latter film informs the new millennium narrative and also shows how a romantic comedy can enter popular culture since the lines 'You had me at hello', and 'You complete me' have been repeatedly used on American television and many films elevating *Jerry Maguire* to the status of classic rom com. In addition, the use of shots of the classic *The Graduate* (1968) in such different films as the mainstream *It's Complicated* (2009) and the independently produced *(500) Days of Summer* (2010) are instances that involve the older audience in an intelligent and playful game of irony and narrative information but also introduce the younger generation to an important cinematic text they would probably not have a chance to 'meet' otherwise.

Finally, romantic comedies are more than often dismissed and/or singled out as specifically addressing a certain part of the audience, that is the female audience. In this way, the narratives that place a woman or a girl at their centre become instantly the 'Other' to a norm that is never actually articulated in the reviews. There is no written evidence that claims that male-centred blockbusters, such as superhero and/or action–adventure films, or male-centred critically appraised dramas are the canon to which the female romantic narratives should compare. In addition, there is no mention of male-driven films as targeting their own specific audience. Therein lies a socially and at the same time theoretic impasse because for as long one keeps isolating female cinematic narratives with the use of adjectives (i.e. female), or nouns (i.e. chick flick), thus isolating and also categorizing the 'female' film as a 'mistake' or a 'deviation' from a standardized recipe and a profit-inclined industry, the dichotomy between the dominant/male and the subservient – however commercially successful – female cinematic tales will unfortunately be perpetuated. At the same time, this imbalance will keep producing scholarly work in an effort to examine more closely gender representations in these films showing that these predominantly 'female' stories hide a complex level of meaning which goes unnoticed if one is to just look at their carefully polished and shiny wrapping.

The corpus

The corpus comprises 162 Hollywood romantic comedies (both mainstream and independent) which were released internationally between 2000 and 2010.[5] The criteria based on which each film was accepted were its international distribution, North American production, and year of release. These criteria ensure that the films are among the most popular cinematic texts of the genre and can consequently constitute a fecund terrain for discussion, but by definition exclude, among others, the very successful British rom coms *Bridget Jones' Diary* (2000), *Love Actually* (2003), and *Bridget Jones' Diary: The Edge of Reason* (2004). Also excluded from the corpus due to the absence of international distribution are three rom coms focused on African-American romantic entanglements (*Brown Sugar*, 2002, *Breakin' All the Rules*, 2004, and *Just Wright*, 2009), and *Something New* (2006), a rare instance of an interracial relationship. Interestingly enough, there were films which found their way overseas but not domestically, such as the Uma Thurman vehicle *The Accidental Husband* (2008) and Catherine Zeta-Jones' *The Rebound* (2010), which are also not part of the corpus.

Two additional factors allowed the inclusion of a given film in the corpus: First, each film had to be acknowledged as a romantic comedy by major internet databases, such as imdb.com and boxofficemojo, and/or publications, such as *Variety* and the *New York Times*. Most importantly, however, all the films' 'dominant' feature had to be the 'journey' of the couple – whether two people trying to get together or two people trying to stay together – in a narrative that accentuated the comic side of interpersonal relationships. According to the Russian formalist, Roman Jakobson (1981, p. 751), 'The dominant may be defined as the focusing component of a work of art: it rules, determines, and transforms the remaining components'. It is the building block which 'dominates the entire structure and thus acts as its mandatory and inalienable constituent dominating all the remaining elements and exerting direct influence upon them'. Based on Jakobson's theory of the dominant, some films which are considered romantic comedies by the press are not included in the corpus. For instance, I contend that the *Devil Wears Prada* (2006) and *Morning Glory* (2010), both scripted by Aline Brosh McKenna, belong to another category; the writer herself refers to these two films as well as the 2011 production *I Don't Know How She Does It* 'as "the BlackBerry 3" because the women in them are forever clutching their phones or chucking them or eyeing them longingly or putting them in the freezer' (Susan Dominus 2011). Dominus observes that '[w]hat feels modern about McKenna's version of the romantic comedy is that, as she explains it, the women have goals that are not strictly speaking romantic'. However, I argue that these films are not a new version of the romantic comedy since the first two films' dominant feature is the heroine's journey towards a successful career and not towards the perfect family life in the suburbs. For instance, in *The Devil Wears Prada* it is Anne Hathaway's relationship with Meryl Streep and in *Morning Glory* it is Rachel McAdam's relationship with Harrison Ford that constitute the building blocks of the narrative. Both heroines' romantic relationships are secondary plots, and as such the films could not be considered romantic comedies. In other words, while Deleyto sees a western (*Rio Bravo*) or a suspense thriller (*Rear Window*) as 'secret' instances of the rom com genre, I would suggest that not all films that adopt the semantic and syntactic ingredients we have come to recognize as indispensable to the genre (the urban landscape, the independent heroine, recognizable melodies of the past and present, comic situations) are necessarily romantic comedies.

The corpus may not be exhaustive in the sense it cannot include every single romantic comedy produced in the USA between 2000 and 2010; yet it can provide a broad and sufficient starting guide of the Hollywood romantic comedy production during this decade, while it can be used as an efficient methodological tool which could lead to a number of interesting conclusions. First, the corpus confirms the continuing popularity of the genre during the beginning of the new millennium; the numbers of films may oscillate from 11 in 2006 (the lowest) to 19 in 2009 (the highest), but the average number of 14.7 demonstrates that the genre is among the film industry's production priorities. The second observation concerns the gender politics at play 'behind the scenes' and corroborates the male dominance in what is perceived a female genre. From the 123 directors of the 162 films, only 15 were women (12.1 per cent). These 15 female filmmakers directed only 19 films

(11.7 per cent) – Nancy Meyers directed four films, while Anne Fletcher directed two. The writing department showed an improvement regarding the directorial gender 'gap', as 51 (31.9 per cent) romantic comedies were written or co-written by female writers. This apparent gender discrepancy does not only concern the romantic comedy genre but is unfortunately a canon in the film industry. 'According to a study by the Center for the Study of Women in Television and Film at San Diego State University, women made up 18 percent of all directors, producers, writers, cinematographers and editors working on the top 250 highest-grossing movies' in 2011. However, '[o]nly 5 percent of directors were women', 'a decrease of 2 percentage points from 2010 and approximately half the percentage of women directors working in 1998' (Rebecca Ford, 2012). Regarding female writers, according to the 2011 Hollywood Writers Report, published by the Writers Guild of America, '[i]n film, female writers make up 17% of film writers' (Melissa Silverstein, 2011). Silverstein explains that '[a]s the nation grappled with the worst economic downturn since the Great Depression, the few hopeful signs for women and minority writers discussed in the previous report either disappeared or seemed considerably less encouraging by 2009'. Although these numbers are certainly disappointing, a more detailed discussion on the role of women in film production and distribution exceeds the goal of the book and should be reserved for the detailed study it deserves.

The book

The book is made up of ten chapters: the first seven chapters focus on seven romantic comedy cycles, and the last three examine three broader groupings of the genre. Usually, cycles emerge within a film genre, in an industry attempt to capitalize 'on the (often unexpected) success of a film that offers a new twist on an old genre' (Glitre, 2006, p. 20) by investing in similar films marked by what Rick Altman calls 'common features' and Jakobson calls 'the dominant', thus gradually 'associating a new type of material or approach with already existing genres' (Altman, 2006, p. 60). For instance, the 'new career woman' cycle focuses on a number of films whose central narrative stratagem is how the heroine manages her professional aspirations vis-à-vis her love life.

Each chapter focuses on two paradigmatic examples of the genre cycle or cluster in question, based on commercial success and/or artistic excellence. Through textual analysis, I examine each film as a unique instance of a dialogue mainly between the sociopolitical context during the production of the text and the genre conventions, against a theoretical background informed by gender, genre, star and political theories. The first four chapters examine four cycles, three of which have a history that dates back to the 1930s.

Chapter 1 focuses on the 'battle of the sexes' cycle, which represents a recognizable narrative stratagem of the genre and has had a long history. The two films examined in the chapter, *Intolerable Cruelty* and *The Ugly Truth*

(2009), will serve as paradigms of how neoliberalism tries and eventually succeeds in penetrating into the sexual relationships of modern couples, and even controlling their most private moments.

Chapter 2 also centres on another familiar cycle of the romantic comedy, the career woman comedy. After a brief presentation of its cinematic history, I study two millennial examples of the 'new' career woman rom com, using *The Proposal* and *New in Town* (both, 2009) as case studies. The aim of the chapter is to show how the two filmic texts empower women through professional ambition, but also advocate that their female heroines can find a balance between work and a male companion and/or family, without compromise.

In Chapter 3, I summarily trace the history of another undervalued genre, the fantasy genre, and I discuss the history of the hybrid fantasy romantic comedy. The chapter views its two films, *Enchanted* and *Ghost Town* (2008), as instances of imaginative and/or 'unreal' texts, which serve to comment on specific sociopolitical circumstances.

Chapter 4 explores a cycle that was born in the mid-1980s, the action romantic comedy. The two case studies, *Date Night* and *Knight and Day* (both, 2010), released at the end of the first decade of the new millennium, are used to examine the dynamics of the heterosexual couple faced with danger. The chapter discusses if and how the active-male/passive-female dichotomy is transformed, the several instances of male objectification and the subtle comments on American political corruption, as well as the nation's sovereign inclinations.

Finally, in Chapter 5, I turn my attention to the teen rom com, and discuss *Chasing Liberty* (2004) and *Sydney White* (2007). I believe that the two films address significant societal issues, except from the representation of female adolescence in the new millennium. *Chasing Liberty* presents an interesting reading concerning the tensions between Europe and the United States in 2003, while *Sydney White*, a new take on the Snow White fairy tale, is critical of the collegial fraternity system and its rules of exclusion, and inclusion, mirroring what happens in the actual US political landscape.

Chapter 6 presents a romantic comedy cycle that emerged in the new millennium; the heroines and heroes 'of a certain age' cycle. Although the romantic comedy genre, as well as most genres for that matter, opt for young female protagonists, the new millennium witnessed the emergence of romantic narratives that placed women and men in their 40s, 50s, and even 60s, in starring roles, creating new and exciting narratives. After a brief presentation of the reasons that may have led to the birth of the cycle, I focus on the three sub-cycles that include representations of mature heroines and heroes. I first examine the 'cougar' cycle (*I Could Never Be Your Woman*, 2007, *The Rebound*), which deals with a reverse May–December romance. Second, I focus on the 'troubled marriage' cycle (*Couples Retreat*) and finally, I study the cycle of the 'single mature' woman (*It's Complicated*), which depicts female sexuality after 50.

In chapter 7, the discussion revolves around another new cycle of the genre, the 'baby-crazed' romantic comedies; that is films whose heroines go to great lengths to have a baby even though they begin their narrative journeys without a male partner. In this chapter, I examine the changed patterns that motherhood has undergone in the last decades due to medicine and celebrity culture, and through the analysis of *Baby Mama* (2008) and *The Back-Up Plan* (2010), I also associate motherhood with the effects of neoliberalism.

Chapter 8 focuses on the cluster of what I call 'man-com', that is a great variety of romantic comedies which centre on the male perspective. The chapter examines the dominant masculinity model which 'circulated' in popular culture during the Bush administration, its impact on male cinematic representations, and its relation to the Reagan years. Through the mainstream *Made of Honor* and the 'auteuristic' *Whatever Works* (2009), I aim to show how the concept of a single masculinity model cannot account for the abundance of male performances, even by the same male individual, as well as its association with a specific sociopolitical context.

Chapter 9 looks at the independent romantic comedies, which constitute a fecund terrain for the discussion of genre evolution and gender performativity. I discuss *(500) Days of Summer* and *Happythankyoumoreplease* (2010), two cinematic texts that capture the angst of the 20-something generation. In addition, both films were shot and/or released during the economic recession, and can therefore provide valuable insight into the effects of neoliberalism on these younger men and women.

Finally, chapter 10 looks into 'the other' in the rom com, a genre which is still dominated by white, heterosexual heroines and heroes. The chapter focuses on two stars, Will Smith, and Jennifer Lopez, whose romantic comedies have had an impressive worldwide success. I argue that the popularity of these films constitutes the proof of how stardom can transcend racial, ethnic and/or gender barriers through careful media construction of the star's image. Finally, I maintain that Will Smith and Jennifer Lopez are examples of the neoliberal discourse of colour blindness which is inaccurately considered as the only way to completely eradicate racism, while at the same time it perpetuates consumerism and submission to the law of the market.

2 The battle of the sexes rom com: to be continued?

In *Adam's Rib* (1949), one of the last classic screwball comedies, Amanda Bonner (Katharine Hepburn) and Adam Bonner (Spencer Tracy) are pitted against each other 'as opposing lawyers in an attempted murder case that soon becomes a comic treatise on woman's equality' on the part of Amanda (Gehring, 2002, p. 132). The defendant of the case, a young woman, shot her philandering husband, and Amanda seized the opportunity, as her lawyer, to turn the case into a cause for women's rights on the one hand, and a battle of the sexes on the other, since Adam is the prosecuting district attorney on the same case. Amanda and Adam's inherent competitiveness may result in most amusing scenes but at the same time complicates their marriage as they both do their very best, even resorting to unnecessary and questionable actions, to win their case. When the final verdict acquits the defendant, Adam's male ego is seriously wounded while Amanda's legal triumph is equated with the deterioration and possible dissolution of her marriage. However, the ending finds the two protagonists together in bed talking about the case, their professional future, and the difference between men and women. The final repartee is intriguing:

AMANDA: What I said was true, there's no difference between the sexes. Men, women, the same.
ADAM: They are?
AMANDA: Well, maybe there is a difference, but it's a little difference.
ADAM: Well, you know as the French say [...]
AMANDA: What do they say?
ADAM: *Vive la différence!*
AMANDA: Which means?
ADAM: Which means hurray for that little difference.

It could be argued that the fact that it is Adam who not only has the last word but has managed to prove that men and women are different and by extension men are superior has a double function: it obscures Amanda's previous legal victory and appeases the 1940s audience who were mostly used to 'the one-sided battle of the sexes with its inevitable male triumph' (Harvey,

1987, p. 417), despite Harvey's conclusion that *Adam's Rib* proposes that the battle 'is at least a draw' (ibid.). Adam's comment on the biological difference is important insofar as during the 1940s, 'sexual inequality in the US was repeatedly explained in terms of biology, even by groups representing women' (Glitre, 2006, p. 93). However, Glitre adds that the 'connection between social inequality and biological difference' is ultimately a capitalist construction which 'had [initially] defined wage labour as a male prerogative', and continued by controlling women's employment by sex-typing – at least before World War II – which 'reflected and reinforced dominant beliefs about the "natural" differences between men and women, seeming to probe that a woman's place was in the home, even when she was at work' (ibid. p. 94).

More than seven decades later, these 'natural' differences still constitute part of popular culture as evidenced by a number of book titles, such as James D. Mallory's 1996 *Battle of the Sexes: How Both Sides Can Win with Honor*, Brant Wenegrat's 1996 *Illness and Power: Women's Mental Disorders and the Battle Between the Sexes*, Kate Taylor's 2003 *The Battle of the Sexes* and Wynn Wheldon's 2006 *The Battle of the Sexes: Men v. Women – The Truth Once and for All*, board games, such as *The Original Battle of the Sexes*, *Battle of the Sexes Simpsons*, and *Battle of the Sexes IQ Game* and of course romantic comedies.

A number of scholars view the battle of the sexes as an essential structural building block of the genre. Roberta Garrett (2007, p. 11) remarks that the genre's construction contains an 'inherent "battle of the sexes"' element, while Cherry Potter notes 'that the battle of the sexes constitutes the romantic comedy's *raison d'être*' (in Kyle Stevens, 2009, p. 137). Similarly, Jeffers McDonald (2007, p. 57) writes that the first part of the contemporary romantic comedy 'will often detail the battle of the sexes embodied in two individual protagonists, before moving to a more romantic comedy narrative in the second part.' However, although I also believe that the genre often uses 'the essential opposition of male and female', in order to better service the progression of the plot (Jeffers McDonald, 2007, p. 57), I would argue the following: the millennial romantic comedies are not by definition based on the differences that are claimed to exist between men and women and that the above generalizations fail to explore many cinematic examples that show an opposite structural tactic and prove the diverse narrative paths these genre films may choose. First of all, a number of millennial productions present the 'obstacle' as external and not internal. For instance, in *Summer Catch* (2001), it is a class difference that generates friction between the couple; in *My Big Fat Greek Wedding*, it is the heroine's father that creates the problem the couple has to overcome; in *Over Her Dead Body*, it is the ghost of the fiancée that hinders the hero's eventual union with another woman; and in *Going the Distance* (2010), it is actually the great distance between the cities where the two protagonists work that delays the evolution of their relationship. Secondly, even when the narrative impediment is internal, it is very often irrelevant to the characteristics of the battle of the sexes. Thus, in *American*

Sweethearts (2001), it is Julia Roberts's shyness that prevents her from revealing her romantic feelings to John Cusack; in *Life or Something Like It* (2002) and *View from the Top*, it is Angelina Jolie's and Gwyneth Paltrow's career ambitions that keep them away from their respective relationships; in *50 First Dates*, it is Drew Barrymore's amnesia that poses the problem; in *Prime*, it is Uma Thurman's age difference with her much younger boyfriend that leads to her decision to break up; and in *Eat, Pray, Love* (2010), it is Julia Roberts's journey to self-discovery that postpones her long-term commitment to a man. It can be, therefore, argued that the battle of the sexes represents one of the tropes of the genre but it is not present in every narrative.

This chapter will then focus on those films that centre on the stereotypical differences between men and women and try to impose the perception that men are indeed from Mars and women from Venus, perpetuating the discourse of both biological and gender dissimilarities. The 'dominant' element of these romantic comedies is the witty verbal exchange targeted mainly at the differences of the sexes between the hero and the heroine who begin their narrative journeys as enemies of some sort only to end up together and in love. This cycle comprises films such as *Someone Like You* (2001), *Down with Love* (2003), *Intolerable Cruelty*, *How to Lose a Guy in 10 Days*, *The Ugly Truth*, *The Bounty Hunter* and *Leap Year* (2010). The obvious tension and animosity that are at first created between the man and the woman is a prolific terrain for the discussion of whether or not men and women actually seek different things regarding love, commitment, relationships and marriage. This chapter will not only examine the evolution of the cycle but will mainly focus on the representation of the stereotypical male and female 'flaws' as registered in the various film texts of the cycle and their possible resonance in the real world. The two films that constitute the focus of this chapter, *Intolerable Cruelty* and *The Ugly Truth*, were chosen not only because of their considerable commercial success, but because they best exemplify the influence the sociopolitical situation exerts on the protagonist couple. The battle of the sexes will be placed in a political context in order to examine how capitalism manages to infiltrate and to an extent regulate its subjects even in their most intimate relationships.

Intolerable Cruelty

Intolerable Cruelty was directed by Joel and Ethan Coen, two of the most important contemporary American filmmakers. Therefore, this film is one of the few instances of the current romantic comedy universe, where the directors' names carry 'an aura of auteur-celebrity', (Jon Lewis, 2002, p. 109) and can consequently lead a different part of the audience to the theatre. This observation also draws attention to the almost non-existent academic interest to those contemporary directors whose career has mainly been tied to the genre. Successful directors, such as Ken Kwapis, Marc Lawrence, Robert Luketic, Garry Marshall, Nancy Meyers, Donald Petrie, Rob Reiner, Andy

Tennant and Marc Waters do not constitute the subject of academic examination not only because of the general undervaluation of the genre but
because of the definition of expert cinematic direction. Writing about the
prominence of dialogue in screwball comedies, Sarah Kozloff (2000, p. 170)
astutely observes that 'if one defines expert filmmaking only as breath-taking
long shots of scenery, dramatic use of light and shadows, or rapid editing of
action sequences', then one could conclude that the camera does not 'do
much' in these films. However, Kozloff (ibid.) adds that

> these movies feature long takes that allow the scenes' tension to build,
> wide shots that permit us to see the characters in spatial relation to one
> another, lighting that flatters the stars and the expensive sets, and subtle
> reframings to emphasize a line or a reaction shot. The prominence of
> 'talk' in screwball comedies leads to an understated, but by no means
> inartistic, visual style.

Kozloff's observations can be applied to millennial romantic comedies as well
and can to an extent account for the 'silence' that accompanies the majority
of directors responsible for how we watch the heroes and heroines fall in love
on the big screen, with rare exceptions such as Woody Allen or directors who
may not be exclusively associated with the genre but are regarded as having a
personal visual style, such as Paul Thomas Anderson (*Punch-Drunk Love*,
2000), Robert Altman (*Dr. T and the Women*, 2000), James Ivory (*Le
Divorce*, 2003), Jim Jarmusch (*Broken Flowers*, 2004), Ridley Scott (*A Good
Year*, 2006) and the Coen brothers.

Thus, the Coen brothers' attempt at the romantic comedy genre was first
regarded as a deviation from the acclaimed duo's usual thematic preoccupations. Not only did it become 'their first movie to emerge from a script not
their own, but it was their first venture into the mainstream – a romantic
comedy with top-notch stars' (Ryan P. Doom, 2009, p. 136). Starring George
Clooney as Miles Massey, a nationally famous lawyer for drawing up the
presumably ironclad 'Massey Prenup', and Catherine Zeta-Jones as Marylin
Rexroth, a gorgeous woman who marries rich men to ensure her financial
security, *Intolerable Cruelty* became the Coen brothers' most commercial film
to that time, earning more than $120 million in admissions worldwide and
today is number three in the directors' filmography surpassed by *No Country
for Old Men* (2007) and *Burn After Reading* (2008). More importantly, however, the film uses the classical screwball comedy as its main inspiration,
imbuing it with elements of black comedy and even film noir, confirming one
of the directors' most recognizable traits, their 'habit of looking at reality
through the lens of earlier genre films' (William Rodney Allen, 2006, p. xii).
Finally, *Intolerable Cruelty* is 'the first Coen movie to decidedly focus on the
haves instead of the have-nots', and establishes 'a conversation about the
morality of the country, a discussion about the state of marriage, ethics, and
true love' (Doom, 2009, p. 128).

The film 'opens with an establishing shot of modern Los Angeles with the discovery of an affair between a woman and her producer husband', a humorous prelude 'which alludes to the infidelity, disillusion, and the social satirical tone to come. The state of marriage in America has become an industry all its own, which leads us to Miles', who decides to defend the wife even though she is clearly the adulterer (Doom, 2009, p. 127). Miles is presented as the perfect embodiment of the corporate attorney. Extensively knowledgeable, experienced and powerful, he plays with justice and interprets the law according to his client's wishes, enabling him to win yet another case. Miles is also a vain character – he has an obsession with whitening his teeth and looking at them in every reflecting surface – and a bored individual despite all his power and accumulated material possessions. His challenge soon comes in the form of Marylin, a strikingly beautiful and sexual woman, who enchants men with incredible effortlessness. Her main occupation is marrying rich husbands with the sole purpose of divorcing them to get half of their assets, which as she admits onscreen is her 'passport to wealth, independence and freedom.' Her man-eating habits are immediately spotted by Miles, her first husband's lawyer. Marylin unwillingly stumbles upon a worthy adversary, and the rest of the narrative, which pays tribute to the tradition of the 1930s screwball comedies and includes the major characteristics of that cycle (rapid exchange of witty dialogue, surreal situations, slapstick moments, luxurious sets and costumes), follows her trials to finally get her 'passport', while avenging Miles who left her penniless after her first marriage.

The plot is therefore constructed upon the binary opposition of two equally worthy adversaries: an intelligent professional male and an equally intelligent female. This battle of the sexes, however, is not isolated from the social context of the beginning of the 2000s, which informs the gender representations and performances of the opposing duet. As was stated above, Miles is driven by his need to conquer Marylin, whereas Marylin is determined to exterminate the man who dared interfere with her plans for wealth. However, both characters are actually motivated by the same desire – greed, one of '[t]he animating drivers of neoliberalism' (Michael Fielding and Peter Moss, 2011, p. 48). Fielding and Moss (ibid.) argue that 'under the hegemony of neoliberalism […] [p]ersonhood has become both atomized and collectivized and thus, despite its ideological protestations and first appearances, totalitarian in its propensities and inclinations.' Fielding and Moss (ibid.) also add that under neoliberalism, we are all 'encouraged to see ourselves as atomistic, acquisitive and inveterately hard-wired into exponential consumption', and 'we are required to do so through perpetual personal reinvention, the self as entrepreneur of the self, thus necessitating new products and patterns of consumption' (ibid.). Miles's greed is evident in his insatiable need for material possessions, his perfectionism regarding his external appearance and his supposedly inherent need to win at all costs. Marylin's greed presents the same desires as Miles's with the difference she does not use her professional knowledge to win but her sexuality.

Although Marylin is clearly a very bright woman – the narrative dictates she use all her mental capabilities for intrigue, deception and hypocrisy. Conveying the old message that a beautiful woman is conniving and manipulative, the film perpetuates the myth of the inherent evils female sexuality carries. At the same time, *Intolerable Cruelty* uses the generic conventions of the screwball comedy to promote the battle-of-the-sexes scenario and assigns stereotypical attributes to the male and the female 'opponents'. On the one side, the narrative presents Miles as the ultimate alpha male, despite some weird idiosyncrasies (mainly his teeth obsession) as well as a propensity to 'bend' the law as he sees fit, but shows his vulnerable and more humane side when he genuinely falls in love with Marylin. On the opposite side, Marylin is the embodiment of the film noir's femme fatale, albeit in a lighter and more genre appropriate manner, and her reciprocating Miles's emotions remains doubtful even after the last sequence which celebrates their union. Thus, whereas even when a screwball comedy such as *The Lady Eve* (1941) portrayed the heroine as a con artist, interested in acquiring wealth, it ended leaving no doubt as to whether the female protagonist was transformed through love. Marylin is not given the same opportunity for transformation and until the end she exists 'as a vacant character without romantic interests, without ethics, and without any real personality' (Doom, 2009, p. 132). Although Doom also notices that both the protagonists are 'morally corrupt, leaving the audience no one to root for or care for' (ibid. p. 127), Miles is 'saved' by the power of love and thus becomes the more likeable character.

Despite the negative portrayal of both Marylin and Miles, one could argue that they are both the perfect incarnation of the society that helped 'produce' them. As Doom (2009, p. 128) underlines, the plot of the film mainly 'takes place in plastic Los Angeles, a city many see as the downfall of man where sin, sex, a lack of ethics, a lack of character, selfishness, and violence all run rampant' and thus the entire narrative serves as an indirect condemnation of neoliberalism's persistence on generating avid consumers. Indeed, although the ending of *Intolerable Cruelty* finds Miles and Marylin married and reconciled, it also finds them partners in a new and seemingly successful television show, thus increasing their combined wealth and consequently securing the longevity of their marriage through financial prosperity.

The Ugly Truth

The Ugly Truth was released in 2009 and became a worldwide commercial success. With a modest budget of $38 million, it earned more than $205 million in admissions. The film's international appeal is also another instance of star power as *The Ugly Truth* stars Katherine Heigl and Gerard Butler, two actors who have seen their careers rise in the 2000s are today among the studios' most sought-after 'investments.' After her role as the sensitive doctor Izzie Stevens in the acclaimed dramedy *Grey's Anatomy* (ABC, 2005–present), Heigl successfully crossed over to the big screen with a number of romantic comedies (*Side Effects*, 2005, *Knocked Up*, 2007, *27 Dresses*, 2008, *Killers* and *Life as We Know it*, both 2010), allowing for the possibility to be considered as the 'new queen of the rom com' (see among others, Evan Fanning 2008, and Claude Brodesser-Akner and Adam Stembergh, 2010). Indeed, along with *The Ugly Truth*, and not including Heigl's latest contribution to the genre, *New Year's Eve* (2011), the actress's romantic comedies returned more than an impressive $892 million worldwide. At the same time, the Scottish Gerard Butler rose to stardom after portraying King Leonidas in *300* (2007). Butler's later filmography includes roles in various genres: he portrayed the dead sensitive husband in the romantic comedy *P.S. I Love You* (2007), the crook in the British crime film *Rocknrolla* (2008) and the family man who takes the law into his own hands in the thriller *Law-Abiding Citizen* (2009). However, with the exception of the actor's participation as the voice of the village chief in the animated *How to Train Your Dragon* (2010) – which grossed almost $495 million – his three romantic comedies (*P.S. I Love You*, *The Ugly Truth* and *The Bounty Hunter*) are the actor's most commercially popular films. This observation not only validates the popularity of the genre in the new millennium but also confirms that certain A-list thespians, such as Butler's co-stars (Katherine Heigl in *The Ugly Truth* and Jennifer Aniston in *The Bounty Hunter*,) constitute 'a form of capital' (Paul McDonald, 2000, p. 11) for the Hollywood industry, which seeks to capitalize on their established connection to certain genres which have already led to significant profits in the past.

The Heigl–Butler pairing in *The Ugly Truth* not only focuses on the battle of the sexes but imbues the central characters with recognizable characteristics from their previous roles, multiplying the intertextual references but also assisting and anchoring the association of the particular actors with the genre. Thus, Heigl plays Abby, an intelligent, responsible, resourceful yet sweet and sensitive television producer of a morning show in Sacramento, a role which has been repeated by the actress in *27 Dresses,* where she played an assistant to the director of an eco-friendly firm, and in *Knocked Up,* where she was a television journalist. Butler, on the other hand, plays Mike, the presenter of a local show called *The Ugly Truth*, where he shares his 'expertise' on heterosexual relationships, and offers 'advice' on relationships to mostly female callers without any regard to propriety, manners or the use of appropriate language. Butler uses his 'macho' image and virile physique to portray a cynical, misogynistic male character whose philosophy is that '[m]en have penises, and women should accommodate them any which way they can, preferably in push-up bras and remote-controlled vibrating panties' (Dargis, 2009).

Despite the obvious irony in Dargis's comment, it is true that *The Ugly Truth*'s approach regarding the sexes is explicitly coarse. In the opening credits, for instance, Heigl's name is accompanied by a simple, white cartoonish figure designating a female individual, while a red heart approaches the figure and settles in the head. Butler's name is also accompanied by the same, male this time, figure but the heart settles in the area of the figure's supposed genitalia. The same connotation is included in the film's poster which features the two protagonists separated by a wall, each holding a red paper heart, Heigl near her head and Butler right under his belt. The message is therefore made clear: women love with their mind, and men love with their penis. The strict binary opposition between men and women is the centre around which the relationship between Abby and Mike progresses. Abby first notices Mike when her cat accidentally pushes the remote and the TV turns on the show Mike is hosting. Appalled by his cynical, phallocratic and obviously derogatory comments towards women, and his conviction that men are only interested in sex, Abby calls in to express her strong disagreement. Mike asks her to describe the man she thinks is capable of love and Abby starts listing a series of attributes the perfect companion has. Mike soon understands the man she is referring to (intelligent, handsome, successful, with a taste for red wine, picnics, classical music and cats) exists only in her head and confronts her instantly, leaving Abby unable to reply.

The next day, however, her boss, Stuart (Nick Searcy) informs his staff that due to *The Ugly Truth*'s popularity, they have hired Mike to become part of their morning show, presenting his own segment twice a week. Despite Abby's protests about the lowering of their product's ethical standards, Stuart retorts and tells her, 'We're news people. We don't have to like it', as if he were referring to an interview with a foreign dictator, a terrorist group or a criminal, that is threatening and dangerous individuals who are and in some cases should become the subject of news. Stuart's comment, however, also serves as a reminder of the use of sensationalism in American television and press as a means to attract more viewers and/or readers – and advertisers, thus increasing both ratings and revenue (Jim Willis, 2010, p. 17). In addition, Stuart's reaction places the film in a wider category of narratives that explores what happens behind the scenes of the news world. This filmic tradition started in the late 1930s and 1940s and the newspaper world (*Nothing Sacred*, 1930, *His Girl Friday,* 1940, *Woman of the Year*, 1942) and then moved into the world of television. From the satirical yet poignant *Network* (1976) to *Broadcast News* (1987), *Switching Channels* (1988), *He Said, She Said* (1991), *Up Close and Personal* (1996), *Someone Like You* (2001), and *Life or Something Like It* (2002), the comedy genre has often used the television backstage not just as a suitable terrain for the battle of the sexes, but as an appropriate ground to critique the contemporary sociopolitical status quo. Nevertheless, the common thread of all these films and many more that use the same subtext is that truth, integrity and honesty are not necessarily the priority of the majority of people, and especially the decision-making individuals working in the mass media. What these narratives imply is that since their survival depends on circulation and ratings, then their aim is the attraction of more readers and viewers at any cost. Therefore, although Abby has no desire to work with someone who disparages everything she has worked hard for and stands for, she is obliged to accommodate her boss's wishes for fear of being demoted or let go.

Indeed, Mike appears the same morning as a commentator on the show. The hosts, married for quite a long time, Georgia (Cheryl Hines) and Larry (John Michael Higgins), begin their introduction, as instructed by Abby in the control room, by observing that Mike's show is offensive, especially to women. However, Mike not only accepts the otherwise insulting characterization but immediately replies that the truth is offensive as well. He then continues his monologue by explaining that marriage is an institution based on social pressure, status and sex, and then he comments on the anchors' marriage. He openly shares his opinion on national television about how Georgia slept with Larry when she was a young, ambitious woman to advance her career and how Larry became emasculated by Georgia's eventual higher popularity and subsequent higher income in their professional field, and became a weakened man with no desire, and more importantly, no actual ability, to have sexual relations with his wife. Despite Mike's disparaging anatomy of a long-term marriage on-air and the fact he blames Georgia for the deterioration of the relationship, his words seem to resonate with both Georgia and Larry, who kiss upon his prompting on air as if he were the professional counsellor who magically provided them with the 'ugly truth' that instantly liberated them. At the same time, however, Mike's misogynistic attack on financially successful career women, and especially wives whose income is the main driving force of their household, reverberates with current trends in family life.

Hanna Rosin (2010) notes that '[r]esearchers have recently begun scrutinizing a new kind of family ruled by "breadwinner wives" or "top income wives," defined as women who make more money than their husbands', and whose percentage in 2010 accounts for approximately '22 percent of American marriages of people over 30', and is a significant increase compared to the 4 per cent of marriages in 1970. Rosin adds that although 'demographers expect the number of such marriages to grow, as women continue to attain more college degrees than young men and to outearn them', this will happen in a socio-politically ambivalent ambiance. 'In a recent Pew Research Center survey, 67 per cent of Americans said that in order to be ready for marriage, a man should be able to support his family financially, while only 33 percent said the same for women' (ibid.) Additionally, '[a] 2007 Pew survey found that working mothers increasingly say they would rather not work full time' while a 2010 poll showed Americans are divided as far as changes in the family structure are concerned (ibid). D'Vera Cohn and Richard Fry (2010) explain this gender reversal trend in the American family and note that apart from the rise in the number of educated women, the main cause is that the economic recession 'hurt employment of men more than that of women.' Cohn and Fry also underline that '[m]ales accounted for about 75% of the 2008 decline in employment among prime-working-age individuals (U.S. Bureau of Labor Statistics, 2009)', and that '[w]omen are moving toward a new milestone in which they constitute half of all the employed', with a 'share increased from 46.5% in December 2007 to 47.4% in December 2009' (ibid.).

This recent female financial 'superiority' may strengthen women's roles in society as well as serve as a paradigm to be followed by younger generations, but can also create tension between the two sexes. In a 2010 *New York Times* article written by Sam Roberts, Professor Stephanie Coontz expressed a concern regarding the men's reaction due to their 'increasing dependence on their wives, especially if they are laid off', in what she considers 'truly a sea change in gender relations within marriage'.

Following Mike's societal observations, Larry's fictional erectile dysfunction is exclusively attributed to his being 'financially destroyed' by his wife, while no other factors, such as lack of desire, physical and/or emotional problems are taken into consideration. Through Mike's dynamic presence and his absolute view on the inherent differences between men and women and the catastrophic consequences of female emancipation, *The Ugly Truth* endorses in a way a return to the 1950s, the superficially peaceful time of men at the office and women in the kitchen.

Despite the animosity between Mike and Abby, heightened by Mike's constant sexual innuendos, the two protagonists are forced to spend time together initially at work. Still, when Abby meets the man of her dreams, she inadvertently shares the news with Mike who offers to help her 'get him' if she follows his rules. When his first tip proves a success, Abby agrees to be guided, enticed by Mike's intention of quitting if he fails in his task. The narrative does not satisfactorily explain Abby's sudden and complete trust in Mike, despite a silent acceptance perhaps due to her feelings of despair regarding her love life, and their agreement is followed by a makeover montage, a very popular romantic comedy convention that most frequently involves the female character (*She's All That*, 1999, The *Princess Diaries*, 2001, *My Big Fat Greek Wedding*). Male makeovers are quite rare in the genre with *Tootsie* (1982) and *Mrs. Doubtfire* (1993) serving as primary examples of an intentional gender masquerade. However, 2011 witnessed two 'traditional' male makeovers in the romantic comedies *Larry Crowne* and *Crazy, Stupid, Love*, perhaps acknowledging the fact that men are also in need of a change in appearance which can be followed by a change in attitude.

The Ugly Truth's makeover, however, does not include the transformation of an ugly duckling into a swan (*She's All That*, *The Princess Diaries*) or the updating of a middle-aged man's wardrobe (*Larry Crowne*, *Crazy, Stupid, Love*). Instead, it involves the transformation of an already beautiful woman into a sexual object. Mike 'orders' Abby to buy the tightest dress possible, lingerie that can accentuate her breasts, and to add extensions to her mid-length hair because 'men like something to grab on to other than [the woman's] ass'. His vulgarity and borderline obscene comments about her body parts as well as the way she should behave around men seem not only grossly exaggerated but insulting to both men and women. Although the battle of the sexes has a long and rich cinematic tradition in the genre, as was stated above, and has permutated reflecting each specific socio-historical period, in *The Ugly Truth* it is presented as 'a natural, inevitable conflict abstracted from historical and systemic conditions', and 'suggests a power struggle for the supremacy of one x over the other', perpetuating 'the misogynist stereotype of the feminist as a castrating bitch' (Aspasia Kotsopoulos, 2010, p. 311). In this battle, Mike is a man unlike the usually strong yet sensitive leads of the millennial genre paradigms. As portrayed by Butler, known for his role as the almost invincible and mythical King Leonidas, he mostly represents the mythopoetic men's movement which claimed the public attention after American poet, author and activist Robert Bly published *Iron John: A Book About Men*, a Brothers Grimm fairy tale refashioned as a commentary on the deteriorating state of masculinity in the late 1980s and early 1990s', caused by 'the perceived "feminisation" of society, and feminism' (Peberdy 2011, p. 99). The influence of Bly's words created a men's movement that celebrated nature and men's connection to it as the only way 'to re-establish the male ideal in the contemporary period' (ibid.). However, although Bly did not intend to attack women, a number of feminists viewed his ideal of the Wild Man with scepticism and argued that this male model represented 'misogyny', and was 'indicative of the damaging effect of patriarchal masculinity' (ibid. p. 100).

Mike's use of foul language and continuous debasement of the female sex does not stop even when he is forced by genre conventions to fall in love and end up with Abby. Nevertheless, his character stays true to his beliefs throughout the narrative, whereas Abby's character may confuse the audience. Although her philosophy of life is in no way similar to Mike's, Abby follows his advice to the letter with almost no objection and succeeds in 'getting' the man she has been fantasizing about. Her transformation into a sex object, a woman who suppresses her individuality to win the heart of a man, comes in complete contrast to Abby's set of values, which not only weakens the fictional character but implies that masquerading and/or performing is the way women can enter a relationship. On the other hand, Abby's initial attraction to Mike seems to be purely sexual and is primarily justified by her 11-month abstinence from sex.

The Ugly Truth provides a surprising version of a female orgasm in the tradition of the classic scene in *When Harry Met Sally* (1989). Abby climaxes by mistake at a restaurant, during an important meeting, when the remote control of the vibrating underwear Mike bought her as a 'joke', is found accidentally by a little boy who starts toying with it without knowing the effect it can have. Abby's public sexual expression may be an empowering representation of a woman who is secure and confident to use a device in order to satisfy herself, but it should be noted that the underwear came from Mike when Abby earlier disclosed she does not masturbate. Thus, this confession minimizes the empowering dimensions of the climax scene and allows only for the possibility of Abby's reuse of the device in the private space of her home.

Although *The Ugly Truth* was written by three women and its five-member production team was made up of three women and two men, it fails to treat and/or update the battle of the sexes convention to the new millennium. Instead, it shows a strong, independent, career-oriented woman led by the advice of a macho cynical man to turn into an erotically attractive object and a docile female in order to attract the attention of an appropriate male. Despite Abby and Mike's differences regarding the ways men and women form relationships, their proper likes and dislikes, they have one thing in common. Just like Miles and Marylin in *Intolerable Cruelty*, who view money and financial security as vital to their existence, Abby and Mike never forget about their professional and by consequence financial gains from their cooperation. For instance, after Mike's first television appearance, a colleague of Abby's informs her that the station received more than 1,000 calls and 300 e-mails of viewers expressing their approval, and he leaves her office asking her to 'keep him happy' in order to 'get their contracts renewed'. The next day, Abby forgets that she considered Mike's show to be at least morally challenging, and while Mike is on the air playing with some girls covered in strawberry-flavoured gelatine, she orders him to lick one of the girls' fingers, pushing the segment into an even more provocative and sexually charged path. Abby's justification for her change of direction is direct, sharp and derives from the rules of the market. 'If we're going to do this, we might as well milk it', she tells her assistant and crew in the control room, and her demeanour shows no remorse whatsoever about abandoning her moral standards to secure and perhaps advance her career. Even when she later admits what she did was 'cheap titillation', she keeps on working with Mike.

In the films discussed in this chapter, the battle of the sexes has a winner but it is an unlikely one as it is neither the man nor the woman. I would suggest the winner is the capitalist system, which will ensure the financial security of the couple and therefore their durability. It should be noted that Mike and Abby's final confrontation and eventual acknowledgement of mutual erotic feelings begins on air when they both cover a big exposition of hot air balloons. Their aggressive repartee is captured by the camera and the producer of the show asks his cameraman to keep rolling, instead of going to commercials, because he knows this fight will draw in more viewers. More importantly, however, Mike and Abby are also aware they are being filmed and neither suggests they should continue what is clearly a private and intimate conversation off the air. Miles and Marylin of *Intolerable Cruelty* and Mike and Abby of *The Ugly Truth* add another characteristic to the battle of the sexes in the new millennium; love may conquer the differences of men and women by the end of the narrative but only if they are accompanied by money and professional success.

3 The 'new' career woman rom com

When Tess Harding (Katharine Hepburn), a prominent, upper-class feminist and 'serious' political journalist, is bestowed with the Outstanding Woman of the Year award, her husband of just a few weeks, middle-class sports journalist Sam Craig (Spencer Tracy), enraged by being more of a secretary and a helper than an equal partner inside a marriage exclaims: 'The outstanding woman of the year is no woman at all' before leaving Tess and her lavish Fifth Avenue apartment. This scene from the career woman comedy *Woman of the Year* (1942) exemplifies how the films of this cycle glorified and at the same time exorcised the working female, even during a social climate that witnessed 'more than 350,000 women [...] donning military uniforms and six million more who had taken jobs in defence plants and offices as part of the war effort' (Steven Jay Schneider, 2006, p. 84).

The history of the career woman film is so long that it cannot possibly be exhausted in a single chapter or even a whole book for that matter. However, before I proceed with how the millennial Hollywood rom com views the contemporary working girl, I believe it will be useful to briefly go back to those fictional heroines and the cinematic texts that showed the way and provided the narrative skeleton for the contemporary cycle. Even before Clara Bow starred in *It* in 1927, perfectly embodying the 1920s flapper, the ultimate independent working girl, American society had to deal with women earning a salary and not having to be entirely dependent on men. This fictional move away from the Victorian housewife feminine ideal was represented onscreen by 'flapper actresses such as Colleen Moore, Clara Bow, Louise Brooks, Virginia Lee Corbin, Madge Bellamy, and Joan Crawford', while the films centred on 'the flapper's pursuit of modern life – independent from parental and other authoritarian control – and a modern romance in which her defiant actions, unruly behavior, and daring dress are either obstacles or catalysts, or both'. (Lori Landay, 2002, p. 224).

The screwball comedy, which mainly focused on wealthy and/or spoilt heiresses, such as Ellie (Claudette Colbert) in *It Happened One Night* (1934), Irene (Carole Lombard) in *My Man Godfrey* (1936) and Tracy (Katharine Hepburn) in *The Philadelphia Story* (1940), had to give way to a new cycle, following America's entry into World War II in December 1941. World War

II led the Hollywood industry to invest 'in an enormous array of Hollywood's genres, from war films, spy films and musicals to Tarzan films, westerns and horror films' (Steve Neale, 2000, p. 211). According to Glitre (2006, p. 28), 'The innocence and irresponsibility so vital to the screwball comedy sensibility simply could not survive in this atmosphere of patriotic duty'. Thus, the romantic comedy genre responded to the new sociopolitical climate with the cycle of the career woman comedy, which 'was primarily concerned with the changing role of women in the public sphere' (Glitre, 2006, p. 29). Potter (2002, p. 44) notes that during 'the Second World War more women than ever before were required to prove their abilities in every conceivable kind of men's work: from farm labour to shipbuilding and "manning" the munitions factories'. Potter (ibid.) adds that there were also women in the army who despite their placement in offices had to spend months and/or years away from home and deal with the horrors of war on a daily basis. The impressive extent of female participation in the workforce was mirrored in the romantic comedy genre and films such as *Woman of the Year, They All Kissed the Bride* (1942), *Lady in the Dark* (1944), and *She Wouldn't Say Yes* (1945). However, despite the representation of the importance of female professional achievement, most 'films usually suggest that [the heroine's] success in this man's world comes at a cost: no social life and *No Time for Love* (1943)', as Glitre (2006, p. 30) perceptively observes. Leger Grindon (2011, p. 40) places the career woman comedy in what he calls *The World War II Cluster* (1942–46) and argues that this group of films 'came under increasing attack for jeopardizing [the heroines'] femininity and inhibiting romance' reinforcing gender discrimination contrary to what the screwball comedies attempted to subvert a few years earlier. Consequently, the overwhelming majority of career woman comedies warned 'women that pursuing a long-term professional career would jeopardize their love life', sending mixed messages to the great numbers of women that society was actually recruiting, remunerating and celebrating during the war.

Later cycles of the genre continued to include working girls: the sex comedies of the late 1950s and early 1960s (*Pillow Talk*, 1959, *The Thrill of It All*, 1963), the nervous romances of the 1970s (*The Owl and the Pussycat*, 1970, *Manhattan*, 1979), the new romances of the 1980s (*Broadcast News* and *Baby Boom*, 1987, *Working Girl*, 1988) and the rom coms of the 1990s (*Sleepless in Seattle*, 1993, *The Mirror Has Two Faces*, 1996) reflected the realities of the workforce that saw women increasing their numbers as professionals. Work was seen as a normal and creative facet of the heroine's character in the genre in contrast to films such as the erotic thriller *Fatal Attraction* (1987) and the female friendship thriller *Single White Female* (1992) which tried to pathologize the career woman and turn her into a monstrous figure (Garrett, 2007, p. 166). Functioning on a different narrative level and with different goals, the romantic comedy of the 1980s and 1990s explored the difficulties and obstacles faced by working, middle-class, white women, 'offering different perspectives and ideological discourses' (Deleyto, 2009, p. 42). Women in these narratives were shown as pressured to 'have it all' by a patriarchal society which 'may have grudgingly accepted their social and sexual equality but still expected them to continue doing what they were doing before' (ibid.). For instance, J.C. Wiatt (Dianne Keaton) in *Baby Boom*, a hard-core power Manhattan executive, 'is schooled on the virtues of maternal generosity, a lesson that arrives via the inheritance of an unexpected child', an upheaval which 'results in her eventual relocation to Vermont, the abandonment of a lucrative corporate career, and a rugged, masculine boyfriend' (Suzanne Leonard, 2009, pp. 80–1). Although J.C. manages by the end of the film to finance and become the owner of her own production line of baby food, enjoying simultaneously the joys of motherhood and coupledom, her fictional colleague Katherine Parker (Sigourney Weaver) is punished for her ruthlessness and is left unemployed and without a lover by the end of *Working Girl*. One could argue that Katherine stole an innovative business idea from her assistant, Tess (Melanie Griffith), and was rightfully fired and scorned by her boyfriend who discovered her fraud at the end. However, Jane Craig (Holly Hunter), a dedicated television producer, whose ethics cannot be questioned in *Broadcast News* follows Katherine's single existence during the end credits. In other words, it seems that the more powerful the woman is in these 1980s films, the less likely it is for her to achieve balance between her love life and the office. Noting this backlash in different genre films of the same period, Leonard (2009, p. 81) maintains that female achievement 'can best be resolved by denying the ambitious woman permission to continue as she is, either because she is forcibly recuperated into traditional patriarchal structures through shame or embarrassment or, conversely, because she is killed', as it happened in *Fatal Attraction* and *Presumed Innocent* (1990).

Despite the 'suspicion' and the more than often unfortunate fate that awaits the working woman in various Hollywood genres, the cycle of the career woman comedy still constitutes part of the new-millennium romantic comedy. Although most of the films in our corpus depict working heroines, the films of the cycle and this chapter focus on and organize their narratives around the female need for professional fulfilment and achievement and the romantic male object that 'gets in the way'. Films such as *The Wedding Planner* (2001), *Life or Something Like It*, *Two Weeks Notice* and *Sweet Home Alabama*, (all three, 2002), *View from the Top* (2003), *The Proposal*, *New in Town* and *My Life in Ruins* (all 2009) are 'dominated' by heroines who start their fictional journeys as confident, high-powered career women who prefer to achieve their professional goals than to search for Mr Right.

The representation of women at work is naturally mirroring one of the main characteristics of the contemporary woman and as Garrett notes, 'single working women are hardly a novelty' (2007, p. 104). Indeed, according to 2010 statistics, and 'for the first time in American history, the balance of the workforce tipped toward women, who now hold a majority of the nation's jobs' (Rosin, 2010).[1] Yet, despite the notable ratio of women in the workplace, Rosin emphasizes that it is still women who also predominantly take care of the home and children while the best jobs are still occupied by men. At the same time, the career woman rom coms respond to the social climate created after 9/11 which witnessed 'a return to hearth and home' (Diane Negra, 2008, p. 55), by either insisting on the values of the small town and/or the heterosexual couple.

Talking about the heroines of contemporary rom coms, Garrett argues that '[d]espite having a career and material aspirations, being able to support themselves financially and having supportive friends, there is a persistent sense of lack associated with their singleton status' (2007, p. 94). Garrett also points out that

> [w]hat has shifted is the social status and cultural fantasies concerning the newly identified figure of the 'singleton', rather than spinster or traditional maiden aunt. The fictional singleton is still haunted by the low status of the traditional spinster (hence the continuing preoccupation with pair-bonding) but the emergence of a generation of educated, independent women with far greater choices concerning relationships and marriage creates a tension between the old pressures and new pleasures and aspirations (2007, p. 104).

Similarly, Negra argues that '[i]n the contemporary chick flick, professional women are misguided at best and troubled at worst' (2008, p. 53). However, I contend that what these films try to convey is that professional ambition is a significant and empowering part of the millennial woman, and that the romantic relationship that completes the narrative cannot a priori be considered as a lack, a compromise or an innuendo of the female protagonist's eventual withdrawal from the rat race.

The 2000s started and ended with commercially successful rom coms where the heroines' work was the focus of the narrative and did not simply constitute a structural ingredient that could have been left out and/or not dealt with in depth. The decade began with *The Wedding Planner* in 2001 (which grossed around $95 million worldwide), continued with *Two Weeks Notice* (which almost returned $200 million), and *Sweet Home Alabama* (with more than $180 million) in 2002, *View from the Top* in 2003 ($19 million), and drew to a close with *The Proposal* (with more than $317 million), *New in Town* ($29 million) and *My Life in Ruins* ($20 million) in 2009.

New in Town and *The Proposal*

New in Town and *The Proposal* are the two focal points of the chapter – although references will be made to other films of the cycle – as I believe they are exemplary instances of the career woman cycle even though the first belongs to the top ten of the most commercial successes in the history of the genre, grossing over $317 million worldwide with a cost of $40 million while the second returned a little over $29 million worldwide with an estimated budget of $8 million.[2] What is interesting is that the two films which were both released in 2009 present so many narrative similarities that I could not help but wonder what made the first a huge success and the second go almost unnoticed despite having two superstars at the helm. Of course, the question of why some narratives appeal to film viewers and similar others do not does not have an easy answer and is a theoretical query that goes back more than two thousand years ago, that is when Aristotle first posed it in his *Poetics*.

One could hypothesize that Renée Zellweger's decision to portray a completely different character than what she used to could have played a major role in the film's quite indifferent reception by the audience. According to Susanne Kord and Elisabeth Krimmer (2005, p. 75), Zellweger's characters are more than often 'the exact opposite of the highly educated, impressively competent, and usually (over-) ambitious professional woman of many Hollywood films', and 'tend to be uneducated or undereducated and work in lowly positions, if at all'. Indeed, in *Jerry Maguire* and the two Bridget Jones films, Zellweger's characters were very sympathetic and adorable working girls but they lacked professional ambition and dynamic drive. Therefore, it is possible the audience could not identify with a ruthless, decisive and high-maintenance character from an actor they had associated with gentleness, passivity and sweetness whereas at the same time they rewarded Sandra Bullock for playing a different version of *Two Weeks Notice*'s Lucy Kelson, the clumsy yet high-powered and socially conscious lawyer in *The Proposal*.

In *New in Town*, Lucy Hill (Zellweger), a commanding executive in the food industry, has to move from Miami to a cold, small Minnesota town in order to oversee the restructuring of a small food plant while fighting with the union representative Ted Mitchell (Harry Connick, Jr.) and eventually warming up to the town, the workers, her quirky assistant Blanche (Siobhan Fallon Hogan) and, of course, Ted. In *The Proposal*, Margaret Tate (Bullock), a Canadian tough editor, faces deportation and decides to marry her assistant, Andrew Paxton (Ryan Reynolds). To do that, however, she has to spend some time in his small Alaskan hometown and meet his relatives before 'softening up' and falling in love.

Both films' credit sequences depict the heroines' morning ritual before they head to work. *New in Town*'s Lucy is jogging while *The Proposal*'s Margaret is exercising on a stationary bike while editing a manuscript at the same time. Their apartments are modern and comfortable and order appears to reign everywhere. Both women are then seen showering and dressed in tight suits and high heels before heading to work. Lucy is wearing a silver suit and red high heels, shoulder-length, sleek hairstyle while Margaret sports a total black look and a severe ponytail. However, this small colour discrepancy can be attributed to their environment. Lucy is working in Miami, a more colourful and 'sunnier' city than Manhattan, Margaret's workplace, which demands a more conservative business attire. Both sequences are accompanied by vibrant, energetic songs – Perk Badger's 'Do Your Stuff' and the Gabe Dixon Band's 'Find my Way' respectively – that function diegetically, intensifying both women's dynamism, vitality and power.

Lucy and Margaret don their 'costumes' at the beginning of the films in order to be able to brave the food and the publishing industries respectively. Like another type of superhero, these women would probably not dare show themselves in trainers or without having their hair done in the man-dominated world they have to tackle. It is worth noting that Lucy is the only female executive among four other male colleagues in the meeting she attends and Margaret has to answer to two male superior execs in her work. Their costumes are therefore necessary in that while they do not deny their femininity as both heroines wear tight skirts and jackets that accentuate their well-toned bodies, they are also quite severe in that they are not overtly sexual – the skirts are long, there are not any plunging necklines – and their light make-up and carefully styled hair suggest both women try not to command attention to anything but their professional skills. In other words, Lucy and Margaret's clothes are not just present as a part of Hollywood's effort to combine film and consumerism, but do indeed have a narrative function as they add to character information. In her study on costume in Hollywood, Jeffers McDonald notes that film costumes are today considered as narrative signs by both academia and film costume designers alike which either complement or contradict the totality of a film character (2010, p. 15).

Through the use of costume, acting and dialogue, both women are initially shown as high-powered, humourless and without scruples; When Lucy talks about the fate of a small Minnesota food plant, she agrees with a 50 per cent cut in personnel and has no problem with the families that will be left without a job. She is finally put in charge of the restructuring of the plant, and during her first dinner at her assistant's house in the cold town of New Ulm, she enters into a fight with Ted about positive female role models and then the economic situation of the United States. Their dialogue is revealing:

LUCY: Industrial competition in a free-market economy is what built this country.
TED: No, robber barons built this country, and they did it from the blood of working folks. Hell, you steal somebody's car, you get thrown in jail, you steal somebody's life savings, you get to be a CEO.
LUCY: I'm planning on being a CEO.

Lucy is not afraid of voicing her opinion and stating her desire in life is to reach the top of the corporate ladder. Her intense stichomythia with Ted is also a welcome gender reversal; no longer is the man placed in the position of the ambitious and restless career-oriented individual; here he is replaced by a softer, yet dynamic, person who moved to a much smaller town after his wife's untimely death, and tries to raise his teenage daughter and avoid the negative influences of big urban centres – even though he exaggerates – he does not allow his daughter to listen to pop star Fergie's music as he considers her 'sexy and provocative' and not a suitable role model. On the other hand, Lucy is depicted as a traditional alpha male, defending the US free economy ideology and disclosing that her desire is to reach the top of the corporate world. Susan M. Roberts (2004, pp. 136–7) distinguishes four ways in which neoliberalism frames women as objects: as 'individual market actors', who are free to consume as they please, as 'human capital', who can be educated and consequently 'productively participate in (formal) labor markets', as 'political subjects' with rights and responsibilities, and 'as important components of "social capital" as members and organizers of formalized civil society'. In other words, whereas Lucy's devotion to her career and her knowledge are empowering, her absolute views on free economy distinguish her as a neoliberal subject of human capital. Thus, she is negatively portrayed as she seems to advocate for an impersonal system which uses individuals as either objects or subjects without actually caring about the welfare of those people.

The Proposal offers an even more radical take on gender commentary. The first time Margaret enters the office, all the computers light up once an employee sends the message 'It's here' and everybody panics and starts looking busy as Margaret walks steadily and without even talking to anyone towards her office. The 'It' of the message underlines that Margaret is seen as a gender-less individual; she is rather considered by her subordinates as a robotic version of a person who as her personal assistant, Andrew, later cynically notes is allergic to '[p]ine nuts, and the full spectrum of human emotion'.

As is typical of the reaction the genre receives, Lucy and Margaret are not applauded for their perseverance, hard work and education, factors that must have gotten them to their positions. Instead, Lucy is dismissed as 'a shark in spike' (Stephen Holden, 2009) and Margaret is described as 'a Type A (rhymes with) witch' (Manohla Dargis, 2009). Although *Wall Street*'s (1987) venomous Gordon Gekko (Michael Douglas) was also characterized as a 'predator, a corporate raider', and 'a Wall Street shark' (Rogert Ebert, 1987), it seems that no leniency can be attributed to equally authoritative female professionals even in a 'benign' fictional narrative such as that of the rom com or maybe because of that since '[i]f a film threatens to be mildly interesting in cinematic or ideological terms then it cannot possibly be a romantic comedy' (Deleyto, 2009, p. 3). Writing about powerful female literary figures, Harriet Hawkins concluded that 'the more successful and brilliant and ambitious and glamorous and famous [a woman] is in her own right, and the more she enjoys her success, the more she must be morally anathematised as a *femme fatale*, a vampire, an unnatural monster, a superbitch' (1990, p. 55). Therefore, Lucy and Margaret's lack of sensitivity, softness and humour and their dedication, drive and decisiveness to doing their best on the career front, traits that men in business are by definition congratulated upon, are characteristics that make these two fictional characters be considered neurotic, misguided and 'miswanting', that is, wanting the wrong things in life.

In the level of story in its formalist sense, Lucy and Margaret's trajectories are identical. Lucy has to move from Miami to a little town in Minnesota and through a long process resolve a work problem while she finds the man of her dreams, whom she initially detests. Similarly, Margaret goes from New York to a small town in Alaska in her attempt to solve her immigration issue while she also falls in love with a man she would never consider a likely candidate. Both romantic narratives present the inverted scenario of many film noirs and westerns of the past where a man is transformed in the hands of a woman. Deleyto astutely observes in his claim that *Rio Bravo* (1959) is both a western and a romantic comedy that 'Chance's [John Wayne] evolution as a character […] will happen through a process of apparent male humiliation at the hands of the woman' (Deleyto, 2009, p. 15). However, despite *Rio Bravo*'s celebration as one of the most important westerns in the history of the genre, its hero's transformation through a female touch is viewed positively as it suggests Chance's entrance into the civilized world. On the other hand, Lucy and Margaret's 'inverted' transformation in *New in Town* and *The Proposal* is condemned as traditional manipulation, compromise and eventual female disempowerment.

In writing about rom coms that depict working girls,[3] such as the British productions *Bridget Jones's Diary* (2001) and *Bridget Jones: The Edge of Reason* (2004), or the US productions *Sweet Home Alabama* (2002), *How to Lose a Guy in 10 Days* (2003), and *13 Going on 30*, (2004), among others, Deborah Barker (2008, p. 113) believes that

> work is the impediment to successful romance because the inappropriate man is a co-worker/boss, and/or because the demands of work preclude a social life. But, more important, work threatens to turn women into the vicious caricature of the 1980s evil career woman.

Barker adds that '[t]ypically, the heroine must give up her successful job […] and choose the simple life in order to find love', and that these representations entail the risk of becoming caricatures of the evil career woman of the 1980s (ibid.). However, in none of the films Barker refers to does the heroine lose her job in order to create the perfect nuclear family. Bridget Jones, for instance, quits and finds a better job in the first film while she gets a promotion in the second, and Kate Hudson in *How to Lose a Guy in 10 Days* also quits from *Composure*, a women's magazine in the tradition of *Cosmopolitan* and *Elle* to pursue a more 'serious' journalistic career. Finally, in the focal films of this chapter, Lucy in *New in Town* becomes the manager of the plant in Minnesota and *The Proposal*'s Margaret does not lose her job as she is really getting married to Andrew and consequently getting the green card she needs to continue working in the United States.

In the same vein as Barker, Negra (2009, p. 19) observes that quite a few romantic narratives in the early 2000s 'conjoin self-discovery with the rejection of the city'. In the new career woman cycle, this does constitute one of the preferred resolutions. Thus, Melanie (Reese Witherspoon) returns home to her ex-husband in *Sweet Home Alabama*, abandoning her promising career in

New York; Donna (Gwyneth Paltrow) in *View from the Top* (2003) resigns from being an international flight attendant and settles in Cleveland but having been promoted to a pilot; and Professor Georgia (Nia Vardalos) in *My Life in Ruins* decides to stay in Greece as a tour guide with Prokopis (Alexis Georgoulis) and rejects an offer for a teaching position from the University of Michigan. However, none of these women actually lose their job. Only Kate (Meg Ryan) in *Kate & Leopold* actually leaves not only her job but the twentieth century to live with Leopold (Hugh Jackman) in the late nineteenth century, but this film belongs to the fantasy cycle as its dominant feature is time travel. On the other hand, there is no relocation and/or job abandonment in *The Wedding Planner, Two Weeks Notice*, or *The Proposal*. Negra adds that these films 'routinely depict urban professional women whose crises of identity are linked to a dawning realization that they cannot truly be at home in an urban milieu' (2009, p. 19). However, she only discusses the film *Win a Date with Tad Hamilton* (2004) as an example 'of the kind of equation made in recent popular culture between idealized femininity and the hometown films' while her link of the female 'crises of identity to a dawning realization that [the heroines] cannot truly be home in an urban milieu' does not apply to all the new-millennium career woman rom coms (ibid.). Both Barker and Negra place the romantic comedies of the early 2000s in a postfeminist context which as Negra argues 'informs and is informed by a cultural climate strongly marked by the political empowerment of fundamentalist Christianity and regnant paradigms of commercialized family values' (2009, p. 6).

However, both *New in Town* and *The Proposal* do not ask their female protagonists to give up their jobs and/or start giving birth to a number of kids in the suburbs. Rather, the two narratives suggest there is a space for the couple to coexist without having to compromise their work. On the other, a closer inspection of the films shows how the two heroines overcome significant obstacles at work and may serve as positive role models for the viewer. When Lucy first arrives in the small town of New Ulm, she is greeted with suspicion and even hostility by Stu Kopenhafer (J. K. Simmons), the hard-working, yet whimsical and honest foreman, and the mostly male workers. Nevertheless, she does not give up and even despite being made a fool by the small community on a couple of occasions, she does not shy away from confrontation and shows she cannot be intimidated by anyone. When the nearby lake freezes up, she drives on it to confront the foreman who called a strike. When the Miami office informs her that they decided to close everything up, Lucy does not abandon the people she has come to know and like and comes up with a brand new product and only four weeks to produce it and present it to the board members. She decides to produce and market Blanche's tapioca, in a montage which reminds the 'older' viewer of J. C. Wiatt's (Dianne Keaton) idea to produce applesauce in *Baby Boom* when she finds herself alone in an old Vermont house.

Lucy does save the day and gets the promotion she wanted. When faced with the dilemma between her personal life and her job, the latter takes precedence and Lucy goes back to Miami. This decision may constitute the last 'obligatory' narrative obstacle before the heterosexual couple's final reunion but it is significant in that it shows that a woman may find fulfilment in her professional arena and may not always choose the dream guy over her dream job. It is true that one cannot be sure whether Lucy would have stayed had Ted asked her to, but even his resistance and perhaps fear and insecurity to commit to a dynamic woman, especially after his wife's untimely death, show the softer masculine side of this cycle's male protagonists. A parallel montage show both Lucy and Ted going about their everyday life, a little sadder and more thoughtful. No one, however, initiates a reunion. What is going to save their relationship is none other than Lucy's work. When the Miami branch decides once again to close the now successful Minnesota plant and move it somewhere else, Lucy steps up. She once again flies back to New Ulm and proposes a group of investors initially buy the plant and help until it is 'entirely owner-operated', on the condition she can return as the CEO. No female compromise closes the narrative as Lucy still retains the top job, but this time she also gets to go back home to a man and a teenage girl. At the same time, Margaret in *The Proposal* refuses to compromise and does not go through with the fake wedding she needs to hold on to her job. She leaves the Alaskan town of Sitka and decides to return to Canada as after having met and grown to like Andrew's family, not to mention her romantic feelings for her assistant, she does not feel she can be dishonest towards them and herself.

The Woman of the Year ends with Hepburn trying to make breakfast and ending by making a fool of herself and a mess of the kitchen, in an effort to reconcile with her estranged husband. Jeanine Basinger notes that '[a]s Hepburn destroys the kitchen, Tracy shows us how to see her incompetence, and then he rescues her' (1993, p. 200). This scene has been interpreted as epitomizing the core of the career woman cycle: 'the high flying independent woman brought finally and comically to ground by the solid, complacent, implacable man' (James Harvey, 1998 p. 409). However, the film ends with Tracy asking Hepburn: 'I don't want you to be Tess Harding any more than I want you to be Mrs. Sam Craig. Why can't you be Tess Harding-Craig?' In other, words, even as far back as 1942, there were men who believed that a marriage should be a more or less equal partnership and not a master–slave patriarchal structure.

The millennial male partners of Lucy and Margaret present an evolved male side. Both Ted and Andrew are depicted as understanding, kinder and more socially sensitive than their female counterparts. Ted is the union representative, trying to fight for the rights of the workers and at the same time a widower and a single father who tries his best to raise a teenage daughter. His decision to settle in a small town and his aversion towards sexually charged pop culture female icons is perhaps a response to a general post-9/11 tendency to return to a simpler time, a simpler place and avoid urban settings. On the other hand, Andrew's on-going fight with his father who wants him to quit his job and run the family empire and his firm decision to stay in the job that 'makes him happy' is simultaneously an act of assertiveness and a rejection of the 'law of the father', and by consequence every kind of authority. Individual choice is therefore what is celebrated in both *New in Town* and *The Proposal* as all four protagonists choose their job and their partner without having to compromise.

It can therefore be argued that the 'new' career woman cycle reflects and celebrates the social climate of neoliberalism characterized by 'a current of individualism that has almost entirely replaced notions of the social or political, or any idea of individuals as subject to pressures, constraints or influence from outside themselves' (Gill and Scharff, 2011, p. 7). The subtext of neoliberalism through individualism is also reinforced by the absence of either male or female sidekicks, at least in the majority of the films in this cycle, and is particularly more apparent in the films which were released towards the end of the decade. Deleyto has already underlined that during the last decades of the genre's evolution, 'heterosexual love appears to be challenged, and occasionally replaced, by friendship' (2003, p. 168). However, this cycle uses the job itself as the narrative stratagem which threatens the heterosexual union and depends on secondary characters for the necessary comic relief, such as Blanche and Stu in *New in Town* or Andrew's irreverent grandma (Betty White) in *The Proposal*. Of course, laughter also comes from the protagonists and mainly the female stars as they both excel at physical comedy. Zellweger falls off her porch in a drunken attempt to seduce Ted after being trapped in the snow while Bullock is at her funniest when she runs after an eagle that grabbed Andrew's granny's beloved poodle and loses her 'beloved' cell phone in the process. Both women are known for being funny and versatile and most importantly not afraid to tamper with their otherwise impeccable public image. Zellweger put on a lot of weight to portray the hilarious Bridget Jones and Bullock was the tomboy in the beginning of *Miss Congeniality* (2000). The two thespians follow the tradition of those beautiful and glamorous screwball actresses such as Carole Lombard, Claudette Colbert and Katharine Hepburn whose timing, physical comedy and presence could at times become more important than the story itself, and it is unfortunate there are only a few books and/or articles in the field of film theory that study the impact particular performances by particular female stars have had on this particular genre.

Although the career woman cycle is not the dominant paradigm of the genre in the new millennium, mainly because working girls cannot be considered an originality any more, it follows a tradition that has lasted for more than 70 years. *The Proposal*'s director Anne Fletcher has stated in an online interview that she was inspired by the screwball tradition in bringing these characters to life. Mixing screwball elements, quick dialogue and physical comedy, these narratives show that women can combine their demanding careers while sharing their lives with a companion. Although Kord and Krimmer noted in 2005 that '[t]here are almost no romantic comedies in which women struggle to combine family and career', (11) the 2011 production *I Don't Know How She Does It*, a romantic comedy centred on the life of a finance executive who tries to find a balance among her work, her husband and her two kids, proves the cycle can still evolve in interesting ways that could both enlighten and entertain.

4 The fantasy rom com

Fantasy is a genre with a very long history which has produced a great number of celebrated literary works, such as J. R. R. Tolkien's *The Hobbit* (1937), *The Lord of the Rings* (1954–55) and more recently J. K. Rowling's Harry Potter book series. However, the delineation of the literary genre has been proven a difficult task. Summarizing the most significant definitions of the past thirty years, Joshua David Bellin (2005, p. 14) notes:

> Rosemary Jackson sees fantasy as that which subverts the status quo; Eric Rabkin understands fantasy as that which violates its own internal rules; Tzvetan Todorov views fantasy as that which engenders a momentary hesitation concerning whether an inexplicable event is real or not; Brian Attebery regards fantasy as that which contravenes what the author considers natural law (*Fantasy Tradition*); and Kathryn Hume, in the most expansive of modern definitions, conceives of fantasy as any departure from consensus reality.

The similarities and simultaneous deviations of these theoretical approaches confirm the inherent complexities scholars face when in the presence of a significant body of work that may share common structural elements but can be also differentiated according to time of production, style and theme(s). These theoretical speculations can be further exacerbated when the question turns to fantasy film, which must be separated from horror and science fiction. For instance, James Walters (2011, p. 3) notes that its definition is challenging 'as fantasy is an especially broad genre'. Moreover, fantasy films are not considered as important as other generic categories such as the film noir, the melodrama, etc. because '[a]s a rule, fantasy tends to favor happy endings, and eschews not only tragedy, but cynicism, providing solace and redemption in a world of evil and violence' (Katherine A. Fowkes, 2010, p. 6). Although Fowkes remarks that 'J. R. R. Tolkien characterized fantasy as a literature of *hope*, a sentiment echoed by numerous fantasy scholars, and widely celebrated by fans of the genre', it is exactly the genre's 'emphasis on hope, happy endings, and a rejection of cynicism' which 'has only encouraged scholars and critics to ignore or vilify fantasy' (ibid.), just as they do with the romantic comedy genre, which also focuses on the 'brighter' side of life.

The combination of fantasy and romantic comedy dates back to the late 1930s and *Topper*, a 1937 screwball romance whose protagonist couple, the Kerbys (Constance Bennett and Cary Grant), die in a car accident, become ghosts and decide to have fun with their situation. Billy Mernit (2000, p. 27) classifies these 'fantastic' romantic comedies under the heading 'supernatural/fantasy' and further divides them into three smaller groups: films that include ghosts, such as *Topper* and *Dona Flor and Her Two Husbands* (1947), films that he labels 'More than Human', such as *I Married a Witch* (1942) and *Splash* (1984), and films that deal with the afterlife, such as *Heaven Can Wait* (1978) and *Defending Your Life* (1991).

Mernit (ibid. pp. 27–8) claims that this cycle

> is rich in imaginative conceits: girl meets ghost (*The Ghost and Mrs. Muir*), boy meets mermaid (*Splash*), girl meets reincarnation (*Chances Are*). Whereas conflicts revolve around issues typical of the genre norm, climaxes often involve an obligatory 'recognition' scene (e.g., the revelation that his date *is* a mermaid provokes *Splash*'s penultimate crisis). Where the ghostly and unhuman sub-cross-genres are typified by scenes of spooky trickery (how did she/he do *that?*), the afterlife romantic comedy, or populist fantasy, tends to dig a little deeper, generally employing love-is-stronger-than-death themes that lend poignancy to the wildest conceptual contrivances (e.g., *Heaven*).

Mernit also underlines that these cross-genre romances are very popular and the Hollywood output of fantasy romantic comedies in the first decade of the new millennium proves him right: from *Down to Earth* (2001), a remake of the 1978 classic *Heaven Can Wait*, the time-travel *Kate & Leopold*, *13 Going on 30* and *17 Again* (2009), to the ghost rom coms *Just Like Heaven* (2005), *Over Her Dead Body*, *Ghost Town* (2008), and *Ghosts of Girlfriends Past*, the 'magical' fairy tales *Ella Enchanted* (2004), *Enchanted*, and *Bewitched* (2005), the cinematic adaptation of America's favourite television witch, *My Super Ex-Girlfriend* (2006), the comical side of the superhero genre that flourished in the 2000s, to *Just My Luck*, 2006, and *When in Rome*, 2010, two films whose plots revolve around wishes that magically come true and complicate the heroines' lives, fantasy rom coms seem to be among the audience's and the industry's list of priorities.

However, the mating of two genres, both of which are more often than not undervalued and/or even dismissed as pure escapism, poses an additional problem for an examination of the sociopolitical dimensions of this cycle. Bellin (2005, p. 4) rightly observes that although studies on genres related to fantasy, such as science fiction films, have demonstrated the genre's intrinsic association with its cultural context:

> [C]onsiderable resistance remains to historicizing films that appear to elude or resist the sci-fi label, films such as *The Wizard of Oz*, the 'fairy-tale'

fantasia of Tim Burton's *Edward Scissorhands* (1990), or Peter Jackson's screen adaptation of J. R. R. Tolkien's epic swords-and-sorcery trilogy, *The Lord of the Rings* (2001–3).

Indeed, just as Deleyto argues that if one is to evaluate a romantic comedy based on its boy-meets-girl, boy-loses-girl, boy-gets-girl in an affluent urban environment formula, he/she will inevitably snub the genre as conservative and conventional, Bellin (2005, p. 5) similarly notes that 'if one accepts the common-sense definition of *fantasy* as that which "could never have been, cannot be, and can never be within the actual, social, cultural, and intellectual milieu of its creation" (Schlobin in Bellin, 2005, p. 5)', then it follows that the genre is of no interest to a serious examination of its sociopolitical connotations, comments, and/or subversions of the status quo. However, such an approach does 'a disservice not only to the films but to the culture that bred them and the audiences that view them' (ibid.). Bellin (2005, p. 9), therefore, proposes another approach and argues that

> fantasy films *frame* social reality: they provoke a perspective, provide a context, produce a way of seeing. As such, if these films function as mass-cultural rituals that give image to historically determinate anxieties, wishes, and needs, they simultaneously function by stimulating, endorsing, and broadcasting the very anxieties, wishes, and needs to which they give image.

It is therefore from this perspective that this chapter will investigate the fantasy romantic comedies in order to discern the sociopolitical tensions that can be revealed under the guise of the magical element that fantasy carries and its combination with a light-hearted romance. The films that will be explored in this chapter are *Enchanted* and *Ghost Town*. The first is among the most profitable romantic comedies of all times and combines animation and the Disney fairy-tale legacy, and the second is an interesting take on the ghost plot which draws elements from the screwball comedies of the 1930s and 1940s. *Enchanted* is a female-centred fantasy rom com while *Ghost Town* is a man-centred romance. This gender difference constitutes the main criterion based on which the filmic texts were chosen since it is interesting to explore how the fantastic, however dissimilar, elements in the two narratives represent femininities and masculinities.

Enchanted

Released in 2007, *Enchanted* is not only a hybrid rom com which returned more than $340 million worldwide but also one of the few millennial romantic comedies that were favourably received by the press. Dargis (2007) and Todd McCarthy (2007) praise Amy Adams's performance, Disney's revisionist interpretation of its fairy-tale tradition, the production values and especially the Central Park musical extravaganza, while Ebert (2007) notes that the film 'is a heart-winning musical comedy that skips lightly and sprightly from the lily pads of hope to the manhole covers of actuality'.

Enchanted combines animation and live action to tell a love story. The first ten-minute sequence is animated and the film begins by paying homage to many animated Disney classics, such as *Snow White and the Seven Dwarfs* (1937), *Pinocchio* (1940), *Cinderella* (1950), *Sleeping Beauty* (1959); a fairy-tale book with the title of the film engraved on the cover opens and an omniscient narrator provides the audience with the necessary information about the place and the main characters. Thus, film viewers are transported to the land of Andalasia where Queen Narissa (Susan Sarandon) dreads losing her throne to the maiden that her stepson, Prince Edward (James Marsden), would decide to marry. So obsessed with power is the queen that she has ordered a servant, Nathaniel (Timothy Spall), to be with the prince at all times to distract him from finding a wife. The audience is then introduced to Giselle (Amy Adams), a beautiful maiden, who along with her friends of the animal kingdom, is singing about finding her 'True Love's Kiss', longing to meet her Prince Charming like so many Disney fairy-tale heroines before her. Giselle's beautiful voice interrupts the prince's favourite pastime – capturing trolls – and despite his servant's pleas not to pay attention to something so frivolous, Edward orders his white horse, appropriately named Destiny, to take him to where the voice is coming from. However, Nathaniel frees the troll, who is also bewildered by the voice and reaches Giselle's dwelling first. A fight ensues and naturally Giselle is saved by Edward when she falls from a tree right into his arms. The prince tells Giselle they will marry the next day but he plans his wedding without considering the queen's evil plans. Indeed, when Giselle arrives in the castle, 'all dressed in white,' Narissa, transformed into an old crone, deceives the bride into following her and banishes her to another land far, far away or as she ironically puts it: 'To a place where there are no happily ever afters', present-day New York.

This first sequence sets the first themes of the narrative: the innocence of love, the pursuit of the 'one', and the issue of power. Giselle is an innocent young woman waiting to get married to her true love while Narissa is the older woman in control, who will do anything but relinquish the power she possesses. The fact that both these characters are women means that Narissa is not only 'evil' but is also guilty of betrayal of sisterhood. Writing about films where women exploit other women, such as *Working Girl* (1988) and *Dangerous Liaisons* (1989), Palmer (1993, p. 298) underlines that 'sexploitation is an exercise of power, but irony accrues when one woman is exerting exploitative power over other women', and that '[w]omen should not use other women as objects in their power games'. This power play constitutes *Enchanted*'s driving narrative element as it is Narissa's antagonism against the younger and innocent Giselle that leads to the New York adventure that will ensue.

Despite the queen's fixation with the throne, one could argue that her actions may also stem from the fact Giselle represents her lost youth. In his insightful study of the Disney tradition, Douglas Brode (2005, p. 172) links Snow White's appearance with the Evil Queen's looks and notes that the Queen's make-up, especially the 'eyebrows arched high—resembles the two reigning European imports who dominated 1930s screens, Greta Garbo and Marlene Dietrich. Such stars caused a revolution in fashion, owing to their harsh—indeed, "ludicrously" so—glamour, which became a "standard."' On the other hand, 'Snow White – in her total lack of self-consciousness about appearance – recalls the period's most popular American star, Shirley Temple' (ibid. p. 173). Brode (ibid. p. 174) argues that with the use of this precise iconography, Disney promoted the ideal of inner beauty and also underlined the Queen's narcissism. *Enchanted* continues Disney's legacy; the Queen's make-up is as dark and sinister as Snow White's wicked stepmom and Giselle is presented as a naturally beautiful young woman as unaware of the importance of external appearance as her cinematic predecessors. If one were to 'translate' this fairy-tale rivalry between the two female subjects, it could be assumed that Narissa symbolizes the rigid capitalistic system which does not like change and wishes for its perpetual existence and accumulation of money and material possessions while Giselle epitomizes the everyday person who must stand against the system and through his/her ingenuity and resourcefulness manage to realize his/her goal and dreams, despite the system's constant obstacles. This David and Goliath battle may seem uneven but *Enchanted* proceeds by providing an alternative scenario when the action is carried on in New York.

First, Giselle's transformation into a human and her transportation into a foreign place do not take away her personality traits. As soon as she removes a sewer lid, she emerges in the middle of Times Square at night. Looking amazed and confused by all the lights and the crowds, she is almost hit by passing cars and shouted at by angry drivers. Never having experienced such behaviour in the utopian Andalasia, Giselle is drawn away by the crowds into the subway only to come back up on the surface on the Bowery. On an empty and dark street, she spots a homeless person, whom she approaches happily as she thinks that an old man would certainly help her find her way back. Little does she expect that the man would steal her tiara and run away or that the rain will start pouring down, leaving her wet and distraught. Giselle bears almost no resemblance to the usual romantic heroines of the genre. She is not a career woman (*Rumor Has It*, 2005, *The Holiday*, 2006), a 20-something woman finishing her studies or starting work (*Loser*, 2000, *Going the Distance*) or even an ugly duckling in need of a makeover (*America's Sweethearts*, 2001, *My Big Fat Greek Wedding*). Her human persona retains all the attributes her magical origins have endowed her with (innocence, truthfulness, optimism and sweetness) and thus she is initially presented as the medieval damsel in distress in need of a male saviour.

Indeed, Giselle is soon saved by Robert (Patrick Dempsey), a divorce lawyer and a single dad of a six-year-old daughter, Morgan (Rachel Covey), who is about to propose to his girlfriend, Nancy (Idina Menzel). Robert represents a responsible, mature individual who does not believe in a 'lovey-dovey version' of love, which Giselle speaks of but in rational relationships where the two individuals 'understand [their] strengths and weaknesses'. Robert also tries to impart his mentality to his daughter, and as they drive home he gives Morgan a book as a present. The little girl is not very happy with the book and becomes even more disappointed as she sees that it is not a fairy tale but a book entitled *Important Women of Our Time*. Robert tries to interest her in Rosa Parks and Madame Curie but he soon understands that Morgan would rather have gotten a toy or a doll. However, he does say that Nancy is 'a lot like the women' in the book and reveals to Morgan that he is going to ask her to marry him. While Morgan is mostly worried about whether or not Nancy will take her room in the apartment, Giselle has found a billboard that looks like the entrance of a palace and climbs up to ask for help. Morgan sees her and the moment the taxi stops at a traffic light, she opens the door to approach her. Robert, scared for his daughter, also runs after her and he ends up saving Giselle who falls from the roof she had climbed. Giselle falls in Robert's arms the same way she fell in Edward's in the first animated sequence of the film. However, this 'live' rescue is not followed by a marriage proposal.

Although in Giselle's world, a maiden in a wedding gown would not constitute a strange sight, in contemporary New York, she is viewed as a rather curious spectacle or even a dangerous person. That is why, although Robert allows Giselle to make a phone call from his apartment, he denies his daughter's request to let the 'princess' spend the night, until the exhausted Giselle falls asleep on his couch, and Robert decides to let her be after he asks Morgan to sleep in his room. Although Robert considers his guest 'a seriously confused woman', after she tells him her story about Edward and the 'true love's kiss' she awaits, he cannot but feel engaged in her adventure and her unique way of talking, behaving and viewing things. Her innocence, inexperience and naiveté are enchanting, especially to little Morgan, who is utterly fascinated by her fairy-tale qualities and seems quite indifferent to her father's girlfriend, who is representative of the modern, strong, independent and career-oriented New York woman.

Negra (2009, p. 14) explains Morgan's fascination with Giselle by claiming that she is not only a princess, an adorable figure promoted by the media – and the toy industry – as 'an alternative to the troubled terms of "real world" female achievement', but also more of a girl on the verge of womanhood than an adult female who is in charge of her life. Giselle may be a young Andalasian woman who will become a princess once she marries Prince Edward, but she can be considered a privileged individual in that she has no financial worries or professional preoccupations in her animated world. Negra (ibid. 48–9) remarks that this fixation 'on privileged young women and girls is in keeping with these temporal and consumerist habits' and cites Princess Diana's celebrity, the 'plethora of princess-related marketing directed to young girls to the celebrity of super-rich young women promoted as stars in a culture of fully destigmatized nepotism', a number of films, such as *The Princess Diaries* narratives (2001, 2004), *What A Girl Wants* (2003), *The Prince & Me* (2004), and reality TV series such as *Rich Girls* (MTV, 2003) and *The Simple Life* (Fox, 2003–7) to demonstrate 'an efflorescence of popular culture material glorifying feminine exemplars of inherited wealth and (spending)'. Negra (ibid. p. 49) is critical of 'the princesshood phenomenon' which she views as 'another way of reinforcing the centrality and value of youth to femininity' and as a means of customizing 'aristocratic fantasies for an America in which (particularly when combined with wealth) the precise combination of youthfulness, beauty, and style approaches the function royalty possesses elsewhere as valued social capital'.

Indeed, *Enchanted* supports the princesshood fantasy by having Giselle seduce everyone she meets with her enchanting qualities, her girlish approach and her persistence to the ideal of the love that conquers all. As such, the filmic text promotes the model Negra considers post-feminism's effort to manipulate women into following the neoliberal demands of continuous consumerism. However, *Enchanted* also presents the negative side of princesshood in the form of Narissa, whose attempts to vanquish Giselle do not stop after the latter's presence in New York. Once Prince Edward arrives in the city to locate Giselle, so does his servant, Nathaniel, who is secretly working for the queen. Narissa is exploiting Nathaniel's affection for her and has hinted the two could come together once Giselle is dead. Therefore, while Edward is trying to find his future bride, Nathaniel is trying to poison her and win Narissa's love. As was already argued, Narissa embodies the perfect neoliberal subject, an accomplished and wealthy individual who will stop at nothing in order to maintain his/her position. However, Narissa was most probably also once a princess before she became queen and thus can serve as a cautionary tale to the whole princesshood fantasy that is simultaneously endorsed in the same narrative.

Thus, *Enchanted* presents the following paradox: while it supports the innocence and kindness of a privileged young woman, it hints at the dangers that lurk once this individual reaches maturity and has probably accumulated power – the possibility of her becoming a greedy, cruel person in a vain attempt to defeat time and/or preserve what she has gathered through the years. *Enchanted* celebrates youth, advantage and kindness; yet it does so from a privileged vantage point in that all the protagonists, both in the real world and Andalasia, are wealthy. When, for instance, Giselle has to go to a ball and realizes she has nothing to wear, Morgan gives her one of her dad's credit cards – which she is to use only in case of emergency – and the two 'girls' are seen coming in and out of some of New York's finest and most expensive boutiques. This brief montage comes to an end with a traveling shot that shows almost two dozen shopping bags before the camera stops at Giselle and Morgan sitting at a hairdresser's salon, underlining that while Giselle may have been able to do her own hair and make her own dresses up to that point – even if that meant the destruction of Robert's apartment curtains – a shopping spree is the only way for her to get appropriately ready for the climax that follows. More importantly, the narrative goes as far as to suggest that consumerism is also a form of bonding between a mother and a daughter. Once at the salon, Morgan asks Giselle if that's what it's like going shopping with your mother, implying that the time they spent shopping was something enjoyable and an activity she misses doing with her mother, who the audience learnt in an earlier scene abandoned her husband and daughter. However, this mother–daughter bonding time is linked to materialism and purchase power since shopping cannot be realized without money, something that neither Giselle nor Morgan seem to understand either in terms of what it means or how it is earned.

It becomes clear that *Enchanted* glorifies the ideal of youthfulness, naiveté, chastity and love, but only in the context of a 'healthy' consumerism and a limitless cash flow. The ball sequence is exemplary of the upper-class diversions as it features a great number of affluent guests dressed in period costumes and dancing in an impressive ballroom in the Empire State Building, a New York symbol and by extension a landmark of the American capitalist entrepreneurial spirit. Robert is dancing with Nancy, and Giselle makes her appearance dressed for the first time in a contemporary gown that makes her stand apart from all the other women who are wearing costumes from another era. Giselle's metamorphosis into a city girl is not only signaled by her external appearance but by her reluctance to go back to Andalasia with Edward, her unexplained feelings for Robert and her attraction to what New York has offered her.

However, just before Edward and Giselle are about to leave, Narissa appears in the form of the old hag and offers the young woman an apple which would erase her feelings for Robert. Giselle falls to the floor unconscious, Narissa assumes the form of the queen and her wicked ways are revealed by the betrayed Nathaniel. The climax sees Narissa turn into an enormous dragon and escaping to the top of the Empire State holding Robert hostage. In a reversed damsel-in-distress scenario, Giselle, who was awakened by Robert's 'true love's kiss', and not Edward's, saves her 'Prince' and the dragon/Narissa falls off the building and dies. Robert and Giselle kiss, but the wedding that ensues is not theirs but Edward and Nancy's in Andalasia. The brief animated sequence further critiques the contemporary and dynamic female with the complete invalidation of Nancy's character and her reduction to a literally two-dimensional caricature.

First, Nancy flees to Andalasia without even exchanging but a few phrases with Edward, a gesture which implies that Nancy has always been a romantic soul who was in search of the 'one,' but had to settle with what Robert had to offer. Second, when Edward and Nancy's first kiss as a married couple is interrupted by the sound of an incoming call, Nancy takes out her cell phone, a symbol of her past life, her career, her family and friends, and smashes it without a second thought, proving that nothing can compare to a white wedding dress. The last two scenes transport us back to New York where Giselle has started her own business – 'Andalasia fashions' – and is seen with

Robert, Morgan and a group of little girls in princess-like dresses while the final shot shows the three of them dancing and playing around Robert's apartment. Despite the film's charms, which include Adams's delightful performance, a solid supporting cast, remarkable cinematography and Disney's classic and captivating animation, *Enchanted*'s happily ever after spreads the message that as long as a woman behaves more like a girl and has spending power, then she will definitely meet a wealthy, handsome man, who will sweep her off her feet and make her the queen of his heart. At the same time, the film condemns maturity as a synonym of vindictiveness, evil and manipulation, and thus annuls the possibility of re-inventing the fairy-tale formula by perhaps introducing a new kind of villain who is not necessarily the evil queen. Despite its traditional message, the film's impressive commercial success proves the power of neoliberalism to disguise into easily assimilated forms of popular discourse and diffuse its message by superficially benign narratives. *Enchanted*'s escapist element, combined with the likeability of its protagonist, Amy Adams, the elaborate settings, costumes and the inclusion of the mostly endearing Disney animated sequences provide a smokescreen which can deter the audience from acknowledging the messages hidden underneath the superficially pleasant and joyful veneer, perpetuating an unjust and even perilous political status quo regarding gender relations as well as the place of both female and male individuals in the public sphere.

Ghost Town

Like *Enchanted*, *Ghost Town* is set in New York City. However, this New York is not filled with runaway princesses, princes and their servants or evil queens, nor is it bathed in glorious spring sunlight. Instead, it is New York during the last days of fall, a city inhabited by myriads of ghosts who wonder through the streets trying to find that special person who will help them finish what they were not able to do when they were alive and finally pass over. Even though this kind of paranormal activity is not exactly the traditional context of a romantic comedy, *Ghost Town* draws elements from a number of earlier Hollywood productions that deal 'with the afterlife, including *Topper*, *The Canterville Ghost* (1943), and *The Ghost and Mrs. Muir* (1947)' (Fowkes, 1998, p. 18), to tell the story of how an Englishman learns how to interact with people anew and fall in love. Lee Kovacs (2006, pp. 1–2) argues that the 'small cluster of romantic ghost stories' Hollywood released in the late 1930s and 1940s, offer a 'different and compelling view of society', and 'that the ghost story is not merely a window into the beyond, but actually a reflection of human nature, a pathway into the mind'. Despite the success of these films, ghost stories did not make a comeback until 1978 and the release of *Heaven Can Wait*. Fowkes (2010, p. 25) adds that

> The trend in supernatural stories of a dramatic or comedic bent would return to haunt US cinema in the 1980s and 1990s with films like *All of*

Me (1984) and the sleeper hit *Ghost* (1990). A handful of these were remakes, including *The Preacher's Wife* (1996), a remake of *The Bishop's Wife* (1947), and *City of Angels* (1998), a remake of German filmmaker Wim Wenders' *Wings of Desire* (1987). [...] Many of these later films employed ghosts and angels as vehicles for dramatizing dilemmas of gender identity and romantic or domestic relationships. Invariably, ghosts and angels proved handy devices for stories of redemption, forgiveness, and second chances.

The 2000s has yet to stop the production of ghost films and leaving the horror genre aside, spirits appeared in a number of films such as the animated *Corpse Bride* (2005) and *Coraline* (2009), and the romantic comedies *Just Like Heaven* and *Over Her Dead Body*. *Ghost Town*, therefore, belongs to a long tradition of films, which uses supernatural elements in a specific cultural context in order to comment on a number of social issues that range from gender politics and romance to a flawed human nature.

As was stated in the introduction, *Ghost Town* is a fantasy man-com with a twist in that the main character's sidekick is no longer alive. The two male characters present two distinct masculine types. Bertram the dentist (Ricky Gervais) is the obnoxious, antisocial Briton, who steals taxis and never holds the elevator for his neighbours and seems at peace when his patients are unable to talk on his chair. Frank, the ghost (Greg Kinnear), is the adulterer alpha male who dies and still thinks he can control the universe. The pre-credit sequence starts with a tuxedo-clad Frank, who walks in the street while reprimanding his real estate agent on the phone for contacting his wife with information about a new apartment which was intended for his mistress. Nervous and angry about the situation, he avoids an air conditioner that accidentally falls from an apartment building only to be hit by a bus the very next instant. Although the audience concludes that Frank must be dead, the character appears as elegantly dressed as before, looking at what one can assume is his dead body until two people pass right through his body, making him realize that his life on earth has ended.

The credits appear without any further explanation as to Frank's fate and we are then introduced to a series of dental instruments and Bertram, who is trying to treat a patient. Bertram's interactions with the patient and later with his partner, Dr Jahangir Prashar (Aasif Mandvi), show a man with an antipathy towards people and an inclination to introversion. As portrayed by Ricky Gervais, who rose to prominence, as the co-creator and central character of the critically acclaimed British sitcom *The Office* (BBC Two, 2001–2), Bertram is a quite unconventional romantic hero. Not as handsome or as fit as Hugh Grant, Hugh Jackman, Ben Stiller, Ryan Reynolds, Patrick Dempsey, Gerard Butler or Matthew McConaughey nor as amusingly vulnerable as Steve Carell nor as transparently funny as Adam Sandler and Vince Vaughn, Gervais portrays Bertram with the Brit's notoriously dry (and hilarious) sense of humour mixed with restrained acting that allows for the tiniest exaggerated expression and/or clever line of dialogue to stand out and cause laughter or make the audience recognize the character is hiding many more 'secrets' that will be slowly revealed.

Nevertheless, Bertram is initially seen as an unsociable and distant individual, content in his solitude that is presented as a personal choice. Even when he has to be admitted to hospital for a minor procedure, Bertram is alone and there is not a glimpse of a relative and/or friend, nor is there a hint that the character would have preferred and/or needed some company. However, once he leaves the hospital, everything is changed. When he makes a remark to someone whom he considers a hospital nurse, he finds that the surprised girl starts to follow him. Commenting on this unwanted presence, Bertram almost stumbles upon an elderly couple. The couple are also surprised that the doctor can see them and soon Bertram is followed by more than a dozen ghosts that roam the New York streets in need of closure, providing a traditional motif in the representations of ghosts in film; 'the person who dies having left a task unfinished and returning to see its completion through another' (Tom Ruffles, 2004, p. 82).

Trying to evade all these people and their demands, Bertram returns to the hospital to enquire about the cause of these 'hallucinations'. His doctor informs him that during the procedure, he died for seven minutes but he was fortunately brought back. The narrative's explanation for Bertram's ability to communicate with the dead causes the hero confusion but not disbelief. Trying to rationalize and accept the fact he died, he goes to a bar accompanied by Frank, who wants to ask him for a favour; he wants Bertram to stop his wife from marrying the man she has been seeing and in exchange, he will ask all the other ghosts to leave him alone.

The ghost of Frank seems to be the leader of the New York ghost community and as his filmic antecedents he retains all the characteristics from the time he was alive. However, he is not the playful George Kerby (Cary Grant) in *Topper* or the loving and helpful Sam (Patrick Swayze) in *Ghost*. Frank remains a fast-talking, selfish and arrogant man who defends his adultery and does not care whether the other ghosts have been waiting for many years for someone like Bertram to help them. Fowkes (2010, p. 49) maintains that some ghost films 'explore relations of gender, power, and powerlessness through the device of a hero's ghostly return,' and that '[t]he revenant male is stuck in a role that strips away the simplest tools of power, utterance, and action, and is forced to develop more "feminine" techniques to solve his problem and move on'. However, the case of Frank differs to an extent. Although he does lose some sort of power in that he cannot get good reception on his cell phone, he has still managed to become the leader of the New York ghosts by preserving his persuasion skills. One could argue that Frank is not the central male character and as such dramatic change is not as expected from him as it is from Bertram, but it is still interesting to underline the irony of the narrative, which seems to confirm the popular adage of 'once a cheater [...] always a cheater'.

Both Frank and Bertram initially represent two negative aspects of masculinity: the handsome, suave yet manipulative liar and the plain-looking, antipathetic neurotic. Despite their differences, Frank and Bertram share something in common. They basically both dislike people; the former uses them to achieve whatever goal he has set while the latter simply chooses not to interact with them. Frank and Bertram's selfishness serves as a paradigm of contemporary society's promotion of success based on individualism and the disregard of other people's feelings. According to Herbert Schui (2005, p. 160) '[i]n the neo-liberal world human behavior is determined by the exchange of utility units as a matter of simple arithmetic. The motive for relationships between people is reciprocity in the reduced sense of taking advantage of somebody and to be used in return'. If we apply Schui's comment to Frank and Bertram, we can deduce that Frank uses people for acquiring professional power or sexual pleasure and Bertram views people as providers of the money he needs to enjoy his solitary existence. Although these characters seem dia-metrically opposed on the surface, they are driven by the same principle and decide to join forces in order to benefit from each other. Thus, a kind of oral contract is established. Bertram will assist Frank in stopping his widow's imminent nuptials and Frank will convince the other ghosts to leave the dentist in peace.

This odd couple soon becomes a triangle with the introduction of Gwen (Téa Leoni), who works as an Egyptologist and has been living in the same building as Bertram. Gwen is presented as a dedicated professional who is working on an Egyptian mummy and has trouble discerning the cause of death. When Bertram first sees her during a lecture, he is instantly attracted by her physical beauty and proposes to Frank that the best way to stop her wedding would be to 'present her with an alternative'. Although Frank initi-ally laughs at Bertram's offer to become the 'suitor', he finally concedes and also suggests providing some 'inside' information the dentist could find useful. However, despite Bertram's awkward attempts at flirting and Gwen's dislike of him because of his past un-neighbourly behaviour, she does appreciate his theory about the mummy dying from an uncared for dental abscess and asks him to examine the corpse at the museum. Their time together at the museum and their walk home function therapeutically for Bertram and help him open up after what seems quite a long time. The audience learns that he moved from London to Manhattan when his girlfriend abandoned him and married another man and can thus attribute his aversion towards people to his defence mechanism and fear of getting hurt. Gwen and Bertram's relationship becomes even friendlier, when her dangerous-according-to-Frank fiancé, Richard (Billy Campbell), invites him for dinner. However, once Richard leaves on a work-related emergency, and Gwen and Bertram share a drink and intimate details of their lives, Bertram returns to his apartment and tells Frank that he cannot complete his mission. Not only did he find Richard an exceptional human being, a human rights lawyer who defends the underprivileged of the world, but his feelings for Gwen would not allow him to deprive her of the happiness she deserves. For the first time, Frank seems uncertain and nervous as he realizes his unfinished business may not be Gwen's breaking up with Richard.

Nevertheless, Gwen does break up with Richard of her own accord and decides to take a job offer to spend six months in Egypt. Bertram tries to get closer to Gwen but Frank sabotages their relationship because he does not want her to be with another 'heartless' person. Bertram's transformation, however, is not complete until he decides to help the ghosts who start approaching him again and ask for his help. A moving montage shows Bertram visiting the ghosts' relatives and completing their business while one by one the ghosts finally pass over. By allowing himself to help others and forget about his ego and his individual needs, Bertram realizes the futility of his carefully calculated and lonely existence and confronts Gwen. Although he had earlier tried unsuccessfully to prove that he communicates with her dead husband, Bertram succeeds in making Gwen understand she is still clinging to her dead husband's memory. While they have a heated discussion, Bertram is hit by a bus the same way Frank was in the pre-credit sequence of the film. It is while Bertram's body is lying on the pavement and Betram's ghost converses with Frank that the latter realizes that Gwen's tears over the dentist's body signify feelings he never thought could exist. The moment Frank's arrogance and sentiment of superiority are finally replaced by the acknowledgement of his action's true repercussions when he was alive and his genuine regret is the moment his soul is freed to pass over as his unfinished business was to learn how to empathize with the people who mattered in his life.

Fowkes (2010, p. 42) remarks that although ghosts are said to constitute 'expressions of what we cannot or will not consciously acknowledge', she notes that the main characteristic of many ghost films of the late 1980s and 1990s that 'feature ghosts and/or angels in domestic or romantic relationships' is the introduction of 'a male character (often the ghost itself) who has difficulty expressing emotions or romantic sentiments to his wife or girlfriend' (ibid. p. 83). What is interesting about *Ghost Town* is that both the ghost and the central male character share the same inability to associate with people, sympathize with their problems and/or help them without waiting for something in return. Frank enters Bertram's life not to assist him with his anti-social tendencies or improve his love life but because he wants to use him as an instrument to continue to haunt Gwen's life. At the same time, Bertram agrees to Frank's plan because he is promised to be left alone by the end of the 'mission', but also due to Gwen's attractiveness. Both Frank and Bertram act initially as the paradigms par excellence of an egocentric society which measures its subjects by their status and wealth. The afterlife element in *Ghost Town* functions as a wake-up call for both Bertram and Frank, but only when Gwen's presence enters the equation, underlining the transformative power of love. Although the film provides an open ending with Bertram accepting to fix Gwen's tooth in his office, hinting at the possibility of a romantic relationship that may develop, it does emphasize Bertram's newfound respect for the people around him (his patients, his partner, the doctor who treated him at the hospital) and his willingness to let a special person into his heart again.

It is claimed that the main function of fantasy 'is the vanquishing of despair and restlessness through imagination and hope' (Fowkes, 2010, p. 173). Indeed, both *Enchanted* and *Ghost Town* use their fantastic elements as signs of hope in a society driven by individualism and the powerful laws of the market. However, both romantic comedies do more than just use fantasy as an instrument for the audience's reassurance and escapism. Produced and released on the verge of the 2008 financial meltdown, *Enchanted* ends by promoting the ideal of a girly femininity and encouraging consumerism and self-entrepreneurship through Giselle's new career as a fashion designer. However, although the characters of *Ghost Town* operate in the same societal circumstances, the narrative supports that solidarity and compassion are the values individuals should return to if they want to form long-lasting relationships and lead a meaningful life. The use of ghosts in *Ghost Town*, however, also functions metonymically as a post-9/11 relief, albeit indirectly. Pamela Robertson Wojcik (2010, p. 273) observes that although the film never explicitly addresses the attacks or implies that someone in the ghost community died on 9/11, it nonetheless 'conjures the memory of 9/11 and its aftermath, when the city was filled with images and reminders of loved ones on flyers and other memorials'. In addition, the ghosts themselves serve as grief counsellors not only to their fictional relatives but as an audience reminder 'that death might not be the end' (Ruffles, 2004, p. 1).

It, therefore, becomes evident that the similarities in structure, form and setting and the simultaneous differences in the use of the fantastic of *Enchanted* and *Ghost Town* highlight the complexities of the romantic comedy genre which may suggest various and often contradicting solutions to contemporary social dilemmas, proving not only that the same sociopolitical context and the same industry can offer different and exciting voices and opinions through the use of the same formula.

5 The action rom com

It is true that action/adventure cinema is still associated with male heroes and considered first and foremost a male genre by both film viewers and recent scholarly work (Jose Arroyo 2000, Yvonne Tasker 2004, Eric Lichtenfel 2007, Barna William Donovan 2010) despite the considerable female 'invasion' of at least the last two decades. As I have argued elsewhere, the new millennium witnessed a plethora of action/active heroines in both television and film who proved they 'are just as capable as men to tackle any kind of threat and any villain with a God syndrome and/or world domination plans' (Betty Kaklamanidou, 2010, p. 61). These include television shows such as *Alias* (ABC, 2001–6), *Charmed* (WB, 1998–2004) and *Buffy the Vampire Slayer* (WB, 1997–2003) and such films as *Charlie's Angels* (2000), *Lara Croft: Tomb Raider* (2001), *Lara Croft: Tomb Raider: The Cradle of Life* (2003), *Kill Bill Vol. 1* (2003), *Charlie's Angels Full Throttle* (2003), *Underworld* (2003), *Kill Bill Vol. 2* (2004), *Resident Evil: Apocalypse* (2004), *Catwoman* (2004), *Aeon Flux* (2005), *Elektra* (2005), *Underworld: Revolution* (2006), *Resident Evil: Extinction* (2007), *Salt* (2010), and *Kick-Ass* (2010). However, despite their increasing numbers, and the fact that the majority returned an impressive amount of money (Alice in Wonderland [2010] grossed $1.024 billion world-wide on a budget of $200 million, Salt grossed $295 million with a cost of $110 million and *Wanted* (2008) made $341 million, on a sensible-for-the-genre budget of $75 million), these female-driven action films perpetually struggle to get made.

Robert J. Elisberg (2011) argues that Hollywood 'has a convenient short-term memory when it fits their purposes', and thus avoids female action films if just a single one fails to fulfil its box-office potential. Elisberg (ibid.) notes that the simple 'reality is that bad action movies with women will do poorly,' listing Ultraviolet (2006) as a prime example, but rightly adds that 'so will bad action movies with men', and refers to the meagre $15 million The Assassination of Jesse James grossed worldwide. In the same vein, it should be noted that the action/adventure film genre is not the only generic category that Hollywood hesitates to associate with a female star or stars. The success of almost every kind of filmic narrative that centres on women seems always to come as an unexpected surprise to industry executives. Lynda Obst, producer of diverse films such as the romantic comedies *Sleepless in Seattle* (1993) and *How to Lose a Guy in Ten Days* (2003), the sci-fi *Contact* (1997) and the television show *Hot in Cleveland* (TV Land 2010–present), observes, for instance, how the global commercial and critical success of the female comedy *Bridesmaids* (2011) reawakened the industry's interest in women's projects. However, Obst also notes on an online interview that '[i]f the next [female-driven film] flops, who knows? Two action movies flop and it means nothing; one women's movie flops and it's the end [...] Every time a woman's movie does well, it's a brand-new fact. Every time we rediscover the female audience, it's astonishing' (Obst, 2011).

The continuing application of this gender double standard in Hollywood notwithstanding, film theorists continue to examine those cinematic texts that do get made and represent, not only the evolution of well-established genres, but also offer significant input in the on-going gender dialogue in academia. For instance, the introduction of the action heroine protagonist in the action/ adventure cosmos, stereotypically recognized as a male-dominated genre, has been the subject of academic investigation, best exemplified in Tasker's *Spectacular Bodies* (2002), where the author introduces the term of 'musculinity' to explain 'the extent to which a physical definition of masculinity in terms of a developed musculature is not limited to the male body within representation' (p. 3), showing 'the way in which the signifiers of strength are not limited to male characters' (p. 149). Tasker (2004, p. 4) recognizes that the definition of the genre is problematic and although she recognizes the hybridization process adopted by Hollywood to imbue action narratives with structural elements from other genres, she does not include the romantic comedy among these influences.

Nevertheless, the romantic comedy genre, one of the few female genres par excellence, has also sought to hybridize in order to appeal to male viewers as well.[1] The combination of action and romantic comedy is considered to have started in 1984 with the release of *Romancing the Stone*, starring Kathleen Turner as a lonely New York romance writer who finds herself in Colombia trying to help her sister. In South America she meets the adventurer Michael Douglas, and together they face innumerable dangerous situations while falling in love at the same time. The success of this mixture gave birth to a sequel, *Jewel of The Nile* (1986), as well as several 'adventurous' romantic comedies, such as *Bird on a Wire* (1990), *Grosse Pointe Blank* (1997) and *Six Days Seven Nights* (1998). According to Mernit (2000, p. 22), 'The romantic comedy/adventure movie is distinguished by exotic locales and elements of high-stakes (i.e., life-and-death) drama. It features action set pieces, and it's a good genre for getting protagonists involved superquickly – thrust together in big jeopardy that forces intimacy upon them'. However, the academic examination of this hybrid film type is almost non-existent and is limited to Deleyto's discussion of *Out of Sight* (2009, pp. 1–3) and Mary Beltrán's brief but insightful comments on the same film from the perspective of the ethnic background of its female star, Jennifer Lopez (2004, pp. 192–3).

The last decade included several mainstream action/adventure romantic comedies: *Head Over Heels* (2001), *Serving Sara* (2002), *Gigli* (2002), *Mr. and Mrs. Smith* (2005), *Fool's Gold* (2008), *The Bounty Hunter, Knight and Day, Killers* (2010) and *Date Night*. With the exception of *Gigli* and *Killers*, which did not attract the audience to the theatre, the majority of the remaining films were proven quite commercially successful worldwide, taking their budgets into consideration, (*Fool's Gold* returned $111 million, *The Bounty Hunter* made $134, while *Mr. and Mrs. Smith* earned a staggering $478 million).

This chapter will focus on *Date Night* and *Knight and Day* for the following reasons. First, both films were released at the end of the decade, which witnessed a new interest in this specific hybrid rom com sub-genre; it would be interesting to examine the relationship of the couple in each film to see whether the cycle introduces new narrative elements to the well-known structure which was outlined by Mernit. Second, the films were chosen because of the contrast they present; while *Knight and Day* includes all the ingredients of Mernit's definition (the exotic and/or foreign locales, the progressive intimacy born between the two protagonists), *Date Night* presents a married couple who face death in the heart of New York City, the most recognizable setting of the romantic comedy genre and therefore not an exotic or even 'foreign' backdrop even for the international audience. In addition, *Knight and Day* presents the falling-in-love trajectory of two strangers, whereas *Date Night* features a married couple who rediscovers and/or openly realizes the qualities that have kept them together for many years. As such, the latter film presents an interesting variation on the action rom com cycle, not only because it examines a stable and long-term traditional union in the new millennium, but also because this marriage 'anatomy' is provided through the perspective of two actors who do not conform to the usual standards the cycle imposes (actors with fit bodies, with previous experience in action/adventure films, etc.).

Through these narratives, I want to explore the dynamics of the heterosexual couple faced with danger and more often than not death. Whether the couple is already married (*Fool's Gold, Date Night* and *Killers*), divorced (*The Bounty Hunter*) or has just met (*Knight and Day*), it would be interesting to see whether the female assumes a passive or active role and/or acts as an equal to her male counterpart. I will be, therefore, mostly concerned with what happens during the 'chase' and/or 'at gunpoint' moments which occur during the middle of the narrative. Deleyto (2009, p. 27) observes that one of the two problematic premises upon which recent scholarly work on the genre is based on is the fact that 'the happy ending is the only location of the film's ideology'. Therefore, if one is to examine the action romantic comedy focusing on its ending, he/she will be faced with happy endings which celebrate the return to normal family life: in *Fool's Gold* the heroine not only decides to remarry her ex-husband but is also pregnant; in *Killers*, a baby is also on the way for the protagonist couple; in *The Bounty Hunter*, the hero not only solves the mystery but wins the heart of his estranged ex-wife; while in *Date*

Night, a somewhat boring, mature couple with kids returns to the suburbs after facing corrupt policemen and politicians. In other words, without diminishing the importance of the happy ending, it should be noted that insistence on it distracts attention from 'the vicissitudes of the emotional and sexual relationships between the characters', (Deleyto, 2009, p. 29) which can lead to significant observations regarding gender relations in a specific sociopolitical context.

Date Night

In *Date Night,* Tina Fey and Steve Carell play Claire and Phil Foster, a quiet, suburban couple who live in New Jersey with their two small children. The first sequence of the film establishes their everyday routine with a view to surprising the audience with the action that will follow. However, a more careful reading shows that the couple is already facing quite an adventurous or at least oppressive everyday life. The first shot of the film shows the feet of a child walking in a narrow corridor. This constraint on the audience's point of view through the framing of the shot is a technique amply used by the thriller in order to intensify the viewers' reactions. In the context of *Date Night,* this carefully edited shot accompanied by the Ramones' 'Blitzkrieg Bop', a wildly energetic and popular hit song from 1976, leads to laughter as the boy is just the couple's son who goes to his parents' bedroom to ask for breakfast. Both Claire and Phil are sleeping but as soon as their son asks them to go to the kitchen, their youngest daughter jumps abruptly on the bed and violently wakes them up before she disappears with her brother. Half awake and visibly worn out, Claire and Phil sit on the bed at 5 AM without even having the physical strength to say good morning to each other. Claire says: 'Here we go', to which Phil replies: 'It begins'. What they both refer to is their efforts to responsibly get through another day. The brief scenes that follow show that both Claire and Phil are not very satisfied with their line of work; she is a real estate agent who deals with clients she could never please and he is a New Jersey tax consultant trying in vain to persuade a young couple to take their tax returns more seriously and start acting in a mature and appropriate manner. When Phil returns home exhausted, Claire is on the computer working while the children are playing. This brief sequence, which lasts less than two minutes, is meant to present Claire and Phil as a mundane modern couple who go through life as if on automatic pilot. However, I would argue that this first reading could be a little misleading. Claire and Phil are indeed presented as ordinary people if one is to forget the intricate web of activities and decisions everyday life entails, however repetitive and trivial most of them can be. Ben Highmore (2002, p. 1) notes that the everyday 'might be experienced as a sanctuary, or it may bewilder or give pleasure, it may delight or depress'. The first sequences of *Date Night* connote that the Fosters' everyday is neither a pleasant addition of repetitive actions, nor a depressing assortment of meetings and conversations but instead, a mostly tiring and futile collection of obligatory actions that have to do with child-care, work and taking care of the house. However, the audience soon discovers the protagonist couple attempts to escape this monotonous schedule, at least periodically.

As many modern couples, Claire and Phil have set one evening aside a week, the infamous 'date night', as a chance to spend some quality time together, away from home and their kids. The dinner sequence presents them at their usual restaurant but also shows that despite their routine, they still make each other laugh and enjoy each other's company, connoting that their marriage is solid and their union is not simply something they have grown accustomed to. However, their date does seem like a perfectly choreographed repetition of their past nights out and this is underlined by the longing and somewhat sad expressions both Claire and Phil take when they see what they believe is a married couple across from their table behaving as if they were on their very first date. The protagonists choose not to say anything but the next day, they find out that a couple of their friends are getting divorced. Brad (Mark Ruffalo) summarizes the reasons behind his decision: 'We are just excellent roommates,' he confides to Phil. With the assistance of a parallel montage, his wife Haley (Kristen Wiig) tells Claire that she is tired of 'the same things', confirming recent studies which show that '[t]he butterflies of early romance quickly flutter away and are replaced by familiar, predictable feelings of long-term attachment' (Tara Parker-Pope, 2008). Both Brad's and Haley's reactions to the imminent dissolution of their union actually reverberate their perhaps unspoken thoughts about their mundane life and especially their marriage, which has also turned out to be a series of predictable conversations, actions and even thoughts.

Shocked by the news and alarmed by the idea they could be next, Phil decides their next date night should be spent in one of Manhattan's trendiest restaurants while Claire dresses up in an elegant dress and high heels. Their decision not only constitutes the narrative catalyst which will push the plot forward but also conforms to social psychology professor Arthur Aron's argument about how date nights should be tailored 'around new and different activities' in order to rekindle the sparks in a marriage since '[m]ost studies of love and marriage show that the decline of romantic love over time is inevitable' (Parker-Pope, 2008). When they are denied entry without a booking, Phil decides to show he can take control of the situation and please his wife. Therefore, he decides to take another couple's reservation ('The Tripplehorns') and act as a decisive and traditional male. Indeed, the couple is enjoying themselves, drinking wine and eating the exorbitantly expensive food. However, they are soon interrupted by two men who ask them to follow them, thinking they are the Tripplehorns. Claire and Phil go out with them in a dark alley only to find themselves at gunpoint when the men ask them to surrender a flash drive. Phil does the manly thing and when one of the men takes out a gun and points at them, he gets in front of his wife. When he realizes the men will never believe they are not the couple they are looking for, he makes up a story and tells them they have hidden the flash drive in Central Park. It is at this moment that the heart of the Fosters' everyday life is interrupted by '[t]he non-everyday (the exceptional)' (Highmore, 2002, p. 3) and the film is transformed from a marriage comedy into an action romantic comedy, a structure that goes back to

> the romance of medieval literature: a protagonist either has or develops great and special skills and overcomes insurmountable obstacles in extraordinary situations to successfully achieve some desired goal, usually the restitution of order to the world invoked by the narrative. The protagonists confront the human, natural, or supernatural powers that have improperly assumed control over the world and eventually defeat them (Thomas Sobchack in Steve Neale 2002, p. 74).

Claire and Phil are therefore obliged to transform from a rather boring suburban couple into two action heroes who have to find and return what has been known after Hitchcock as the action 'MacGuffin,' that is an object to be stolen or retrieved but which is actually unimportant for the plot and serves 'merely as a means to an end' (Michael Walker, 2005, p. 297). In Claire and Phil's case, the MacGuffin is a flash drive with vital information for their enemies. What is interesting in the case of *Date Night* is that neither of the protagonists is an adventurer (*Romancing the Stone, Fool's Gold*), a spy or an agent (*Killers, Knight and Day*) or even very athletic, very appealing and/or sexy. Instead, the action has to be provided by two 40-something, quiet, law-abiding citizens who find themselves thrust into an extraordinary situation and having to do the best they can in order to avoid being killed. Furthermore, as embodied by Tina Fey and Steve Carell, – two of the most celebrated and critically acclaimed contemporary television comedians, especially in the US – Claire and Phil are endowed with the appearance and likeability of people the audience can relate to more easily than the usually gorgeous and fit Hollywood stars.

So after Phil vomits when they escape from Central Park and Claire panics at the thought that the 'bad' guys have their address, they decide to do the sensible thing: they go to the nearest police station trying to explain what has happened to them. Unfortunately, once at the police station, Claire and Phil discover that their persecutors are corrupt policemen and are therefore obliged to become more inventive and thus escape not only their everyday routine but also overcome whatever fears and insecurities they have to protect their family. In their effort to find the Tripplehorns, not only do they 'steal' their phone number from the restaurant, but they break into the real estate office to get the address of one of Claire's former clients who she thinks can help them locate the Tripplehorns and, by extension, find the flash drive.

Claire and Phil's actions and reactions complement each other and present a welcoming balance between the female and the male response to a dangerous situation. For instance, they both have their moments of weakness, but they both show initiative and/or act quickly. When they are in Central Park it is Phil who takes a wooden board and knocks one of their enemies down, but in the real estate office it is Claire who, without hesitation, breaks the glass in order to get the file she needs. When Phil thinks their only way out is to retrieve the flash drive, it is Claire who thinks of the man who can help them get the Tripplehorns' address. Even during their astonishing circumstances, Claire and Phil exhibit a kind of intimacy that can only be found in long-term relationships. According to David R. Shumway, (2003, p. 133), intimacy 'represents a newly emerging discourse that has come to complement and compete with the older discourse of romance'. Focusing 'on a new object, "the relationship" both in and out of marriage' (ibid. p. 136), the discourse of intimacy tries 'to demystify attraction and love itself […] assumes a mono-gamous relationship as its paradigm […] [and] assumes companionship as a condition but does not regard it as sufficient' (ibid. pp. 143–53). Not only do the Fosters exhibit this kind of intimacy but they also conform to most stu-dies on the subject which assume that this kind of 'relationship can exist only between equals' and as such 'do not feel the need to argue against male dominance' or discuss gender relations within the institution (ibid. p. 138). At the same time, the focus of *Date Night* on what seems to be a stable marriage differentiates this action romantic comedy from previous examples of the cycle, since the intervals among the action scenes are not spent on the falling-in-love or the-getting-back-together trajectories and allows for an examination of a relationship that is well past its prime.

Claire and Phil's relationship is only seriously questioned once in the nar-rative. When they visit Claire's former client, Phil comes face-to-face with the younger, half-naked and extremely fit and handsome Holbrooke Grant (Mark Wahlberg), who as an intelligence freelancer has the equipment to help them locate the Tripplehorns. While Wahlberg's well-toned abdomen in a few brief scenes provides fruitful terrain for laughter, especially when Phil keeps asking him to put a shirt on, the presence of the 'ultimate' alpha male (fit, hand-some, smart and rich) makes Phil insecure and provides the catalyst for anger and his subsequent outburst. While trying to drive one of Holbrooke's sports cars, which he has 'borrowed,' he first starts 'attacking' Claire on how she became another person in this man's presence, a 'giggly, flirting, charming person' he could not recognize. He then admits: 'He is super hot. […] And I'm just the husband. I'm just a dork, who doesn't know how to load the dishwasher; I am the guy who needs to work out more.' Phil's insecurities are instantly met by Claire's eruption on how she does a million things every day without anyone's help. Her speech echoes contemporary society's demand and/or encouragement that women 'can have it all.'

In other words, Claire and so many other romantic heroines and real women alike, suffer from what experts have termed the '*Superwoman syn-drome* […] which gained prominence in the late 20th century', and desig-nates a woman who can enjoy 'motherhood, love, fun, confidence, success and the admiration of others' (Paula Nicolson, 2002, p. 12). At the same time,

Phil's 'feminized' masculinity urges him to initiate a discussion about their relationship and forces them both to speak about their fear of turning into their friends Brad and Haley, who are divorcing. They both say they would never leave each other but their looks and their body language exude the nervousness and the acknowledgement of two people who have been long enough in a marriage to know they should take care of it more. Claire and Phil's narrative may include the 'obligatory' action and dangerous sequences (car chases, threats at gunpoint, meetings at shady places) but unlike most action romantic comedies, where one of the protagonists or both are skilled in dealing with extreme situations, the Fosters survive through sheer luck, their quick wit, and perhaps the bliss of ignorance. Despite the couple's obvious intimacy, it is their adventures and near-death experiences that re-ignite the spark in their relationship. Thus, the narrative, which ends by Claire and Phil kissing passionately on the lawn in front of their house, proposes that millennial marriages can avoid stagnation by a mixture of Shumway's honest companionship (2003) with Aron's focus on new and exciting joined activities (Parker-Pope, 2008). More importantly, however, the Fosters' marriage survives to reassure the audience the institution is still one of the pillars of the new-millennium western society and no threat can substantially undermine its strength.

Knight and Day

Knight and Day was released two months after *Date Night*, in June 2010, and stars Tom Cruise and Cameron Diaz, two A-list Hollywood stars who are associated with action: the former through the three *Mission: Impossible* films (1996, 2000, 2006) and the latter through the two cinematic *Charlie's Angels* (2000, 2003). Nevertheless, it is interesting to note that the film 'was Tom Cruise's lowest [spectator attendance] in a leading role since *Far and Away* in 1992 (which had nearly as many viewers from about half the theaters)' (Brandon Gray, 2010). Gray notices that '[o]utside of the *Mission: Impossible* movies, Tom Cruise's pictures generally aren't prone to record-breaking launches, and they often enjoy relatively long runs' and he rightly predicted that '*Knight & Day* is unlikely to reach the $100 million mark that used to be the norm for Mr. Cruise' (ibid.). Indeed, surpassing *Date Night*'s budget by a little more than two times, *Knight and Day* did not attract the domestic audience and grossed around $77 million. However, the film did very well overseas, returning more than $227 million worldwide, confirming how contemporary Hollywood films rely more on foreign markets than the domestic audience.

Gray (2010) holds the marketing and advertising campaign responsible for the failure of the film in the USA. However, I would also argue that the not-so-thriving domestic course of *Knight and Day* can also be linked to Cruise's 'wounded' image after Paramount Pictures fired him in 2006, following his excessive declaration of love for his bride-to-be Katie Holmes while jumping on Oprah Winfrey's couch in 2005; his attack on the actress Brooke Shields for her admitting taking prescription drugs to deal with her postpartum depression; as well as his public support for the controversial religion of Scientology. The public suddenly started to question its long-term admiration for the actor who personified, through most of his roles, and for almost three decades, the ultimate American hero: honest, strong and always victorious. These brief observations show that even though Hollywood superstars 'are a form of investment, employed in film productions as a probable guard against loss […] rarely have [they] ever maintained a consistent record at the box office' (Paul McDonald, 2000, pp. 11–12). McDonald adds that rather than considering 'stars as a mechanism for manipulating the market for films, we can more cautiously suggest that stars act as a means of product differentiation which can only potentially stabilise the market.' (ibid. p. 12)

Leaving Cruise's 'fall from grace' in mainly the eyes of the US audience, and the perhaps unsuitable publicity campaign aside, *Knight and Day* was also the star's first attempt at combining action and romantic comedy in his long career and the second time he ever played the romantic hero since *Jerry Maguire* (1996). One could argue that the choice of this particular role and film was also part of a conscious or unconscious effort on the part of Cruise to publicly redeem himself as the actor 'is unaccustomed to offering public concessions or apologies', and his 'persona does not appear to demand or to accommodate redemption' (Michael DeAngelis, 2010, p. 43). However, his role in *Knight and Day* fictionally echoes his past mistakes through parody. Cruise plays Roy Miller, a CIA agent who tries to protect the next best technological gizmo, a battery that never dies coded Zephyr, from Fitzgerald (Peter Sarsgaard), a former partner at the agency who went rogue, and Antonio (Jordi Mollà), a Spanish arms dealer who wants to buy it. The opening sequence presents the two main characters in the Wichita airport. Roy is trying to find something to hide Zephyr in. He seems perfectly calm, and the audience sees him spending his time eating an ice-cream cone and playing an arcade game holding a fake gun. These mundane, everyday acts, performed by countless regular passengers before boarding, seem unsuitable and therefore funny for an actor who usually plays super heroes involved in life or death situations and does not indulge in any humdrum activity of daily life. For instance, Cruise as *Mission: Impossible*'s invincible agent Ethan Hawke was never represented as anything else than the perfect hero, even in the scene of his engagement in *Mission: Impossible III*. However, the narrative parameters of the action romantic comedy cycle combined with the potential restructuring of Cruise's image allows for a first – albeit subtle – subversion in the image of the all-American powerful agent and imbue the character with a more humane side which can be also considered funny.

At the same time, the sequence introduces Roy's partner, June (Cameron Diaz). An actress with an impressive range of film roles in both the mainstream and the independent industry sectors (from the good girl everyone wants in *There's Something about Mary* in 1997, the weird Lotte in *Being*

John Malkovich, the ruthless co-owner of a professional football team in *Any Given Sunday* in 1999, the street-smart pickpocket Jenny in *Gangs of New York* in 2002, the fit and charismatic Natalie, a Charlie's angel, to the mother of a daughter dying from leukaemia in the dramatic *My Sister's Keeper* in 2009), it is quite difficult to find a pattern in Diaz's characters. However, the majority of her roles tend to stress the female character's independence and internal strength, combined, in the action films and romantic comedies of her filmography, with an inclination for physical comedy and self-mockery. In *Knight and Day*, Diaz as June, restores old cars and her carry-on is filled with Pontiac car parts. June is on her way to Boston to finish the restoration of her deceased dad's GTO so that she could give it to her little sister as a wedding present. Her 'masculine' job and her casual clothes present a woman who is secure and self-sufficient. However, once she literally bumps into Roy – who has enough time to hide Zephyr in her bag – June tries to use her feminine charms in order to catch his attention. She begins a conversation with him on the plane and when she goes to the bathroom to clean herself up after her drink is accidentally spilled on her lap, she starts talking to herself in the mirror about how great Roy seems while she puts on some lip balm, fixes her hair and checks her breath. June's self-examination, and the process of beautification which hint at her nervousness and insecurity are also ironic as they are simultaneously performed by Cameron Diaz, a woman who has been featured in the list of the most beautiful and/or sexy actors/celebrities of the last 20 years. Just as June is preparing for the eternal heterosexual seduction 'tango' – intensified by the actual tango performed by the European group Gotan Project which accompanies the sequence – a parallel montage shows Roy exterminating and/or anaesthetizing the 14 people on the plane, including the pilot and the co-pilot, as the flight was just a CIA effort to capture him, arrest him and expose him as a rogue agent. As soon as June comes out from the bathroom, she walks straight to Roy and kisses him without noticing the bodies that are all over the plane or the open door of the cockpit.

Although the romantic comedy genre focuses on romantic relationships, its contemporary representatives have adopted a more traditional approach regarding the importance of any kind of sexual interaction between the couple. A few kisses or even a single kiss toward the end of the narrative usually connotes and/or implies the beginning of the sexual relationship (*The Proposal, Enchanted, 27 Dresses, The Switch*). The instances of the female protagonist initiating a kiss are especially rare; Tina Fey in *Baby Mama*, Cameron Diaz in *The Holiday*, Rachel Weisz in *Definitely, Maybe* (2008) and Lake Bell in *Over Her Dead Body* are among the rare heroines who kiss their desired male first. The dating rules implied by many contemporary romantic comedies which show that it is still the man who should take charge of asking for a date, the first kiss, etc. combined with the rarity in sexual representation, 'provides a problem for the contemporary film since it is frequently devoted to depicting modern date habits, which realistically must include sex' (Jeffers McDonald, 2007, p. 97). Indeed, most mainstream romantic comedies of the last decade, which Jeffers McDonald calls 'neo-traditional,' 'have to work hard to find ways to explain why sex is not happening for its main couple' (ibid.). Even though heroines who 'dare' to actively show they are sexually attracted to a man are not rejected, they are usually met with male surprise and/or have to explain the reason behind their assertiveness.

Thus, although in *Knight and Day* Roy responds to June's kiss, when it is over, June immediately attributes her 'male' sexual aggressiveness to the alcohol she had previously consumed. However, once Roy nonchalantly explains what happened and leaves her to land the plane, June assumes, once again, the role of the passive, ignorant female who needs to be rescued, screaming and obeying Roy's orders to avoid death. However, throughout the course of the narrative and especially during the spectacular action scenes (including a car chase in the streets of Boston, jumping off a helicopter, eluding death on a train in Austria, running on the rooftops of Saltsburg and escaping dozens of bulls in Spain), Diaz gradually becomes more of an assistant rather than an unfortunate liability. She may scream and be visibly scared, as any ordinary individual would be in such extreme situations, but she progressively learns to handle danger and even help Roy defeat his enemies. June's reaction during the action sequences also confirms Geoff King's (2000, p. 4) thesis about how spectacle – which has been accused of suspending narrative continuity – can also reinforce 'the work of narrative'. In *Knight and Day*, the female character evolves through and during the spectacle, and therefore assists the plot and facilitates the romantic relationship between June and Roy at the same time. By the end of the film, June's transformation into an action heroine is complete: not only is she the one who exposes Fitzgerald as the corrupt CIA agent and finally exonerates Roy, bringing an end to the action 'portion' of the plot, but she also leads the romantic one as well, as she abducts a wounded Roy from a Washington hospital after the final 'duel.' The last scene finds Roy waking up in a haze in June's restored GTO, experiencing what June felt three times during the narrative when she was drugged by him. The car is parked near a beach and the couple's witty repartee is an almost exact reversal of an earlier verbal exchange the two shared in the beginning of the narrative. However, now, it is June who tells Roy that she is the only one who can protect him and the two are seen driving to South America as the end credits appear on the screen. *Knight and Day* ends with a gender reversal, placing June in the role of the male 'saviour,' and simultaneously deconstructing Cruise's image as the undefeatable hero by allowing the audience to see a once-venerated action icon saved by a woman.

The action romantic comedy is a hybrid generic form which saw a revival in the new millennium, culminating in the release of four films in 2010 (*Date Night, Knight and Day, The Bounty Hunter* and *Killers*). However, despite the progress in the depiction of female heroines in the last two decades, the action romantic comedy has yet to change the narrative equation and represent a couple where the female is the initial leader and the male is the ordinary individual caught in extraordinary circumstances with the exception of two equally strong characters in *Mr. & Mrs. Smith* and the representation of two ordinary individuals who accidentally stumble upon adventure in *Date Night*. In *Fool's Gold, Killers, The Bounty Hunter* and *Knight and Day*, the male leads are a treasure hunter, a spy, a bounty hunter and a CIA agent respectively, while the women are an academic, an executive, a journalist and a car restorer. Nevertheless, the new millennium romantic comedies are exhibiting an inclination towards an increasing tendency for the objectification of the male body, which was not so apparent in films of previous decades. In *Killers*, Ashton Kutcher is introduced to the audience and Katherine Heigl in his swimsuit, allowing for everyone to gaze at his virile torso and strong legs. Matthew McConaughey spends most of his on-screen time in *Fool's Gold* in nothing but different pairs of Bermuda shorts, while Gerard Butler in *The Bounty Hunter* is also seen half-naked, wrapped in a towel. Finally, in *Knight and Day*, Tom Cruise, 47 at the time of filming, took off his shirt twice, to exhibit his still robust abdomen for the pleasure of the audience. These 'instances of the erotic display of the male body are rife in contemporary film and media production, and can be shown to be geared to either (or both) male and female spectators in different contexts' (Paul Smith, 2004, p. 46). Although Smith adds that 'this objectification has been evident throughout the history of Hollywood' (ibid.), the multiplication and the frequency with which the male body is being eroticized on screen has led Joe Reid (2011) to characterize the cinematic summer of 2011 as the 'the summer that the male gaze was reflected back at itself'. However, the depiction of the male body as a to-be-looked-at object has become the subject of much academic debate ever since Laura Mulvey posited that the cinematic gaze is male in 1975. Drawing on Richard Dyer's work, Tasker (2002, p. 77) claims that in order for the male body to be displayed, it needs to be associated with some kind of activity. Indeed, in the above-mentioned examples of objectified male bodies, the heroes need to show their torsos because they are either going swimming, looking for a treasure hidden in the ocean, taking a shower, or trying to heal a wound. However, this approach can lead to an impasse because the connection between the objectified male body to an activity is always there, however trivial; for instance Cruise in *Knight and Day* does not need 'really' need to take his shirt off to have a look at his wound, and Kutcher in *Killers* does not 'really' need to walk in the hotel elevator wearing nothing but a tight swimsuit despite his intention of diving into the sea. Nevertheless, one could theoretically assume that the link to these activities repositions the male into his patriarchal, energetic and aggressive role. Unfortunately, this position does not take into account the momentary display of the male body as an erotic object nor the pleasure both the male and the female audiences derive from these images.

The stress on masculine virility in this romantic comedy cycle, however, does not forget the representation of female sexuality or fitness. As Reid (2011) underlines, '[i]t's not like women are suddenly *not* being objectified;

now it's just objectification for all'. Consequently, we do get and perhaps *expect* to see Diaz (*Knight and Day*) and Kate Hudson (*Fool's Gold*) in bikinis, and Katherine Heigl (*Killers*) and Jennifer Aniston (*The Bounty Hunter*) in very tight skirts which accentuate their firm yet feminine curves. The heroines' objectification is also tied to narrative parameters as that of their male cinematic partners. Most importantly, however, their semi-clad scenes are linked to the actresses' celebrity status and the constant interest in female body image. While the heterosexual male viewer may enjoy Diaz's bikini scene or Aniston's running barefoot in the tightest skirt possible, the heterosexual female may look for signs of ageing and/or look up the thespians' dietary habits or fitness regime. This observation does not imply that male viewers do not wish they had the bodies of some Hollywood stars but that celebrity culture, and western society as a whole for that matter, still employs a double standard when it comes to external appearance. Male fitness is increasingly claiming a significant part of celebrity culture, representing youthfulness, virility and health. Nonetheless, while paparazzi and/or publicity photos of half-naked fit actors, such as Hugh Jackman, Ryan Gosling, Ryan Reynolds and Ashton Kutcher among others, are widely circulated online and in the press, men are still outnumbered by photos of female bodies. In addition, it is mostly women who are publicly 'punished' should they gain a few pounds, and/or are photographed in uncompromising positions which may reveal their anatomic 'flaws'. Writing on action heroines, Marc O'Day (2004, p. 205), underlines that

> [t]he circulation of extra-textual publicity and behind-the-scenes materials on the action babe stars, characters and movies draws pervasively on this 'fit babe' discourse, highlighting the ways in which the gendered body of both the star and the action babe heroine are processed through the twin lens of eroticization and active strength.

Similarly, the female stars of the action romantic comedy cycle have to stress both their feminine side, which will eventually lead to the expected formation of a heterosexual couple, and their male abilities as strong, fast and resourceful agents during the action sequences. However, although the male protagonists usually assume the more energetic role via their professional identities, at least in the beginning of that narrative, with the exception of two – albeit quite different as far as their narrative treatment is concerned (*Mr. & Mrs. Smith* and *Date Night*) – the new-millennium cycle of the action rom coms seems to renegotiate the strict active-man/passive-woman equation, and allow for the heroine to stand beside the hero as an equal action partner.

The second significant characteristic that distinguishes the new-millennium action rom com is the escapist ending and/or the return to suburban safety. Commenting on *Romancing the Stone*, Palmer situates the film in a group of several 1980s cinematic narratives which he calls the 'Yuppie Texts', and which usually complete their circle by having their yuppie heroes and/or heroines either 'flee further from the pressures of […] the urban workplace battlefield' or 'set out on mythic quests' (1993, p. 297). The films of the last decade may place their couple in several exotic settings (from the French Riviera in *Killers*, Colombia in *Mr. and Mrs. Smith*, the Bahamas in *Fool's Gold* to Austria and Spain, in *Knight and Day*) but their protagonists are not there to escape their fast-paced lives. Instead, Heigl is on vacation in Nice in order to forget a break-up while Kutcher is completing another mission, Brad Pitt and Angelina Jolie are both working in Latin America, Hudson is working on a yacht for a millionaire who is financing her ex-husband's treasure hunt and Diaz is assisting Cruise in retrieving the miraculous battery and its teenage inventor respectively.

Thus, the foreign and often breath-taking surroundings mainly function as the perfect setting for the action and/or romantic sequences, enhance the viewing process but do not in any way imply the characters are under pressure in their everyday life. Even the oppressed Fosters in *Date Night* are not represented as a yuppie couple, but as two decent and hard-working parents who, as neoliberal subjects, benefit from some of the system's rewards (a comfortable home in New Jersey and decently paying jobs).

However, by the end of the films, the majority of the couples (*Mr. and Mrs. Smith*, *Fool's Gold*, *Date Night*, *Killers*) choose the suburban home, away from the urban centre as their ultimate safe haven, underlining a trend that may have started after 9/11 but was exacerbated by the economic recession. The last decade witnessed an impressive increase in relocation away from big cities, and especially New York (Daniel Massey and Miriam Kreinin Souccar, 2009, Jen Doll, 2011). Thus, even though the Big Apple still remains the preferred romantic comedy site, the action rom com cycle offers another alternative.

In choosing to abandon the city, however, another characteristic of the cycle is made apparent. In the case of *Date Night*, the 'bad' guys, with the exception of the mobster Joe Miletto (Ray Liotta), are exactly those public servants (the two policeman and the city's district attorney) who are supposed to protect Americans and make sure the law is upheld. Thus, the city is transformed into an unsafe environment where unlawful deals are conducted 'under the table', between the criminals and the public officials, and where corruption and secrets – the district attorney is a sexually insatiable individual – have to be carefully kept away from the public eye. Thus, the film turns the attention away from those foreign powers that may pose a threat to American safety to suggest that wrongdoing, illegal actions and/or corruption can also be performed by Americans against Americans, in a society still recovering from a significant collective trauma. The corrupt policemen and district attorney not only echo the several sex scandals that have resulted in the resignation of quite a few political figures in the 2000s, such as the cases of Samuel B. Kent, the Texas federal district judge, the Senators John Ensign, John Edwards, and the Representatives Vito Fossella and Tim Mahoney, to name but a few, but imply that 'all is not well in the land of the free'.

Knight and Day opts for a different approach, as the couple does not choose to settle down anywhere but is seen driving away from every place and every one they have ever known. The audience can only presume June and Roy are driving to South America, as the heroine has earlier stated that it was one of her dreams to drive there in her father's old car. In contrast to *Date Night*, the narrative saw the two protagonists travel in many different European countries and exotic locales to retrieve the supposedly invaluable gadget, secure the safety of its inventor, as well as prevent Zephyr's use as a weapon. The villains of *Knight and Day* include a Spanish arms dealer and an FBI agent who went rogue, thus underlining how evil can have no national identity any more. However, it is interesting to observe how the FBI's jurisdiction travels outside the US borders and imposes its rules on other countries without having to answer to the local authorities. This type of American sovereignty, or should I say complex of superiority, may be justified as the only way to 'get things done', but at the same time, echoes the many instances of US intervention all around the world.

To conclude, the millennial action rom com retains the same structural frame it inherited from the 1980s. Nevertheless, its subtle differentiations allow for new, interesting readings regarding the negotiation of male/female action heroes, the examination of relationships in the context of extreme situations, as well as the complexities and negative aspects of the US political system, its 'imperialist' tendencies and its voracious need to control situations that should obviously be of no concern to it.

6   The teen rom com

I was lucky to come of age in the 1980s, a decade which meant quite different things for Greece and the United States. Greece welcomed its first socialist government in 1981, and the middle class enjoyed unprecedented prosperity. In contrast, the 1980s, characterized as 'the narrative of Ronald Reagan's America' (Graham Thompson, 2007, p. 3), dealt with foreign issues, such as 'terrorism, the nuclear threat, détente', and domestic issues, 'such as the farm crisis, the new racism, and the yuppie phenomenon' (Palmer, 1993, p. xii), AIDS, and homelessness. I was also fortunate enough to grow up watching all the great teen movies of the decade, otherwise known as the John Hughes's films.[1] From *Sixteen Candles* (1984) to *The Breakfast Club* (1985) and *Pretty in Pink* (1986), I was mesmerized not just by the romances between characters approximately my age but also because I was introduced to a new and exciting world. These films were not mere entertainment, but they were actually teaching my friends and me about how teenagers act in American schools, why the 'prom' is so important, and the division of the students into a 'caste' system (the cheerleaders, the jocks, the nerds, the 'bad' boys).

As I moved from adolescence to adulthood, I did not lose interest in the teen films Hollywood continued to release year by year. I came to realize that in almost every respect (personality development, development of tastes in music, fashion, film, educational capabilities and sexual identity among others) adolescence is one of the most significant periods in the life of an individual. It is also during this time that the first 'crushes' or the first 'loves' occur and the concept of romantic relationships is formed. These moments are very important as more often than not, it is these romantic decisions that end up dictating the pattern which the individual will follow into adulthood. In addition to the representation of romantic love, the teen film genre helps us understand 'how successive generations have endured the conflicts of claiming identity and seeking recognition for their actions', and especially in the new millennium represent 'the contemporary coming-of-age process' (Timothy Shary, 2003, pp. 491–2). Like the romantic comedy genre, the teen film remained underappreciated and unexamined at least until 1985 and the publication of David Considine's *The Cinema of Adolescence*, 'the first book-length study of the image of teenagers in American movies' (Shary, 2011,

p. 7). Gradually, scholars have acknowledged the power, variety and societal commentary of the genre and started producing a number of studies (see among others, Jon Lewis, 1992, Roz Kaveney, 2006, and Catherine Driscoll, 2011) which shed light on a genre whose main subject, 'adolescence', was discovered along with motion pictures 'as the nineteenth century was growing into the twentieth', with the publication of G. Stanley Hall's 'groundbreaking study *Adolescence: Its Psychology, and Its Relations to Physiology, Anthropology, Sociology, Sex, Crime, Religion, and Education*', the first study that identified adolescence as a distinct and significant stage of life (Shary, 2011, p. 1).

Most writers (Kaveney, 2006, Shary, 2011, Driscoll, 2011) recognize the 1980s as a turning point regarding a more nuanced depiction of teenage characters. However, as a detailed exploration of the various sub-genres teen film encompasses exceeds the scope of this study, I will limit the discussion to the new millennium cycle of the teen romantic comedy. I will explore how and where these instances of the very first eye contact, the first phone call, the first awkward date, the first physical contact and/or the first relationship happen and how these instances are treated by both the teenagers involved as well as the people around them (family, teachers, friends). However, despite the focus on the romantic aspect of the narratives, I will also place my analysis in a sociopolitical context. In his examination of 1990s teen films, Wood (2003, p. 311) assumes the same viewpoint and questions whether these narratives reflect dominant trends in US culture, 'offer seductive fantasies' or present 'progressive aspects in their treatment of today's teenagers'. Therefore, my analysis will also be complemented by issues of class and parenthood with the view to questioning if and how the teen rom com cycle addresses contemporary adolescence in the specific societal circumstances of the last decade.

However, during the categorization of the corpus, I made a few unexpected findings. First of all, from the 18 US teen film productions of the last decade only 12 can be included in the romantic comedy cycle. When faced with a similar obstacle regarding two Kirsten Dunst teen films, Jeffers McDonald (2007, p. 9) claimed that *Bring it On* (2000) is not a romantic comedy since its focus is 'to expose the problems of incidental daily racism affecting the lives of a troupe of black cheerleaders' while *Get Over It* (2001) is included in the rom com genre since the heroine's actions 'are motivated by her love' for a young boy (ibid.). Similarly, I excluded six teen films from the teen romantic comedy cycle since their dominant feature is not the pursuit of a romantic relationship, despite its inclusion as a sub-plot. *What a Girl Wants* (2003) explores a father–daughter relationship, *Mean Girls* (2004) is a witty comment on the American high school caste system, *Raise Your Voice* (2004) and *Confessions of a Teenage Drama Queen* (2004) are two stories of girly empowerment and defiance and *The Sisterhood of the Traveling Pants* (2005) is an ensemble film about friendship, daughter–parent relationships, love and loss. What is interesting is that the films excluded from the cycle because their dominant narrative ingredient was not the quest for love, were nevertheless all centred on teen girls and vehicles for three of the new millennium teen 'queens': Hilary Duff, Lindsay Lohan and Amanda Bynes, who star in every film except *The Sisterhood of the Traveling Pants*. In addition, of the 12 teen rom coms, eight featured a female heroine while only four were centred on male protagonists.

Interestingly, these four male-driven teen romances were released between 2000–2004 (*Loser, Get Over It, Summer Catch* and *The Girl Next Door*) and there was no male-focused teen romantic comedy released internationally after 2004. The male teen rom com *Love at First Hiccup* was not released theatrically in the United States in 2009 and was, thus, not included in the corpus, while *Tadpole* (2000), the coming-of-age story of a teenage boy had a limited release in both the US and the rest of the world. These observations do not mean male teenagers were absent from the silver screen. On the contrary, they had significant success, but with such teen male-centred films as the *American Pie* franchise consisting of three films (1999, 2001, and 2003) and four straight to video spin-off films (2005, 2006, 2007, and 2009). The *American Pie* films are considered sex comedies in the tradition of the three *Porky's* comedies of the 1980s, which according to Jeffers McDonald (2007, p. 56), use sex 'as the motor to drive the plot forward'.

The female dominance in the new millennium teen movie universe is an interesting finding, since the teen films of the 1990s 'remain resolutely male-centered, the main action (the "plot") invariably initiated by the males' (Wood, 2003, p. 320). The gender reversal in the last decade can be linked to two reasons: first, the impressive turn of teenage boys to video games, and especially console games, whether multiplayer games, such as *Gears of War* and *Star Wars*, third-person shooter games, such as *Dead Space* and *Silent Hill* or first-person shooter games, such as *Rage*, and *Killzone 2*. In the era of synergies and global conglomerates, it is safe to hypothesize that companies with interests both in the film and video game industries, such as Sony, would invest capital in the latter, since teenage boys and/or young men are not, by definition, interested in romantic film narratives and seem to prefer spending their free time playing. Although teenage girls have also begun to constitute a significant portion of the gamer community (see the Video Game Industry Statistics for 2010, and Jennifer Jenson and Suzanne de Castell, 2008), they still constitute a viable target for the film industry. However, the significant number of female-centred teenage romantic comedies in the last two decades can also be explained to a great extent by the rise of girl power and its omni-presence in media culture for the past 20 years. Four important factors are associated with the emergence of this new movement and the entrance of the term 'girl power' in everyday vocabulary after the mid-1990s: first, the back-lash against second-wave feminism and the emergence of the third wave; second, the publication of Mary Pipher's *Reviving Ophelia: Saving the Selves of Adolescent Girls* in 1994, a parents' advice guidebook which investigated why 'girls "lose" an authentic Selfhood in order to become what [American] culture dictates' (Dawn Currie, Deirdre M. Kelly and Shauna Pomerantz,

2009, p. 6); third, the 'Riot Grrrl' bands of the 1990s, which 'challenged the sexism and racism of punk rock', and 'combined an "innocent" girlish aesthetic with what is most threatening to adults: youthful rage and bitterness about the adult world' (ibid. p. 7)[2]; and the fourth factor was 'the short-lived, but overwhelmingly, successful British pop singing group, The Spice Girls', who 'proclaimed that girl power was a way to identify with feminism without having to use what had become a "dirty word"' (Emilie Zaslow, 2009, p. 3). Zaslow (ibid.) adds that 'girl power quickly moved beyond a catchy slogan to represent a cultural moment in which girls not only had an increase in purchasing power but also required industry executives to create a new consumer profile'.

This profile was also employed by the US film and television industries to exploit the female teenage portion of the audience. Kathleen Rowe Karlyn (2011, p. 5) notes that the unexpected commercial success of the teen romantic comedy *Clueless* (1995) and the girl-centred thriller *Scream* (1996) were followed respectively 'by a television spin-off and a wave of romantic teen flicks' and three sequels (1997, 2000 and 2011). Rowe also notices that the television industry sought to capitalize on girl power with shows 'featuring teen-girl protagonists in situations from the everyday (*Felicity* and *Dawson's Creek*) to the fantastic (*Buffy the Vampire Slayer*, based on a 1992 movie)' (ibid.). These fictional representations offer a variety of discourses which negotiate the characteristics of the modern teenage girl in the new millennium. On the one hand, most representations consist of female empowerment through individual choices the teenage heroines make, and on the other emphasize the importance of femininity through the traditional arsenal of make-up and wardrobe. In addition, as these new-millennium narratives are produced and take place in a specific sociopolitical context, they also include comments on several political and cultural issues, such as the high school and college hierarchy which is similar to the hierarchy that exists in the adult world, while they continue to negotiate the meaning of American adolescence. Thus, part of the analysis that ensues will focus on how the structure of teenage life and the high school cosmos can be used either as paradigms that reflect and support the hierarchies and structure of US life and/or offer alternatives to the neoliberal status quo.

The two teen rom coms discussed in this chapter, *Chasing Liberty* (2004) and *Sydney White* (2007) were chosen not only because they can be considered 'classic' examples of the cycle, or because they star two teen 'queens' of the 2000s (Mandy Moore and Amanda Bynes respectively) but also because they address important societal issues, aside from the representation of the millennial female adolescent. *Chasing Liberty* offers an interesting interpretation regarding the tensions between Europe and the United States in the months before the Iraq War in 2003, while *Sydney White*, which re-invents the Snow White fairy tale, and whose plot takes place on a college campus, criticizes the fraternity system with its elaborate rules which include and exclude individuals based on social standing, appearance and/or intelligence but is also characterized by corruption, personal agendas and intrigue, reflecting the larger political system with the powerful lobbies and organizations that may dictate governmental policy.

Chasing Liberty

Chasing Liberty does not take place in a high school context nor does it culminate in a much-awaited prom night. Instead, it is the journey of a runaway teenage girl through Europe. However, 18-year-old Anna (Mandy Moore) is not just a frustrated teenager. She is the daughter of James Foster (Mark Harmon), the President of the United States. As the daughter of the President for six years, and the daughter of a governor for eight years, Anna has never been able to know what it means to walk in the streets without drawing attention. The credit sequence teases the audience with a parallel montage showing Anna trying on outfits in front of her mirror and a boy driving to pick her up for a date. What the viewers perceive as the prelude of a 'normal' evening is interrupted once the camera draws away from Anna's window to reveal that her house is the White House. On the one hand, this shot instantly implies that the ensuing date cannot be ordinary, and on the other it comes in stark contrast with the first sequence which portrays the feelings of impatience, longing and excitement a young woman experiences before a young man knocks on her door, and this contrast can lead to the audience's amusement and subsequent curiosity. Indeed, Grant (Stark Sands) and his car have to go through a rigorous check at the gate, the same rigorous examination both teenagers face at the restaurant at which they are dining. Although Anna seems at ease with the attention and explains she was brought up in the public eye and is therefore used to this life, Grant is overwhelmed. When the couple is approached by three teenage boys, the secret service agents who are surveying Grant's and Anna's every move from strategically placed positions perceive the movement as a threat and the date is brought to an abrupt ending with Grant telling Anna that he cannot see her anymore.

Her unsuccessful date incites Anna's anger and she immediately storms into the Oval Office without noticing the officials her dad, the President is conferring with about the upcoming G8 Summit in Prague. Her outburst and subsequent surprise at the sight of the men and women who are witnessing her teenage eruption is comic even as it provides food for thought. In teen romantic comedies and other genres of teen films for that matter, teenage crises and/or rebellious acts are usually brought about by conflicts with adults and especially parents. For instance, writing about John Hughes's films, Thomas Leitch (1992, p. 44) observes that the writer/director usually holds 'inadequate parents and parent figures' responsible for the adolescent problems he explores in the filmic narratives. However, in *Chasing Liberty*, Dad's 'inadequacy' does not originate from abusive behavior or addiction problems, as in *Breakfast Club* (1985), or depression and abandonment, as in *Pretty in Pink* (1986). James Foster is the President of the United States and his well-being as well as that of his family members is a matter of national security. That is why, at the breakfast scene that ensues after the disastrous date, the President accidentally reveals he had the young man checked by the FBI and that Anna should not be very upset as Grant was not the 'right' candidate for his daughter. Anna is once again furious with the complete lack of privacy but she tries to persuade her father to let her go to a concert without any security when the presidential family goes to Prague and she meets Gabrielle (Beatrice Rosen), the French ambassador's daughter. Naturally, the President does not accept Anna's request but they both compromise and decide Anna will 'only' be discreetly escorted by two agents.

However, Dad never intended to keep his promise and as soon as he sees that Gabrielle has a pierced tongue, he immediately labels her as a negative influence and without his daughter's knowledge, he orders a team of agents to follow her without being noticed. Although Gabrielle belongs to the same social class and is the same age as Anna, she is enjoying freedoms that Anna was never allowed to have. The fact that the President perceives Gabrielle as a 'wild child' and even goes as far as telling the First Lady, 'Thank God Gabrielle found another trashy friend to hang out with', when he sees Gabrielle and another girl – who in fact is his daughter with a new hairdo and dressed in casual clothes – points to a USA–Europe divide that will become a repeated theme for the rest of the narrative.

It should be noted that *Chasing Liberty* was released in early 2004 but was filmed in 2003, the year during which '[r]elations between the United States and its traditional European allies' reached a low point 'in the months before the war in Iraq in early 2003' (Sven Steinmo and Jeffrey Kopstein, 2008, p. 2). Although Steinmo and Kopstein add that the partnership has, since 2003 found a certain balance, they claim that the relationship between Europe and the United States 'has changed' (ibid.). Similarly, Laurent Cohen-Tanugi (2008, p. 214) argues that 'the global shock of September 11, 2001, and one of its principal consequences, the American-led invasion of Iraq' simply exacerbated the deterioration of the Euro–American alliance, since 'tensions had […] been accumulating between the two sides of the Atlantic over a vast range of "nonstrategic" matters such as trade and economic regulation, global warming […] and societal issues such as human rights and the death penalty'. *Chasing Liberty* takes this tension for granted and focuses on the cultural differences between Europe and the United States through specific European characters, such as the 'naughty' Gabrielle from France or the untrustworthy Scottish McGruff (Martin Hancock), who will be shortly discussed.

Anna is finally enjoying what she perceives as relative freedom but she soon realizes her father was lying. Frustrated and betrayed, she changes clothes with a drunken girl in the bathroom, prompted by Gabrielle, and escapes the agents. As soon as she runs out of the concert hall, she asks a young man to take her away on his scooter and the couple skilfully escapes the secret service in the narrow streets of Prague. Ben (Matthew Goode) joins her at the bar she is supposed to meet Gabrielle, and Anna relaxes once again and even drinks beer which she legally can in Europe but not in the USA, where the age limit for alcohol consumption is 21 years of age. Nevertheless, despite her not breaking the law, Anna's drinking may remind the audience of Jenna and Barbara Bush, who were arrested in 2001 for underage drinking and were also involved in several other misdemeanours during the years of their father's presidency. Anna does seem inebriated as she leaves the bar and falls down on the pavement but she soon pulls herself together as she is once again spotted by the two agents. Ben helps her escape again but by now, the viewers have learnt that he is also an agent and that the President assigned him with the protection of Anna in order to give her 'an illusion of independence'. ·

The President's parental strictness may seem excessive but, on the other hand, it can be justified. His daughter is not just an average teenager in that she is recognized all over the world and can be the target of domestic and foreign political enemies as well as terrorists. Thus, the seemingly over-protective measures he takes to ensure Anna's safety can also be considered necessary, especially in a post-9/11 climate. If we apply Cindy Weber's intelligent gender reading on the 2001 drama *In the Bedroom*, through post-9/11 US foreign policy, we could argue that Anna represents 'the unofficial desire [...] to have al Qaeda brought to justice', while President Foster 'represents the official US government view', which asks for immediate justice (2006, p. 112). Thus, Anna metonymically stands for a feminized, disobedient and reckless USA, which requires the guiding hand of the masculinized nation in the form of the (Republican) father.

In addition, President Foster's use of his position as the leader of the free world to control his daughter follows in a long line of cinematic fathers who tried in vain to keep their daughters close to them without realizing their child had turned into an independent young woman. From Spencer Tracy in *Father of the Bride* (1950), Jerry Orbach in *Dirty Dancing* (1987), and Steve Martin in *Father of the Bride* (1990) to Dan Hedaya in *Clueless* (1995) – to refer to just a few dads that appeared in comedies – the relationship between a father and a daughter was almost always represented as a dichotomy between law and disobedience, and absolute control and desire for freedom. In addition, the more recent instances of fatherhood on film reflect 'the emergence of a cultural shift in expectations surrounding fathering, most notable since the 1980s', and more often than not present a father who 'is more emotionally involved, more nurturing', and more sensitive to his children's needs (Glenda Wall and Stephanie Arnold, 2007, pp. 509–10). Nevertheless, even though James Foster is not particularly represented as committed to understanding and/or even really listening to his teenage daughter's problems – he is the leader of the 'last' super power after all – *Chasing Liberty* places him, and not Anna's mother, as the opposition, thus underlining the importance of their relationship, and consequently of fatherhood and masculinity.

On the other hand, Anna's act of rebellion is not instigated by unhappiness, need for attention or anger towards her parents, as is Molly Ringwald's in

Breakfast Club, but by a healthy need to experience life away from the spotlight, doing things she would normally not even dream of, like swimming naked in the Danube or watching an art performance from a rooftop. Anna feels free and happy but little does she know, her unruly behavior is not just constantly monitored by not just one but three of her dad's secret agents. Ben may be by her side, pretending to be a photographer but agents Weiss (Jeremy Piven) and Morales (Annabella Sciorra) are one step behind them at all times. That is why, although Anna planned to return to her duties the next morning and calls her father, she decides to prolong her 'vacation' once the President orders her to come back when he receives naked photos taken when she was ready to dive in the Danube. Like a twenty-first-century Ellie (Claudette Colbert) in *It Happened One Night*, Anna jumps on a train in defiance of her father, and just like Ellie, she is not alone. While in the 1934 classic, the wealthy heiress was accompanied by Peter (Clark Gable), an ambitious journalist, Anna is accompanied by Ben, whose initial purpose is to get her safely back to her father. In fact, *Chasing Liberty* pays homage to Frank Capra's screwball comedy in many respects. It is a story of a young woman who decides to abandon her 'safe' surroundings and experience an adventure. It is also a story of a young woman and a young man from two different worlds who meet under peculiar circumstances, pretend at some point that they are married and fall in love during a long and eventful journey. However, unlike *It Happened One Night*, *Chasing Liberty* is not a 'cross-class romance', nor does it provide an 'extended commentary on the structure of social class' (Beach, 2002, p. 71).

Chasing Liberty chooses to pretend that the story unfolds in a classless society and thus annuls the potential social critique that could have enriched the narrative and also assist Anna's understanding of the world during her few days of freedom. On the other hand, although Ben and Anna meet many friendly and helpful people, the film underlines that danger is never far away in the 'real' world Anna desperately wants to explore. Ben and Anna meet a Scottish backpacker, McGruff, who seems friendly and funny, but after a carefree day the three of them spend in Venice, McGruff steals Anna's wallet. In addition, when Anna finally discovers that Ben is a secret agent during the Love Parade in Berlin, she runs away only to be recognized and terrorized by some American tourists.

Thus, *Chasing Liberty* is not critical of the upper class like *It Happened One Night* but of the middle class implying that one is almost never safe since threatening situations may arise whether you are a public figure – McGruff does not know Anna is the President's daughter – or not – the American youth in Berlin harass Anna because of her identity. The European characters Anna and Ben meet in their adventure are all flawed and stereotypical in one way or another. The French Gabrielle is a 'bad girl', who disregards the etiquette that surrounds her identity as the French Ambassador's daughter and seems only interested in parties. The Italian gondolier Eugenio (Joseph Long) is a 40-something mama's boy with no career aspirations or interest in his love life, who still lives with his mother. His mother, Maria (Miriam Margolyes), is represented as the traditional, oppressive and loud Italian middle-aged matriarch, who is always right and expresses hostility to anyone who may articulate an opinion she does not agree with. Finally, the Scottish McGruff is a thief who masquerades as a friendly guy but is only interested in having fun, even if he does so at the expense of others. Even Anna's object of affection, the born-in-Wales but raised-in-London Ben turns out to be a liar, since he could not reveal his true identity and opted to obey the President than stay true to himself and his feelings. The film's superficial portrayal of several European identities reinforces the Euro–American cultural divide and does not permit a deeper understanding of the richness that the 'old continent' carries in its long history. Only the British Ben is spared from this 'easy' characterization not just because he is Anna's protector, friend, first love and finally saviour but also because of the UK government alliance with the US decision to invade Iraq in 2003. It should be noted that '[t]he controversial election of George W. Bush and the undiplomatic attitudes toward European positions of the first few months of his administration crystallized and increased those tensions and anti-American sentiment in Europe' (Tanugi, 2008, p. 214). However, despite the eventual assistance most countries in the European Union offered in the 2003 Iraq invasion, and despite the especially vocal French and German opposition before and after, the overwhelming majority of European citizens were against their governments' involvement, thus creating a widespread anti-American sentiment. Thus, *Chasing Liberty* can be also read as a political cinematic text that uses a teenage love story as a pretext to comment on and support US sovereignty.

When Anna is carried away from the Berlin parade and into a helicopter, she completes a different journey from Ellie's in Capra's classic screwball comedy. In *It Happened One Night*, Ellie realizes that the world is inhabited by people who suffer, but also people who are decent, hard-working and mostly honest. On the contrary, Anna leaves Europe, betrayed by both her father and the first man she fell in love with, hurt by love and disillusioned with what freedom can be. Back home, she enrols at Harvard and a brief sequence shows her and Ben going about their lives thinking of their time together. Surprisingly, the resolution is provided by the President himself who advises his daughter to attend an exchange program at Oxford and also tells her that Ben is now working in London. Once again, Anna acts responsibly and follows not only her heart but her father's wishes as well and she is reunited with Ben in the British capital. Although the President's sudden change of heart is not plausibly explained, it can be suggested that Anna's melancholia upon her return, and her progress at Harvard, led to his realization that she is no longer his little girl but an autonomous and reliable individual who should be free to make her own choices and her own mistakes for that matter. Anna's obedience to the law, exemplified by her father, the President, is what makes her life functional again. The film may end with her kissing Ben in London, but only after Anna accepts and acts upon her father's suggestion. Therefore, *Chasing Liberty* ends by advocating the discipline of a liberal, feminine character, which could also stand for the US democratic ideology, as was argued above, in favour of the wisdom of the male authority figure, that is the Republican governmental policy. Despite the happy ending, which appropriately completes a teenage romantic comedy, Anna remains a docile neoliberal subject, whose actions will be controlled and/or pre-determined for the sake of her family's stability and, by extension, the nation's global sovereignty.

Sydney White

Sydney White is a free adaptation of *Snow White* starring the teen queen Amanda Bynes (*She's the Man*, 2006, *Love Wrecked*, 2005, *What a Girl Wants*, and *Big Fat Liar*, 2002). However, unlike *Chasing Liberty*, and its fairy-tale source for that matter, *Sydney White* is an intensely political text which addresses issues of class and gender. Sydney is a middle-class girl who is about to start college on a scholarship. Unlike in the fairy tale, her father is not a king or even a wealthy man, but a plumber (John Schneider). The first sequence shows Sydney working with her dad and his crew. All the men are signing a card for her and when her dad presents her with a big box, Sydney, who is working alongside them, asks if it is 'a Stanley 22-ounce Antivibe framing hammer'. Sydney's interest in tools, rather than a beautiful dress or whatever can be perceived as an 'appropriate' present for a girl is intriguing. Right from the start, the film moves away from its literary source and presents its heroine as a tomboy. The voiceover which then accompanies a brief flashback of Sydney's life explains to the audience how she lost her mother when she was nine years old and how she grew up in an exclusively male environment. The lack of female influence has, therefore, assisted Sydney's development of a femininity which does not follow a 'traditional' path but is more in league with current theories that view gender as a social construction. Sydney is therefore presented as a confident, decisive, intelligent and pragmatic young woman who was raised by a caring and loving father and has grown up to be an independent individual and was never drawn to the temptations of a consumerist neoliberal society.

The plot begins as Sydney leaves for college, ready and excited not only to begin a new chapter in her life but also because she will be attending her mother's alma matter and joining her mother's fraternity, KΦN. Sydney arrives at the college and meets her roommate, Dinky (Crystal Hunt), a sociable Southern girl, whose mother was also a Kappa sister. Dinky loans Sydney a dress for their first meeting at the sorority house because the heroine's suitcase is filled with her comic book collection, another sign of her masculine side and her indifference to an entire industry that demands all women, regardless of age, to discover their identity through make-up and clothes. As the two girls walk on the campus, the scenery resembles a suburban town with beautiful buildings and broad streets. Sydney attracts the attention of Tyler (Matt Long) who offers to be their guide.

During their short walk, Tyler points at each building and says that 'each house has a reputation'. He proceeds by explaining the distinguishing characteristics of the different sororities, noting that the ΓΦ 'are [...] perky cheerleaders', the ΠΒΩ girls party all the time, the Vortex, a dilapidated building, houses 'losers' and is soon to be demolished, while the ΚΦΝ are 'intense'. Tyler's classification is an explicit political statement as he and the rest of the student body live in a clearly socially divided environment. The campus society is thus a reflection of a society where 'all men are created equal'. What is interesting and alarming at the same time is that Tyler and both girls accept his description at face value and do not raise any objection to the obvious categorization every student that arrives at the fictional Southern Atlantic University has to go through. One can assume that the reason for Sydney's and Dinky's nonchalance, as well as the young man's casual division of students into different 'categories' originates from their never being a target of any kind of prejudice. Although Sydney comes from the middle class, the brief flashback showed that she was not only brought up in a loving environment but also a well-protected one and that her moving to college is the first time she will experience people from different backgrounds.

The social division is not limited to the general categories students belong to. The film shows that inside every fraternity and sorority there is also a strict hierarchy. The villainess of this version of the classic fairy tale is not Sydney's dad's new wife, but ΚΦΝ's president, Rachel Witchburn (Sara Paxton), an overly ambitious, blonde and wealthy student who runs the sorority and the student council. The viewers are introduced to her in a scene where she parks her sports car outside the sorority's house, walks past everyone to her room and logs on her computer to check the 'Hot or Not' list of the campus, which substitutes for the tale's magic mirror. Of course, Rachel is the 'fairest' of them all.

In Rachel's kingdom, the young women may be accepted based on their family's name and/or wealth but they are then judged based on their appearance. In a revealing sequence, the new pledges pass in front of Rachel who is holding a magnifying glass and insults every one of them for either having visible pores, thicker eyebrows or the wrong hairstyle. Rachel seems to promote a uniform style: rich, thin, blonde girls who are there to obey her every wish and who would not dare question her.

When she realizes that Sydney poses a threat after witnessing Tyler's interest, and her increasing popularity among the rest of her sorority sisters, she systematically tries to sabotage Sydney's efforts to become a Kappa; however, Sydney's authentic personality, her ability to make friends with girls as well as boys with the same ease, her non-pretentious behaviour and her eagerness to help whomever she thinks is in need make her even more popular and earn her a spot on the 'Hot or Not' list, a fact that infuriates Rachel. She then decides to publicly humiliate Sydney during the pledge night and announces to everyone that not only did she violate sorority rules but she is the daughter of a plumber. Not even Tyler comes to her rescue, and Sydney packs her suitcase and leaves the KΦN house. However, she is soon saved by the 'losers' that welcome her in the Vortex. There, she meets the new-millennium seven dwarfs: Lenny the hypochondriac/Sneezy (Jack Carpenter), Terrence the silent genius/Doc (Jeremy Howard), Gurkin (Danny Strong), the video game afi-cionado/Grumpy, Spanky the womanizer /Happy (Samm Levine), Jeremy the uncommunicative one/Bashful (Adam Hendershott), George/Dopey (Arnie Pantoja) and Embele, the Nigerian jet-lagged student/Sleepy (Donté Bonner). Accustomed to being around men, Sydney quickly establishes connections with all her new friends. In addition, she immediately takes the initiative and asks them to repair their dwelling. When she hears that the student council is run by 'Greeks' and that all the money is usually divided among the Greek fraternities and sororities, Sydney signs up Terrence to become a president in an effort to correct the injustice that has been tolerated by the rest of the university student body for years.

From that moment on, *Sydney White* becomes an 'American tale', that is a story which exists 'to explain history, to condone some behaviours and con-demn others, and to pass on the culture of the community from one genera-tion to the next' (Daniel P. Franklin, 2006, p. 24). According to Franklin's categorization of the American 'myths' that are propagated through the silver screen, *Sydney White* belongs to those films that centre on 'the cult of the individual;' that is cinematic texts in which 'a resilient resourceful individual with personal courage and ingenuity overcomes the odds and succeeds with-out help against the grain of an oppressive environment often depicted as the government' (ibid., p. 25).

Sydney begins a campaign to change life at the university while she starts fixing things around the house and also helps her seven friends deal with their problems. She also finds time to do her homework and has a first date with Tyler. While Sydney is a secure female individual who sets goals and goes after them methodically and energetically, she only feels awkward when she is in the presence of Tyler, which not only implies her lack of sexual experience but also the lack or non-realization of her sexual awakening. Sydney's virgi-nity, both literally and metaphorically, may remove the question of teen sex from the narrative, but it can be argued that the heroine channels her repres-sed sexual feelings in her effort to change the university's structure. Her first date, however, is not a traditional night out. Tyler takes her to a church where Sydney and he are going to feed the homeless. Sydney is impressed by Tyler's socially conscious side and agrees to go on a second date. This time, however, Tyler spends the night at the Vortex playing video games with Gurkin, beat-ing him and earning the respect of Sydney's seven friends. Tyler is also impressed by what he thought was a group of 'losers' and invites them to a party at his fraternity. Unfortunately, Rachel decides to destroy Sydney who, by that point, has reached the coveted number 1 on the 'Hot or Not' list, is going out with her future husband and is threatening her seat on the student council. Therefore, at the Beta party, she humiliates Sydney's seven friends, announces that Terrence is disqualified from the presidency campaign because he has already graduated and that she has had the Vortex condemned upon Tyler's advice.

Once again, Sydney has to face a lost battle, as well as a broken heart, since she believes Tyler is responsible for her friends' 'homelessness'. However, a visit from her dad helps her restore her faith in herself and she decides to run against Rachel. A montage sequence shows her planning her campaign after convincing the seven 'dwarfs' that this is something worth fighting for, spending time with the 80 per cent of the school who does not belong to the Greek system, dancing with the school band, joining the Jewish student community and even attending a performance by a transgender student. Sydney's sincerity and genuineness win the hearts and minds of the student body and during the final debate, she is enthusiastically cheered on even by some Kappa sisters when she announces, 'It's time for the rest of the school to take back the school'. Sydney's concluding phrase cannot be easily dismissed as a populist attempt to win more votes as it reflects the similar way the American society, and most western societies for that matter, are organized and administered: the power belongs to the few who control the vast majority. Sydney's campaign, the posters, the rallies, her visits with almost every student and the final debate likens the collegial election system to the nation's real electoral procedure and offers a panorama, however limited and brief, of the process: from the campaign design, the manipulative manoeuvres of the candidates, the need to reach out to every voter whatever their gender, religion or ethnic background, to the continuous effort to address multiple and often contradicting issues.

Sydney White may end on a utopian note, finding all the students from every background united in celebration, but its message about equality is nevertheless potent and optimistic. Furthermore, the millennial Snow White does not have to be kissed by a prince to come alive. She may get a kiss by Tyler to wake up in time for the debate but her victory belongs solely to her ingenuity, efforts and careful planning. Without neglecting the romantic aspect or the comic moments of the genre, *Sydney White* devotes a significant narrative portion to university politics, denoting its importance for the lives of many teenagers who may feel they do not belong to a certain group, and simultaneously connoting the importance of societal pluralism, and the acceptance of difference. Finally, *Sydney White* is a narrative that empowers its female teenage heroine by showing how openness, generosity, sincerity and lack of pretentiousness can lead to real friendships and romantic relationships.

Both *Chasing Liberty* and *Sydney White* depart considerably from the 1980s, as well as several 1990s, teen films. First, unlike their 1990s counterparts, these films centre on girls, and not boys, which can be mostly attributed to the girl power movement of the late 1990s and 2000s. Although, as it has already been noted, teen sex comedies, such as the *American Pie* series, focus on boys and sex, the 'surrender' of the teen rom com cycle to teenage girls instead of boys can be seen as progress in the politics of a male-centred industry and also an acknowledgement of the purchasing power of the female teenage audience. In addition, the representation of Anna and Sydney is an important paradigm of empowerment. It is true that Anna's social status enables her to enjoy publicity and material possessions. However, her being under constant scrutiny every second of every day might have resulted in emotional instability and/or even aggression. Nevertheless, Anna is presented as a responsible, forthright and intelligent 18 year old whose only 'transgression' was her desire to be anonymous for a few days, in a way emulating Princess Ann's (Audrey Hepburn) anonymous 'adventures' in Rome in William Wyler's classic romantic comedy *Roman Holiday* (1953).

On the other hand, although Sydney comes from a middle-class background and is faced with the college's caste system and a cross-class romance, she never feels inferior or gives up, and in this way she is differentiated from Ringwald and Andrew McCarthy's socially forbidden romance in *Pretty in Pink*. These films promote a positive teenage feminine identity, underlining independence, intelligence, resourcefulness, empathy, generosity and responsibility as its key traits. Although both films are placed in a specific sociopolitical climate and negotiate political and social issues, whether implicitly (*Chasing Liberty*) or more explicitly (*Sydney White*), they release their heroines from consumerist obsession and/or class restrictions. *Chasing Liberty* and *Sydney White* do not fall in the trap of the male/female strict dichotomy and allow for a consideration of multiple masculinities and femininities, adhering to contemporary theoretical work which highlights the many facets gender can acquire in its performance. Except for the idea of female empowerment, these teen films also promote family and its importance in a post-9/11 climate, which strengthened the institution as it tried to heal the collective American trauma. That is why the parental figures, when depicted, are represented as stable, caring and protective and differ from the dysfunctional parents of the 1980s films who were in a way held responsible for their children's rebellion.

Nevertheless, the two films differ in one significant respect. The father of *Chasing Liberty* is a powerful, male authority figure who puts the world to rights through his wisdom and discipline. Thus, the whole world, and not just his daughter, is healed when this male is listened to and obeyed. In contrast, *Sydney White*'s father may raise his daughter with the help of his all-male group of workers, but in a feminized, masculine world which carefully nurtures people, who are then able to make their own sound decisions, free from the overarching authority of the male voice. Finally, *Sydney White* updates its fairy-tale source but in the end subverts it by proposing Sydney becoming the president of her college, that is, holding a kind of public office, and not compromising with just winning the heart of Tyler.

Lastly, as most 1990s films of the same cycle, the millennial teen romances continue to avoid discussion about race and/or homosexuality. Although most films include African-American, Hispanic and/or Asian characters, they mostly place them in secondary roles, and in this way they prove to be more conservative in the representation of modern multicultural societies. Despite the fact that the 2000s witnessed a welcome introduction of teenage homo-sexual characters from different races on American television (*Ugly Betty* ABC, 2006–2010 and *Glee* Fox 2009–present), mainstream cinema has yet to embrace this change and thus denies a substantial portion of the audience the pleasure of enjoying a homosexual romance and relate to their own personal experiences, as the heterosexual audience has been able to do for decades.

The millennial teen romantic comedies may seem more traditional and even conservative but a more careful reading reveals the inherent conflicts of a genre which not only focuses on a decisive phase of every person's life, one which is by definition turbulent but also the politics of the society that pro-duces these conflicts, a society which is supposed to uphold and protect free-dom and civil rights but also a neoliberal society which is divided, unequal and is still struggling to achieve balance in almost every sector.

7   The 'mature' rom com: heroines and heroes 'of a certain age'

In a 2010 *Los Angeles Times* article, Rebecca Keegan noted that 'older actresses are gaining ground' in the Hollywood cinematic arena. Citing such female-driven films as *The Devil Wears Prada*, *Sex and the City*, *The Blind Side* (2009) and *Secretariat* (2010), Keegan explained that this trend in the new millennium resulted from the industry's 'growing awareness [...] of the untapped potential of older audiences, especially female ones'. It is true that the new millennium witnessed several female-centred films from various genres enjoying both considerable worldwide success and critical praise. Suffice it to say that the first cinematic version of the HBO series *Sex and the City* (1998–2004) earned $415 million on a budget of $65 million, *The Devil Wears Prada* returned $326 million costing only $35 million, while the mostly favourably reviewed *The Blind Side* was not only the film that earned its star, Sandra Bullock, an Oscar, but became her second most commercially successful film to date, after *The Proposal*, with more than $307 million.

However, despite the obvious and incontestable truth the above numbers prove, recent statistics reveal that the film industry is still a long way from achieving a gender balance in the on-screen representation of men and women. According to the 2005 Statistics on Women and Media, 'women over the age of 40 were cast in only 11% of the roles for women, while men aged 40 and over accounted for nearly 26% of roles cast'. Similarly, the 2010 Department of Professional Employees Fact Sheet noted that 'in 2006, only 26% of all female roles went to women over the age of 40, while men over 40 got 40% of all male roles'.

The 'expiration date' of older actresses does not only revolve around statistics and the media. In 2002, actress Rosanna Arquette filmed *Searching for Debra Winger*, a documentary which includes interviews with 25 actresses (Jane Fonda, Whoopi Goldberg, Sharon Stone and Vanessa Redgrave, among others) who discuss the difficulty they face in securing leading roles and stimulating parts in big productions as they get older (Marie C. Wilson, 2007, p. 136). According to Helen Bushby (2002) Arquette 'feels that Hollywood is over-obsessed with starring young, gorgeous women in its films, and roles "all but dry up" once these female thespians get a few wrinkles and their bodies lose their "perkiness".' In 2010, 66-year-old Helen Mirren received the Sherry

Lansing Leadership Award; in her acceptance speech she spoke about how 'unused' and 'ill-used' women have been through history and remarked that 'not too much has changed in the canon of Hollywood filmmaking that continues to worship at the altar of the 18- to 25-year-old male and his penis'.[1] Hollywood's long-standing obsession with youth is of course not restricted to the romantic comedy genre or even to older actresses for that matter. In March 2011, 26-year-old Amanda Seyfried, one of Hollywood's most promising young stars, revealed that she had already been asked by studio executives to get Botox. In her *Elle* interview with Emily Dougherty, Seyfried explained that she understood the reasons behind such a demand as she believes the new digital cameras are simply unforgiving (Dougherty, 2011). Seyfried's diplomatic answer is indicative of the pressure both younger and older female actors face, both in front of the camera, but, more importantly, of the film industry's 'masculine' politics, which prefer to treat women as second-class citizens.

The romantic comedy genre is no exception to this gender-gap inequality, and indeed until the late 1990s, most films were populated by young, wrinkle-free heroines portrayed by actresses who were in their twenties or thirties. In fact, with the exception of *The Graduate* (1967), which dared show a woman in her forties who could have sexual desires and actually act on them – even though Anne Bancroft was just 36 at the time and a mere six years older than the 'supposedly' 20-year-old Dustin Hoffman – and *The Mirror Has Two Faces* (1996), directed and starring Barbra Streisand, who was 54 at the time, actresses over 40 were almost excluded from the genre. Although Hollywood still deifies youth, the new millennium witnessed a kind of revolution in the depiction of female characters in the romantic comedy landscape and also the representation of couples in their 40s, 50s, and even 60s, in the context of a genre which usually ends with a wedding and does not question what happens after the vows have been spoken and the cake has been eaten.

The representation of mature characters, both male and female, in a genre mostly known for young couples falling in love can be explained to a great extent by the purchasing power that the baby boomer generation has been demonstrating in at least the last ten years. According to a 2009 Survey of Buying Power, people over 50 constitute the most active consumer age group, surpassing teenagers by more than $20 million. Dean Burns adds that baby boomers 'represent the generation with the greatest buying power in the history' of the USA and 'account for a dramatic 40% of total consumer demand – even in a recession'. Hollywood could not leave this powerful target group 'uncared for', and started investing in stories featuring older protagonists, the same way it did in the 1950s, when it recognized the purchasing power of teenagers.

This chapter will, therefore, focus on these representations from the three different perspectives in which they appear. First, I will examine the cycle of the 'cougar' (*Under the Tuscan Sun*, 2003, *Prime*, 2005, *I Could Never Be Your Woman*, 2007, *The Rebound*), which deals with the coupling of an older woman with a younger man, reversing the traditional May–December romance. Second, I will focus on the 'troubled marriage' cycle (*Town & Country*, 2001, *Trust The Man*, 2006, *Serious Moonlight*, *Did You Hear About The Morgans?* *Couples Retreat*, all three 2009, *Sex and The City 2* and *The Kids Are All Right*, both 2010).[2] Finally, I will refer to the cycle of the 'single mature' woman (*Last Chance Harvey*, 2008, *The Answer Man*, 2009, *Something's Gotta Give*,[3] *It's Complicated*), which deals with both female and male sexuality after 50.

The cougar cycle

The word 'cougar' stopped signifying just a mammal of the feline family and acquired an added meaning in the beginning of the new millennium, with the publication of Canadian sex and relationship columnist Valerie Gibson's *Cougar: A Guide for Older Women Dating Younger Men* (2001). Gibson's best-seller includes a series of 'dos and don'ts' for mature women who date younger men and although the term 'cougar' is said to have started 'in the 1980s by Canadian ice hockey team *The Vancouver Canucks*' which used it 'to describe the older [...] women who [...] pursue[d] players sexually' (Lawton and Callister, 2010, p. 4), it was Gibson's notoriety that enabled the widespread use of the word and its appearance next to certain Hollywood stars, such as Madonna, Demi Moore, Susan Sarandon, Kim Catrall, and Courtney Cox (among others), who date or have married younger men. Real celebrity cougars became the new favourite 'it' thing 'leading *Newsweek*'s writer Ramin Setoodeh (2009) to declare 2009 as "the year of the cougar"' (Kaklamanidou, 2012, p. 79). The emergence and popularity of the cougar phenomenon challenges social mores and may seem to adopt the view point that the reverse May–December romance is a choice made by two individuals.

In the context of the third feminist wave, and its endorsement of personal choice, the cougar can constitute yet another means of female empowerment. Karlyn (2006, p. 62) notes that the third feminist wave may continue 'the second wave's critique of sexuality under patriarchy, but more openly explores sexuality and femininity as multidimensional'. In addition to adhering to a contemporary theoretical feminist framework, the cougar, as the possible breaking of yet another taboo in heterosexual relationships corresponded to a real social climate which witnessed an increase of older women–younger men relationships. However, according to a study undertaken by Sandy Caron, professor of family relations and human sexuality at the University of Maine, despite this increase, 'society has far from embraced the idea' and 'most older women still feel the same societal pressures about pairing with a younger man that were evident in studies conducted more than 30 years ago' (Bouchez, 2007). Caron added that 'Pretty much all the couples in our study cautioned that you have to be prepared to deal with the social stigmas, because they are still here, and they can be particularly cruel to women' (Bouchez, 2007).

As is often the case, Hollywood became eager to capitalize on yet another popular social issue and started producing cougar films varying from gross-out comedies such as the *Cougar Club* (2007) to mainstream and independent romantic comedies such as *Under the Tuscan Sun*, *Prime*, *The Weather Girl*, *I Could Never Be Your Woman* and *The Rebound*. The industry may have invested in a fashionable phenomenon but these cinematic texts function not just as simple entertainment or frivolous escapism. As part of popular culture, I argue that these narratives can be explored as sites 'of identity formation and empowerment, providing an abundant storehouse of images and narrative valuable less as a means of representing reality than as motifs available for contesting, rewriting and recoding' (Karlyn, 2006, p. 62).

Of the cougar films mentioned above, only *Prime* was released internationally earning more than $67 million worldwide on a budget of $22 million. *I Could Never Be Your Woman* faltered in the wake of distribution and budgetary problems and despite starring Michelle Pfeiffer and Paul Rudd and being written and directed by the established and successful Amy Heckerling, it went straight to DVD in the US in 2007 despite having been completed in 2005 and earned a little over $9 million in its worldwide release. As was noted in the introduction, the corpus comprises only Hollywood films that were distributed internationally in order to examine narratives that have had a global appeal and reached the widest possible audience. In the case of Heckerling's film, however, we have a film which reached various audiences in Europe and Asia but was not distributed domestically. One could not help but wonder what would have happened if the film was written and directed by a man and not a woman as *I Could Never Be Your Woman* is one of the few romantic comedies which provides a female point of view in both the writing and the directorial stance and also draws from the writer-director's personal life as was stated in an online 2008 interview. Interestingly, when Heckerling was asked if a successful past in Hollywood gives the filmmaker 'any kind of leverage to get what [she] want[s]', she replied: 'It's always a new river every time you stick your foot in' (Heckerling, 2008), which confirms the old Hollywood adage that 'you're only as good as your last picture', and the cruelty of a system which views individuals as mere numbers.

The Rebound, another star-driven cougar film, faced a similar, daedal and frustrating course for the filmmaking team. The film, written and directed by Bart Freundlich and starring Catherine Zeta-Jones and Justin Bartha, was initially released internationally in 2009 and 2010. A 2010 *Variety* article about one of the film's production companies stated that the film would open nationwide in December 2010, and in October 2011, imdb.com claimed the films was scheduled for a 2011 US release. Finally, *The Rebound* went directly to DVD domestically, in February 2012. What these behind-the-scenes reveal are not only the intricacies of the Hollywood system, or the problems both male and female filmmakers face, but the simple fact that there are interesting films that get made and do not have a chance to be seen and consequently participate in a global cultural dialogue. The reason for the inclusion of this information is that both *I Could Never Be Your Woman* and *The Rebound* are much more progressive and interesting narratives than *Prime* or *Under the Tuscan Sun,* which also tackle the older woman–younger man relationship with sensitivity and frankness but decide to end their narrative on a conservative note.

While in *Prime,* 37-year-old Rafi (Uma Thurman) gets involved with 23-year-old David (Bryan Greenberg), the son of her therapist, she decides to leave him at the end, as she realizes David is much too young to become the father of the child she desires. It therefore seems that despite examining a new relationship model, the film finally retreats 'to a social conservatism which still lingers on relationship models of the past' (Kaklamanidou, 2012, p. 85). In contrast, both *I Could Never Be Your Woman* and *The Rebound* allow their protagonist couples to stay together in the end, despite an almost obligatory break-up before the final sequence. In Heckerling's film, Rosie (Michelle Pfeiffer) plays a single mother, TV producer of a teen show, who meets and falls for the much younger Adam (Paul Rudd), the new hot star in her show. The film takes on a satiric tone with insert surrealistic appearances of Tracey Ullman as Mother Nature who delivers caustic lines, such as 'Here's a woman in her forties trying to moisturize her way back to thirty' or 'you can jump and peel and nip and tuck but your insides are still rotting away'. These comments are not only comical but criticize the impossible strains celebrity culture impose on older women who strive to remain youthful at any cost. However, this pressure is mostly expressed in the film through Rosie's ex-husband, Nathan (Jon Lovitz). Nathan's experimenting with hair plugs and efforts to lose weight in order to appear younger is a welcome subversion and a funny intermission in a world where it is only women who are supposed to be continually obsessed with what time is doing to their faces and bodies. Heckerling's decision to represent male vanity and fear of time is not only funny, but reflects the recent increase in the number of men who opt for a visit to a plastic surgeon in order to improve their external appearance. According to the American Society for Aesthetic Plastic Surgery, in 2010, 'men had over 750,000 cosmetic procedures', a number which accounts for 8 per cent of the total. However, although women still constitute the overwhelming remaining 92 per cent, it should be noted that the number of men who decide to surgically alter part of their bodies constitutes a most impressive 88 per cent increase since 1997.

However, despite the narrative's recognition and representation of the fact that the fear of ageing exists in both the male and the female psyche, irrespective of gender percentages, *I Could Never Be Your Woman* mainly focuses on the acceptance of oneself as the indicated way to lead a meaningful existence. Thus, when Rosie finally realizes and acknowledges that, despite the date on his passport, Adam is a man who represents a companion that loves her, makes her laugh and supports her, she is finally free to explore the possibilities that this relationship has to offer. Likewise, at the conclusion of *The Rebound,* new divorcée Sandy (Catherine Zeta-Jones) decides to give her much younger babysitter Aram (Justin Bartha) another chance after a quite long breakup, appreciating his positive qualities and not letting any societal pressure exert influence on their intimate commitment.

Both of these 'cougar' romantic comedies not only underline that a relationship between a mature woman and a younger man can succeed, but they also include representations of how the children of the female protagonists do not even notice their mothers' boyfriends' age and acknowledge that Rosie and Sandy are respectively happy for the first time in a long time. Unfortunately, the already discussed distribution problems of both *I Could Never Be Your Woman* and *The Rebound* films can lead to the conclusion that their more progressive nature validates Hollywood's conservatism. As I have noted elsewhere, the industry's 'ethical' stance 'is as evident as ever in a US social context which has been concertedly promoting "family values" since 2000, in line with the widespread and well-orchestrated pro-family governmental propaganda employed by the Bush administration'. (Kaklamanidou, 2012, p. 85).

The 'mature' single gal cycle

In 2003, writer-director Nancy Meyers's *Something's Gotta Give* proved that a 57-year-old female actress can very well be the heroine of a romantic comedy while a 63-year-old male actor can effectively act as her object of desire. Although the film owes part of its success to both Dianne Keaton's and Jack Nicholson's impressive careers, it also allows the celebration of an older woman's sexual reawakening (Margaret Tally, 2008, p. 119). Moreover, the impressive box-office success of *Something's Gotta Give* – the film grossed more than $266 million worldwide on a budget of $80 million – proved once again the purchasing power of female viewers, and especially baby boomers. However, even though Tally acknowledges that this film, along with other films such as *The Banger Sisters* (2002) and *Calendar Girls* (2003), 'represent[s] a welcome departure from earlier representations of older women's sexuality as deviant and toxic', she also notes that these fictional heroines 'come back into the family fold' by the end of the narrative and that '[n]one […] are shown reveling in their solitude or living alone willingly' (Tally, 2008, p. 130).

Negra also agrees that the representation of '50-something romances' is '[o]ne of the most striking features of the chick flick in recent years' (2009, p. 73). Nevertheless, Negra links this otherwise welcome trend to post-feminism and its insistence to avoid 'the fate of singlehood' (ibid.). Similarly, Radner views *Something's Gotta Give* as an example of what she calls 'neo-feminist' cinema; Radner argues that the film 'proclaims that only the girlish, successful woman has the capacity to surmount the obstacles that life will place in her path as she progresses towards happiness' (2011, p. 183). Although both Negra's and Radner's skepticism towards the film is substantiated through their arguments concerning post-feminism and neo-feminism, they do not take into account either the conventions of the genre nor the whole of the narrative itself.

Unlike other genres, such as gangster films, war films, political thrillers and courtroom dramas, the romantic comedy, along with the science fiction and the horror film, does not rely so much on what Tzevtan Todorov calls cultural verisimilitude (in Neale, 1990, p. 162); that is a kind of plausibility and probability regarding the setting, the dialogue and the actions in a given film narrative. Although most romantic comedies present love stories that could happen in real life, they mix cultural with generic verisimilitude, which in essence represents the conventions of a film genre the audience accepts as probable, and, therefore, true. Generic verisimilitude is, consequently, the reason why many romantic comedy heroes and heroines live in apartments they cannot afford, do not seem to work and/or seem to own entire wardrobes of designer clothes. However, even though this lack of 'authenticity' is the context upon which a romantic comedy is constructed and is expected by the majority of the audience, it is also one of the main or 'certainly one of the reasons why [these genres] tend to be despised, or at least misunderstood, by critics in the 'quality' press' (Neale, 1990, p. 162).

Examining Meyers's 2009 take on the 50-something heroine in *It's Complicated*, I will argue that these films represent more of a progress than a cautionary tale. In 2009, Meyers once again gathered a team of distinguished actors (Meryl Streep, Alec Baldwin and Steve Martin) and created a film targeting, as most film reviewers noted (see Michael O'Sullivan, 2009, Dargis, 2009, Lou Lumenick, 2009), the specific niche audience of middle-aged women. It is interesting to note that just as the whole genre of the romantic comedy is usually dismissed by critics as simplistic, and formulaic, the cycle of the 'single mature woman' is also singled out as specifically addressing a certain part of the audience. The obvious depreciation these films receive not only influences public opinion but often overlooks 'that this most disparaged and allegedly conventional of genres actually provides one of the few spaces in popular culture where older women audiences might encounter a multi-dimensional, appealing representation of themselves' (Deborah Jermyn, 2011, p. 28).

In *It's Complicated*, Streep plays Jane, a woman in her late fifties, divorced for ten years from Jake, portrayed by Alec Baldwin – Streep's junior by ten years in real life – the successful owner of a Santa Barbara bakery. As their youngest daughter drives off to college, Jane has to face the empty nest and decides to redesign her kitchen as her pet project. However, a random dinner at a New York hotel with her ex turns into an illicit affair, since Jake is married to the much younger Agness (Lake Bell), who has a child from a previous relationship. Jane has to struggle between her ambivalence, her children's reaction and the subtle flirtation provided by Steve Martin, who plays her sensitive architect Adam. As in *Something's Gotta Give*, an amusing love triangle is created. Suddenly, single and sex deprived Jane is enjoying a sexual escapade with her married ex-husband while she is delicately wooed by Adam. It has been argued that the majority of the new-millennium romantic comedy 'de-emphasises sexuality' (Jeffers McDonald). However, *Something's*

Gotta Give and *It's Complicated* insist on both its importance but also its representation. When Jane and Jake meet accidentally at a New York hotel, just before their son's graduation, a whole sequence shows them in slow motion dancing and exchanging meaningful glances before the romantic *mise-en-scène* (through editing, the soft lighting, music and close-ups) is abruptly cut transporting the audience to their post-coital sighs. Indeed, sex or even a kiss is not depicted at this time, but both protagonists are seen gasping for air on the bed. A shot from the ceiling reveals Jake smiling with satisfaction and Jane with an expression of disbelief and utter surprise, clinging to the sheets. The viewer sees Jake's naked torso, through his wide open shirt, while Jane is semi-clad, and only her naked leg is placed out of the covers. Their clothing does not denote conservatism but rather their passionate lovemaking, which did not give them time to properly undress. Jake suddenly gropes Jane's genitals and says: 'Home, sweet home'. This line not only provokes laughter but also implies that, first, Jake missed having sex with his ex-wife and, second, that although Jane is not as young as his second wife, she is just as good, or even better, a sexual partner. Although Jane considers their 'indiscretion' a mistake, Jake starts pursuing her and she finally becomes the 'other woman' in her ex-husband's life. Jane enjoys both the sex and the attention and when her girlfriends notice her changed behaviour, which also reflects on her face, she confesses her affair and surreptitiously admits: 'It turns out I'm a bit of a slut'. In other words, Jane knows that this is an illicit relationship which can hurt other people as well as herself but she also finds the irony in resuming a sexual escapade with the father of her children.

The character of Jane has significant implications regarding gender relations. Her actions empower single women over 50 who may think this time of their life simply involves the management of the empty-nest syndrome, the frustrating consequences of menopause and the fact that sex becomes a mere memory. However, *It's Complicated* supports that women of a certain age can enjoy a healthy sex drive and are also considered sexually attractive. After their first two encounters, Jane always covers her body, because she is insecure of her body image. Nevertheless, once the affair progresses, Jane is ready to stand naked in front of the father of her children, having realized that beauty does not necessarily signify what society perceives as bodily perfection. Meanwhile, Jake has no trouble standing up in just his shorts, despite the fact he is overweight and does not even shy away from commenting on his round belly. By including semi-clad shots, and dialogue that addresses body image between the female and the male protagonists, the film tries to overcome the clichéd double standard which allows men to 'gracefully' grow old, have wrinkles and grey hair, as well as put on more weight, while they forbid women of every age group to show any signs of their biological age on their face and body. Meyers comments on this societal pressure and includes a consultation Jane has with a plastic surgeon. In a world that demands women be physically perfect through magazines, and the proliferation of makeover television shows that promise that surgeries, needles, and chemical substances 'will ensure psychological and subjective coherence and the recovery of what has been – apparently – lost' (Estella Tichnell, 2011, p. 87), Jane runs away from the doctor's office and does not give an artificial makeover a second thought. After all, Jane is seen as a vital, energetic, beautiful and desirable woman, whose natural face lines and some bodily imperfections do not deter two handsome and equally virile men from going after her. Moreover, throughout the film, she is portrayed as a successful businesswoman, confident and smart and, more importantly, secure and not needing validation from a man.

In fact, it is the men in her life that expose their insecurities and express 'male angst'. Jake may initially appear as a middle-life alpha male – the wealthy partner in a law firm and the husband of a much younger, beautiful and career-driven wife. However, he cannot help but admit he has become 'a walking cliché'. He verbally shares his dissatisfaction with Jane and prefers to spend time in the peaceful ambiance that reigns in her house rather than be with Agness, who is obsessively trying to have a child with him, and his stepson, who does not allow him to have any privacy. On the other hand, Adam is the sensitive male, who is 'constricted [...] by the dominant myths of what a man should be' (Janet McCabe, 2009, p. 165). Although, he, too is a successful professional, his behaviour, his flirtation, his movements and his general demeanour when Jane is around reveal he has appropriated femininity following the paradigm of post-classical rom com male characters (Rowe, 1995). However, Adam does not proceed to use his feminism, as Rowe (1995) argues, to boost his own authority and then use it to educate Jane. Adam is indeed an honest, caring and gentle man who is in search of a companion after his divorce and whose masculinity is completely antithetical to Jake's aggressive and overtly expressive desires, proving that the concept of masculinity 'is even more complex than assumed by feminist theory' and that reduction 'to monolithic and universal categories' cannot suffice in the twenty-first century (Raya Morag, 2009, p. 25).

Jake and Adam compete for Jane's affection but they are almost powerless as far as the outcome of their advances is concerned. The progression of the plot depends entirely on Jane. It is her decision to redesign her house after her last child leaves for college and not become depressed. It is her decision to feel sexy and 'naughty' and have an affair with Jake. It is her decision to simultaneously flirt with Adam, and it is finally her decision to break up with Jake and give Adam a chance. In contrast to *Something's Gotta Give*, *It's Complicated* does not confine its mature heroine in a family context at the end of the narrative. Instead, the film closes by winking at the audience and implying a relationship will flourish between Jane and Adam. And, in this respect, Meyers pays homage to many screwball comedies of the 1930s and 1940s, a rom com cycle which questioned marriage and preferred to complete many of its narratives (e.g. *It Happened One Night*, 1934, *My Man Godfrey*, 1936, *His Girl Friday*, 1940), without the representation a wedding ceremony. Although these comedies implied a wedding would very soon take place – after all, *My Man Godfrey* ends just before a simple wedding ceremony occurs – Meyers chooses to free her heroine from all the familial constraints and lets her be her own agent. The only things that remain stable are her job and her house. However, the house is in a process of transformation, as is its owner; from the place where Jane and Jake raised their children, shared happy times but also went through a divorce, Jane is turning it into her own home, with the kitchen of her dreams and possibly a new man to share her savoury recipes with.

The 'troubled-marriage' cycle

In 1981, Stanley Cavell examined seven romantic comedies released between 1934 and 1949 (*It Happened One Night*, 1934, *The Awful Truth*, 1937, *Bringing Up Baby*, 1938, *The Philadelphia Story*, 1940, *His Girl Friday*, 1940, *The Lady Eve*, 1941, and *Adam's Rib*, 1949), and defined them as 'a particular genre of Hollywood talkie' which he labelled the 'comedy of remarriage' (p. 1). For Cavell (1981, p. 2), these screwball comedies were distinguished from the rest of their contemporary romantic comedy productions in that the plot was 'not to get the central pair together, but to get them *back* together, together *again*'. Of course, one could rightfully argue that *It Happened One Night* and *Bringing Up Baby* cannot be identified as comedies of remarriage, since in the former, Ellie (Claudette Colbert) and Peter (Clark Gable) only pretend to be married, and in the latter, David (Cary Grant) and Susan (Katharine Hepburn) are single. Furthermore, the word 'remarriage' presupposes a divorce, and that can also exclude *Adam's Rib* and *The Lady Eve* from Cavell's categorization. Despite these observations, Cavell's grouping is important insofar as it distinguishes specific films that place a married, separated and/or divorced couple at the centre of the narrative, which is a rarity in the cinematic romantic comedy universe. Indeed, the last decade witnessed a handful of films which focus on married couples in their early 40s to mid 50s, either separated (*Did You Hear About the Morgans?*) or in the midst of trouble caused by infidelity, work problems or personal issues (*Town & Country*, *Trust The Man*, *Serious Moonlight*, *Couples Retreat*, *Sex and the City*, and *Sex and The City 2*).[4]

The 'troubled marriage' cycle is worth examining since it explores the tensions and strains a long-term marriage can put on the couple and also questions this 'institution' in the twenty-first century. The word 'institution' is in quotation marks because according to a significant part of feminist work on the subject, marriage as an institution implies 'that marriage is a received, relatively fixed social structure that draws women's participation in maintaining, organizing, and reproducing a sexed/gendered order' (Heather Brook, 2007, p. 16). Marriage is, therefore, accused of being a patriarchal construction to subordinate and exploit women. Indeed, it is widely supported that marriage was initially invented 'as a way of exchanging women [...] [and as a way] to oppress them' (Coontz, 2005, pp. 41–2). Throughout its long history, or at least since the eighteenth century, when 'for the first time in five thousand years, marriage came to be seen as a private relationship between two individuals rather than one link in a larger system of political and economic alliances', and 'was increasingly defined as a private agreement with public consequences, rather than as a public institution' (ibid. pp. 146–7), marriage clearly assigned men the role of the breadwinner and women the role of the hearth protector. However, the social and political changes of the twentieth century, such as the invention of the pill, the victories of the second feminist wave that led to new legislation that empowered women, the trends of cohabitation and single parenthood, among others, could not help but bring significant changes to this 'private agreement'. It would therefore be interesting to see what kind of representations the romantic comedy reserves for marriage in the new millennium.

Couples Retreat was released in 2009 and was written by two of its main characters, Vince Vaughn, John Favreau, and the actor/writer Dana Fox. The film was reviewed unfavourably in the press and scored only 23 out of 100 on metacritic.com, based on 27 reviews.[5] However, its commercial appeal was proportionally opposite to its poor evaluation by film critics and *Couples Retreat* grossed more than $170 million worldwide on a budget of $70 million. Brandon Gray (2009), notes that 'Universal Pictures's exit polling indicated that the "humor" and "Vince Vaughn" were the top reasons people saw *Couples* and that 61 per cent of the audience was female and 56 per cent was 30 years of age and older'. This audience data not only shows how the capital of a movie star can sometimes guarantee the commercial success of the film but also that this 'older' portion of the audience could more easily identify with the marriage theme.

Couples Retreat centres on not just one but four troubled marriages each well past the newlywed stage. Dave (Vince Vaughn) and Ronnie (Malin Akerman) are so busy with work and raising their two children that they do not realize they have forgotten how to communicate as a couple. Jason (Jason Bateman) and Cynthia (Kristen Bell) are having trouble conceiving and their obsession has put a strain on their relationship. Joey (Jon Favreau) and Lucy (Kristin Davis), high school sweethearts with a daughter about to go to college, are both cheating on each other and they have decided to separate once their daughter leaves home. Finally, Shane (Faizon Love) has separated from his wife Jennifer (Tasha Smith) and is dating 20-year-old Trudy (Kali Hawk) in a vain attempt to recapture his lost youth and ease his pain. The film is also one of the few instances in the rom com genre that mostly focuses on the male point-of-view on marriage and as such may provide the theorist with interesting observations.

The four men are supposed to have been friends for years, although no background story is provided. However, even though both the actors and their fictional counterparts are in their early to mid 40s, and the fictional marriages are depicted as long-term relationships, Vaughn's and Bateman's fictional brides are portrayed by actresses in their early 30s – Malin Akerman was 31 at the time of the film's release – and late 20s – Kristen Bell was 29.

On the one hand, this casting decision validates that actresses over 40 are considered 'over the hill' by Hollywood standards, with very few exceptions, and on the other, that the pairing of a 40-year-old man with a younger woman creates unrealistic expectations to the female audience, regarding body images.

The credit sequence of *Couples Retreat* is accompanied by the 1983 David Bowie hit 'Modern Love', and a montage of mostly wholesome American couples from the twentieth century starting with the 1900s and ending with pictures of the film's fictional couples. This opening sequence establishes right from the start that the story will not be about how two people meet but rather how two people who have been together for some time deal with whatever obstacle has come their way. The plot begins when Jason and Cynthia, two control freaks who cannot accept they are reproductively challenged, plead with their friends to accompany them to Eden, a luxurious resort that specializes on healing 'wounded' relationships. On the verge of divorce, Jason and Cynthia come to the conclusion that a two-week escape at Eden, 'the ultimate playground for couples', as Cynthia puts it, can help them re-evaluate their relationship and come to a decision regarding its future through a series of counselling sessions in a tranquil environment and away from their everyday routine. Cynthia and Jason may be authoritative and obsessive – after all they have prepared a whole PowerPoint presentation to convince their friends – but they are honest about the problems they are facing and are ready to work on their marriage unlike their friends who despite their unhappiness or their non realization that something is wrong go about their daily lives.

Jason and Cynthia are also honest about their financial situation. They are not asking their friends to accompany them because they simply want their support. They are inviting them because they cannot otherwise afford their two-week getaway, unless they take advantage of a group rate Cynthia found, which will reduce the cost for all of them. Although none of the couples is unemployed or overtly experiencing financial problems, this reference to Jason and Cynthia's inability to realize this trip goes against one of the genre's main conventions: money is almost never an issue in the romantic comedy universe; that is irrespective of the characters' professions and/or class status, they never, or rarely, worry about paying their bills and seem to go through life as if money is not an issue. Therefore, this reference to Jason and Cynthia's money-related problem, anchors the narrative – albeit momentarily – to reality, and indirectly hints at the US 2008 recession, even though the protagonists are at no time in need of financial assistance.

The three couples finally agree to accompany their friends, thinking they are going to have a wonderful and stress-free vacation. However, once they arrive at Eden, they realize they have to follow a strict program devised by the resort's owner, Marcel (Jean Reno). Mixing New Age methods with yoga, exercises and an intensive couples therapy program, the four couples come quickly face-to-face with problems some did not even realize they have.

Seemingly satisfied Dave starts to recognize he cares more about his work and his friends and does not take part in the household while Ronnie feels she has become solely responsible for their children and home. Jason and Cynthia feel their two weeks at Eden should resolve their issues. Joey and Lucy seem resigned to getting a divorce and express their sentiments of hostility and resentment. Finally, Shane starts to recognize that his May–December affair is just a superficial distraction that helps him avoid the serious problems he has with his wife. Alienation, infidelity, impossible demands and juvenile behaviour are the problems the four couples are afflicted with.

These issues have not yet been examined academically within the context of the contemporary Hollywood romantic comedy. One reason is that the well-established conventions of the genre creates narratives that 'deal with love that leads to marriage or love outside marriage, but not love in marriage' and by and large imply that 'marriage will be a continuation of the romantic state' previously depicted (Shumway, 2003, p. 3). Moreover, because of the combination of the comic and the romantic aspects that anchor the romantic comedy narrative, most films that belong to the genre tend to avoid tackling issues such as infidelity and alienation, leaving them to become the subject of other genres, such as the dramatic *Indecent Proposal* (1993), *Unfaithful* (2002), *Closer* (2004) or the black comedy *The War of The Roses* (1989), among others. Even when Shumway discusses issues of marriage, he chooses to examine fiction, and not film, and in particular novels and stories by John Updike and Alison Lurie.

However, the romantic comedy can also be a very rich terrain for the representation and fictional examination of contemporary married relationships. The number and variety of films from the previous decade that centre on married couples – from the action rom coms *Mr. & Mrs. Smith*, *Date Night* and *Killers*; the battle of the sexes *What Happens in Vegas*, 2008; the family-centred *Marley & Me*, 2008; the screwball *Intolerable Cruelty*, the ensemble rom coms *He's Just Not That Into You*, 2009, *Valentine's Day*, 2010, *Sex and the City*, and *Sex and the City 2*; Julia Roberts's comeback to a leading role in the genre with *Eat, Pray, Love*, 2010; to the films of this chapter's cycle – can be attributed to industry and societal reasons.

First, the inclusion of a marriage plot can elongate the careers of female stars associated with the genre, such as Julia Roberts and Jennifer Aniston and still have commercially successful results, while also providing other 'older' actresses with work. Furthermore, the 2000s witnessed a significant decrease in the divorce rate, which in 2005 reached 'its lowest level since 1970', and at the same time a decrease in '[t]he number of people entering marriage as a proportion of the population in the United States' (Betsey Stevenson and Justin Wolfers, 2007, p. 29). Thus, the romantic comedy responded not only to these statistics but also to a new stance regarding marriage itself which is no longer regarded as 'a social obligation' with the exception of 'rightwing public moralists', but as 'the most private of practices and a matter of individual happiness and fulfillment' (Shumway, 2003, p. 188).

And it is exactly this outlook on marriage as an agreement between two people that is explored through the four relationships in *Couples Retreat*. Each couple faces its own problems that stem from being together for years. Their issues are revealed and/or discussed when the characters have their sessions with an analyst. In a sequence that shows the four couples' discussion with the therapist overlapping with one another, Jason and Cynthia's friends realize they have taken their marriages for granted. Lack of communication is exposed as a central issue these couples face, which leads to their different problems, from alienation to unfaithfulness. Even though the cinematic management of these problems is quite simplistic and even naïve at points, and the script includes many an unnecessary cliché, such as the men's infantile attitude when they have to face a handsome yoga instructor or their wasting time playing a video game when they should be searching for Trudy towards the climax of the narrative, *Couples Retreat* does question the agreement two heterosexual individuals make and also provides the male perspective. Although the four men represent different types of masculinity – Dave is the Peter Pan, Joey is the macho cheater, Jason is the sensible one, and Shane is the sensitive one – they all believe in their marriages and by the end of the narrative they become determined to make them work.

The happy end that finds the four couples united in celebrating their renewed trust in one another should not be easily mistaken and/or dismissed as a conservative closure of a traditional genre film. If one is to discard *Couples Retreat* as 'a genially banal message comedy about learning to live with your spouse by staying true to yourself', (Owen Gleiberman, 2009) then one should also disregard the courage, forgiveness, willingness to compromise and, above all, the love, the eight characters show in order to arrive at a happy reconciliation. The heroes' and heroines' eagerness to start anew and keep working on their marriages is not only dictated by genre conventions, but constitutes a prerequisite for the sustainability and longevity of healthy, modern relationships.

8   The baby-crazed rom com

Motherhood, or the desire for motherhood, was never the main subject of Hollywood's mainstream film production. Ann E. Kaplan points out that 'few Hollywood films make the Mother central, relegating her, rather, to the periphery of a narrative focused on a husband, son, or daughter' (2000, p. 468). She adds that '[m]others are rarely single and rarely combine Mothering with work […]. Often, as in *Mildred Pierce*, the Mother is punished for trying to combine work and Mothering […]' (ibid.). From the maternal melodramas *Stella Dallas* (1937) and *Mildred Pierce* (1945), to *Terms of Endearment* (1983), *Postcards from the Edge* (1990), *Stepmom* (1998) and *The Hours* (2003), it is evident that only a few Hollywood cinematic texts decide to deal with the complexities motherhood entails.

Nevertheless, the millennial romantic comedies of this chapter prove that the desire for motherhood – and pregnancy – are no longer unwanted and/or unpopular subjects. *Baby Mama* (2008) is one of the main narratives of this cycle and reveals its intentions right from the start, abiding of course by the genre's conventions. Therefore, the opening sequence presents aerial shots of urban landmarks in Philadelphia, accompanied by the first notes of a whimsical Talking Heads song. A female voiceover starts narrating and the viewers know they have entered the romantic comedy universe. However, this monologue expresses another female anxiety and not the genre's traditional female longing for Mr Right:

KATE (TINA FEY): I did everything that I was supposed to do: I didn't cry in meetings, I didn't wear short skirts, I put up with the weird upper management guys that kiss you on the mouth at Christmas. Is it fair that to be the youngest VP in my company, I will be the oldest mom at preschool? Not really, but that's part of the deal. I made a choice. Some women got pregnant. I got promotions. And, I still aspire to meet someone, and fall in love and get married, but that is a very high-risk scenario. And I want a baby now. I am 37.

The voiceover, which is accompanied by shots of what we assume is the same woman meeting those 'upper management' guys and eyeing babies in the street, is soon replaced by Kate's direct address to the camera. Or so it seems. Once Kate completes what seems to be an anxiety-filled yet well-organized and thought-out speech without even stopping to take a breath, we realize she was talking to a man on a first date. Unfortunately, the man in front of her is a traditional commitment-phobe, who upon hearing Kate's speech, panics at the thought of marriage and children, and leaves instantly from the restaurant, without even saying goodbye to the heroine, who watches him through the window get into a taxi.

Baby Mama, Tina Fey's first lead role in a feature film, is among the romantic comedies that kicked off a new cycle, focusing on heroines who either want desperately to get pregnant (*Miss Conception*, 2008, *The Back-Up Plan*, 2010, *The Switch*, 2010), get pregnant accidentally (*Knocked Up*, 2007, *Baby on Board*, 2008), or are suddenly forced to become a caregiver to an orphan (*Raising Helen*, 2004, *No Reservations*, 2007, and *Life as We Know It*, 2010).[1] The 'sudden' interest in these themes corresponds both to the positioning 'of pregnancy and motherhood at centre stage in mainstream politics' (Imogen Tyler, 2011, p. 21) as well as to the post-9/11 return to family. Tyler (2011, pp. 21–2) substantiates her thesis by referring to the 'global media storm [that] surrounded the French Justice Minister Rachida Dati when she announced her pregnancy as a lone mother', the controversy that took place during the 2008 US presidential election, when 'pro-life Republican vice-presidential candidate Sarah Palin went on the election trail brandishing a four-month-old son and a pregnant teenage daughter', and the simultaneous emergence of 'pro-choice Ivy League educated attorney Michelle Obama' as 'the nation's rightful "mom in chief."' The extensive visibility of motherhood in politics is also linked to the impressive surge in the number of weddings in the aftermath of 9/11, and the consequent rise in the numbers of babies being born in the United States, in an effort for the nation's citizens to cope with the collective trauma through family stability. Anke Geertsma (2011, p. 92) notes that after 9/11, people moved '[f]rom the superficial and illusory comfort of consumerism' towards 'the things that bring real comfort in life: home, love, and family'. After all, and despite its complexities, the family still represents a solid structure and the safe space one usually retreats to in times of need.

The re-discovery of the family, not only as a pre-existent group of people but as a traditional institution that can start with two individuals and multiply led to an increase of births. According to the National Center for Health Statistics, 2007 witnessed a record number of 4,315,000 babies born. Robert Engelman, vice president for programs at the Worldwatch Institute stresses that this number constitutes 'a record, and it's a particularly interesting record because the year it beats is 1957, which was the height of the baby boom' (David Wright, 2008). Nevertheless, the reasons behind this impressive surge in the number of births differ significantly from the post-war social, economic and political euphoria that led to the 1940s and 1950s baby boom. First, as Wright (2008) notes, there has 'been an uptick in the number of women having children later in their lives, whether as a career choice or with the help of technology'. Second, a great percentage of children were born in single-parent families. More importantly, however, immigration became 'the biggest factor contributing to the current baby boom', as '[t]he birth rate is rising fastest among Hispanic immigrants in particular, far outpacing the 2.1 average births per woman' (Wright, 2008).

Despite the above numbers, 2007 did not lead to the beginning of a new baby boom. During the next two years, there was a 'broad-based decline in births and fertility rates' (Paul D. Sutton, and Brady E. Hamilton. 2010), although according to the Centers for Disease Control and Prevention's National Center for Health Statistics (NCHS) the number of births in 2009 was not much lower compared to that of 2007. According to the report compiled by Brady E. Hamilton, Joyce A. Martin and Stephanie J. Ventura (2010, p. 1), 'the number of births and birth rates declined for all race and Hispanic origin groups in 2009', including white, Hispanic, non-Hispanic white, non-Hispanic black and Asian or Pacific Islander teenagers, women in their early and late 20s and women in their 30s. The only increase was observed among unmarried women and women in their early 40s.

What these statistics prove is that motherhood is not perceived anymore as the woman's first goal in life. It is a well-established fact that women, nowadays, and for at least the last two decades, delay becoming mothers in order to establish their careers first, and then decide whether or not a child should complete their life plan. A 2010 Pew Research Center report shows that this postponement does not only apply to white women, but is spread across all ethnic and income groups (Gretchen Livingston, and D'Vera Cohn, 2010).

The changed patterns in motherhood mentioned above are also promoted by today's celebrity culture, which not only seems obsessed by young and well-toned bodies and beautiful faces, but also by stars and famous women who carry children, adopt or have become mothers. The photograph of a seven-months-pregnant and naked Demi Moore on the cover of *Vanity Fair* in 1991 marks 'the "celebrity event"' which broke 'the powerful cultural taboo around the representation of pregnancy' and ushered in a new era which witnessed and is still witnessing 'thousands of high-profile publicity photo shoots of pregnant celebrities' (Tyler, 2011, p. 23). Tyler adds that the recent 'ideology of pregnant beauty reache[d] its apotheosis in the post-partum photo shoot, the aim of which is to demonstrate how rapidly celebrities can shrink back to a pre-pregnant size and shape', marketed by yet another Moore photo for *Vanity Fair*'s cover in 1992 (ibid. p. 27).

Celebrity culture started to venerate mothers. Once an actress was found to be pregnant, the media simply forgot her perhaps 'naughty' past and concentrated on the new life she was living, the sex of the kid(s), the weight she did or did not put on and her maternity clothes. Suffice it to note that both *People* and *Us Magazine* include separate tabs on celebrity babies and mothers on their online editions, while a great number of internet sites are focused exclusively on both the parents and offspring of the 'rich and famous'. After the birth, all interviews included the 'mandatory' questions about motherhood, which almost always make the celebrity mother sound as if she is just this ordinary 'superwoman', who can take care of the house, her newborn(s), her shooting schedule and at the same time fit into a size 2 dress. For instance, Julianne Moore always puts parenting first, stressing how 'she wants to be with her husband and kids as much as she can' (Dahvi Shira, 2011), while Gwyneth Paltrow, mother of two, reveals that when she is home in London, she is extremely hands on: 'I'm at everything and I pick them up everyday, take them [to school] every day, do everything for them, homework, bath [...]. When I'm home, I'm extremely 100% present' (Cele/bitchy, 2010). These celebrity representations replace 'the feminist political dilemmas of housewife versus career woman [...] by narratives of renaissance women who juggle thriving careers [...] with motherhood' (Jessica Ringrose and Valerie Walkerdine in Tyler, 2011, p. 29).

Of course, the images of these perfect mothers who show that they 'have it all' are counteracted by a series of books that demystify this image and try to expose the 'other side'. In *The Mommy Myth*, Susan Jeanne Douglas and Meredith W. Michaels explain how regular working moms are 'getting increasingly irritable about this chasm between the ridiculous, honey-hued ideals of perfect motherhood in the mass media and the reality of mothers' everyday lives' (2004, p. 2). They also underline how much added stress these celebrity representations can impose on the 'other' mothers by citing a recent survey which showed that '81 percent of women [...] said it's harder to be a mother now than it was twenty or thirty years ago, and 56 percent felt mothers were doing a worse job today than mothers back then' (ibid. p. 3). Douglas and Michaels' define 'new momism',[2] as 'a set of ideals, norms, and practices, most frequently and powerfully represented in the media, that seem on the surface to celebrate motherhood, but which in reality promulgate standards of perfection that are beyond our reach' (ibid. pp. 4–5). The more than often photoshopped flawlessness of celebrity mothers, along with the exclusion of the fact that their children are cared for by a team of professional nannies, creates unrealistic expectations for the ordinary working mother who cannot maintain the same svelte figure and look like she has just left from the beautician. Thus, despite the fact that one of the focal points of new momism is that women have choices – a claim in accordance with third-wave feminism – this new version of motherhood can also be understood as organized and exploited by the media and the corporations that control them in order to combine motherhood and consumerism and 'use' yet another niche target group.

Consequently, the tensions over delayed childbirth for older women who put off having children because of work, or who were having difficulty balancing work and motherhood, combined with the idealized celebrity pregnancy/ motherhood promoted by the US media, 'gave birth' to the romantic comedy cycle of the 'baby-crazed' heroine. This group of films is yet another instance of generic film texts that are born out of specific social circumstances, and as such, it validates Rick Altman's thesis about the functionality of genre films.

Altman underlines that '[w]hereas producers and exhibitors see genre films as "product", critics increasingly recognize their role in a complex cultural system permitting viewers to consider and resolve (albeit fictively) contradictions that are not fully mastered by the society in which they live' (2006, p. 26). Altman's view does echo Claude Lévi-Strauss's (1963) view of myth as a narrative which seeks to provide solutions to long-standing societal conflicts. In other words, these popular comedic romances could be viewed as modern stories which reflect the society which produced them and at the same time negotiate the subject of pregnancy and motherhood through various perspectives. Finally, although *Baby Mama*'s $64 million, *The Back-Up Plan*'s $80 million and *The* Switch's $50 million in worldwide admissions do not constitute impressive numbers even for the romantic comedy genre which includes many films which have surpassed the $100 million threshold, they are box-office hits considering their modest budgets, which were respectively $30 million, $35 million, and $15 million, in a way ensuring we will be watching more 'baby-obsessed' rom coms in the coming years.

Baby Mama and *The Back-Up Plan*: Shopping for vaginas or semen

As was mentioned in the introduction, in *Baby Mama*, Tina Fey plays Kate Holbrook, a Philadelphia executive who was just promoted to vice president of Round Earth, a corporation that produces organic products and is run by Barry (Steve Martin), a New-Age magnate. At 37, Kate was probably so driven by her ambition she 'forgot' to have children or maintain a serious relationship. Despite her numerous attempts, her doctor bluntly informs her that her 'T-shaped uterus' and 'advanced maternal age', give her a one-in-a-million chance to conceive. Kate has also thought of adoption, but as she tells her mother and sister, the process 'can take up to five years for a single woman'. In a few well-scripted scenes, the narrative addresses the infertility problems of a great percentage of women over 35, the problems single women face when they decide to adopt and the fact that the desire to have children is something that a significant percentage of American women start to think about or postpone until well after their thirtieth birthday.

Kate may be single but she has a supportive sister, Caroline (Maura Tierney) and a mother, Rose (Holland Taylor), who considers her decision to be a single parent as part of 'her alternative lifestyle'. In a funny but revealing scene, the three women discuss Kate's options while her opinionated mom – portrayed by an actress who specializes in the portrayal of the ruthless boss (*The Naked Truth,* ABC 1995–98) or the eternally disapproving mother (*Two And A Half Men,* CBS 2003–present) – asks her daughter to at least not adopt a baby of another race because 'she's just had it with the movie stars and their black babies'. Rose is most probably satirizing a trend in celebrity adoption which saw many stars welcome a black baby in their family. Angelina Jolie's adoption of a girl from Ethiopia in 2005, Madonna's controversial adoption of a boy and girl from Malawi, finalized in 2008 and

2009 respectively, Mary Louise Parker's adoption of a girl from Africa in 2007, Sandra Bullock's adoption of a black baby boy in 2010, and Kristin Davis's adoption of a black son in 2011 are among the many Hollywood stars who created an interracial family, leading several journalists, such as Luchina Fisher, (2009) to wonder if black babies are Hollywood's new, hottest accessory.

Urged by her sister, Kate decides to visit the Chaffee Bicknell Center of Surrogate Parenting where she meets Chaffee Bicknell herself (Sigourney Weaver) and is told that surrogacy is another way of outsourcing and that a surrogate is nothing more than 'a nanny who takes care of your child before it's born', as opposed to the nanny who will take care of Kate's baby once it's born. Surrogacy is therefore presented as a very expensive yet almost uncomplicated process whereby the surrogate mother undergoes extensive background checks (physiological, psychological, biographical) and carries the client's baby to term. According to Theresa M. Erickson, '[t]hird-party-assisted reproduction, although cutting-edge, has been helping couples and individuals have children when the possibility previously may not have existed for them for many years with positive results, in the world as we know it' (2010, p. 4). Erickson tackles the legal issues that surround surrogacy, which has in recent years become a global business, with India becoming the leader in the so-called 'reproductive outsourcing'. According to Amelia Gentleman (2008), 'Commercial surrogacy, which is banned in some states and some European countries, was legalized in India in 2002'.[3]

Commenting on American parents who opt to have a baby with a mother overseas, Chaffee reassures Kate that her offspring will not be carried 'by some poor, underpaid woman in the Third World', but an American citizen. In the case of Kate, the power does not lie with her and the $100,000 she has to pay but with Angie (Amy Poehler) who interviews prospective parents and has the final say on whose baby she decides to carry. Angie is the complete opposite of Kate. Uneducated, unsophisticated and accompanied by her 'inventor/entrepreneur' boyfriend Carl (Dax Shepard), she sees Kate as an opportunity to earn money she could not make 'reading people's auras', and impressed by her luxurious apartment decides Kate can 'put her baby inside her'.

The 'fertilization' sequence that follows is interesting as it brings change not only to the grammar of the genre but its syntax as well. First of all, the sequence begins with the two women holding hands once Angie agrees to become Kate's surrogate mother and the sunset light covers the shot while the first lyrics of the 1981 famous Lionel Richie/Diana Ross duet 'Endless Love' begins. The popular love song accompanies the sequence of the *in vitro* procedure Angie undergoes while it shows the two women again holding hands and looking deeply into each other's eyes. The sequence parodies the almost obligatory sequence of the 'melodic birth' of love in most rom coms and simultaneously subverts a 'process' which traditionally involves a heterosexual couple. Kate's and Angie's body language combined with a song that celebrates the power of the heterosexual romantic union causes smiles and disrupts gender stability as it 'explicitly frames the relationship between the driven yuppie and the trash-talking trailer tramp as a nonsexual romance' (Carrie Rickie, 2008). The sequence depicts that a strong female bond is forming between the two women who need each other; Kate cannot have a child without Angie, and Angie cannot have a better quality of life without Kate's payment.

In this way, the narrative seems to celebrate and emphasize the importance of the female bond to the detriment of the heterosexual romantic lives of the heroines, although Angie has Carl and Kate has already met Rob (Greg Kinnear) whom the audience expects she will fall in love with. The focus on female relationships did not always constitute a common narrative device in the history of mainstream American cinema. Tasker notes that the majority of American film genres have 'marginalized representations of female friendship, more often favouring glamorous stars seen to exist in spectacular isolation, supportive figures who exist almost exclusively in relation to the hero, or women set in competition with each other' (2002, p. 139). It was not until the late 1980s when films such as *Mystic Pizza* (1988) and *Steel Magnolias* (1989) put female relationships in the foreground, leading to Karen Hollinger's exploration of the 'female friendship' film and its definition as a sub-genre or cycle of the more inclusive woman's film in her 1998 study.

However, the narrative exploration of the two women's relationship takes an interesting turn once Angie moves into Kate's place after leaving Carl. Kate takes immediate control and before Angie wakes up she has already baby proofed the entire house, leaving Angie at a loss on how to 'unlock' the toilet bowl, ending up relieving herself in the sink and causing Kate's rage. Controlling and also concerned about the status of her baby, Kate throws a tantrum once she gets back from work only to find Angie eating junk food, playing with her niece's present and smoking while she should be resting and taking prenatal vitamins. In a way, Kate could be seen as 'mothering' Angie, not deeming her responsible or capable enough to carry her child. This formation of a bizarre mother–daughter relationship can be also explained through Kate's involuntary celibacy. According to Astrid Henry, '[g]iven that the mother is already stripped of her sexuality – in fact, she must be asexual, if not explicitly anti-sex, to represent the maternal – the daughter's rebellion will necessarily centre on sexuality, as it is here where she can most effectively distance and differentiate herself from her mother' (2004, p. 126). Since Kate has been single and is not having sex, one could easily place her in the position of the know-it-all mother. Kate is becoming her own mother, an authoritative and controlling figure, a person she obviously feels uneasy around but also a person she feels 'a deep underlying pull toward [...] a dread that if [she] relaxes [her] guard [she] will identify with her completely' (Adrienne Rich in Henry, 2004, p. 118).

In addition, this female relationship is problematic as it presents a dyadic power structure, with Kate assuming the position of the capital holder and

Angie the role of the subordinate subject who has to obey in order to receive her remuneration for services rendered. In other words, it can be safely assumed that Kate and Angie's difference in education, financial situation and/or class would, in all probability, not have allowed them to meet in the first place, if Kate were able to have a child on her own. Thus, Kate's overbearing behaviour can stem from her silent realization of her 'superiority', which is expressed through suggestions and advice, and soon transforms into direct orders.

The tension in Kate and Angie's mother–daughter or sovereign–subject relationship leads the two women to the surrogacy centre support group where they are advised 'to spend more time together'. Kate and Angie agree to do so; they enrol in a birthing class, they go shopping for the baby's first necessities, they talk about their past and their future, they even go clubbing; and in the process they start becoming friends. Kate learns to loosen up – she even takes the initiative to visit Rob and even kisses him first and has sex with him on their first date – and Angie starts acting a little more maturely. However, as in every love story, an obstacle has to appear to make things harder for the couple. In the case of Kate and Angie, the twist comes when the viewer first learns that Carl forged the pregnancy test and that Angie is not really pregnant. However, Angie is indeed carrying a child but it is Carl's and not Kate's. At this point of the narrative, Angie assumes responsibility for her imminent new role as a mother, while Kate is enjoying her new relationship with Rob.

What is structurally interesting, however, is that a parallel montage shows the progression of Angie's pregnancy and Kate's relationship with Rob, concentrating once again on the two women and using the men in their lives as peripheral distractions. That is why, even though Kate decides to distance herself from Rob, who finds surrogacy 'science-fictiony', the messy breakup takes place between Kate and Angie, during the baby shower Kate's sister prepared, when everything comes out into the open. Kate learns that Angie is perhaps not carrying her baby, Carl finds out he may become a father, and Rob learns his lover was hiding her intention of becoming a mother on her own.

From that moment, the narrative seems to speed up in that it tries in the remaining 15 minutes to tie up all the loose ends and provide an ending that seems quite at odds with what the main female duet was working towards. A few months later, a judge reads a DNA test which confirms Kate is not the biological mother of Angie's baby. However, even though Kate does not want to continue seeing Angie, she drives her to the hospital because her water breaks outside the courtroom. Kate faints during the labour she witnesses only to wake up and learn that she is pregnant with Rob's child. The final sequence takes place at Angie and Carl's daughter's first birthday attended by Rob, Kate and their newborn. The last characters we see are Kate and Angie holding their children while watching a *Tom and Jerry* episode, which Angie had earlier likened to their relationship.

Nevertheless, the film should not be judged just on its conventional ending. *Baby Mama* negotiates successfully the anxiety a career woman in her late 30s faces when the desire to have a child knocks on her door. It also demonstrates that female friendships can be as strong as male bonds and does not succumb to the cliché of antagonism between the two women even though Kate and Angie's relationship goes through many stages before it achieves balance and equality. Finally, *Baby Mama* places two female heroines at the centre of the humorous romantic narrative and thus strengthens their role as friends, mothers and, at the end, lovers and/or wives. If one hastens to argue that Kate finally has a baby with Rob, one should not forget that at the end, Angie does not 'conveniently' pair up with Carl. Instead, having enrolled in a few classes to learn about design, she decides to be a single parent, with all the ramifications raising a child alone entails.

One could argue that a more progressive alternative of motherhood desire is proposed in *The Back-Up Plan*, a Jennifer Lopez vehicle which was released in 2010, directed by Alan Poul and written by Kate Angelo, in her first feature film after a career in television which included *The Bernie Mac Show* (Fox, 2001–6) and *Will and Grace* (NBC, 1998–2006). The plot revolves around Zoe (Jennifer Lopez), a 30-something pet store owner, who is artificially inseminated the same day she meets the right partner she was looking for to start a family. This was Lopez's first starring role after she gave birth to twins in February 2008 at the age of 39 with her third husband, singer Marc Anthony (the couple filed for divorce in 2011). However, *The Back-Up Plan* is not Lopez's autobiographical story about her own pregnancy. The actress explained her decision to 'come back' with this particular film after her two-year cinematic absence saying:

> I just love romantic comedies. It was just the first thing that I wanted to do back. So we started looking for one and this one came up. It was just perfect. I mean, obviously throughout my career I've always felt like certain things come to me at the right time. When I look at the work that I've done, it's always very kind of indicative of where I was in my life at the moment. This was the same thing. It was just very kind of serendipitous that it happened this way. It was perfect (Fred Topel 2010).

Of the 23 feature films Lopez, or J. Lo as she has been renamed by her fans and the media, had released by the end of 2010, only 4 can be considered bona fide romantic comedies (*The Back-Up Plan, Gigli*, 2003, *Maid in Manhattan*, 2002, and *The Wedding Planner*, 2001). With the exception of *Gigli*, Lopez's romantic comedies are among the top ten of the actress's highest grossing films as they were more favoured by the public. Despite the diversity in her filmography (Lopez has played a US Marshal in the crime film *Out of Sight* (1998) and a child psychologist in the sci-fi thriller *The Cell* (2000), among other parts), it was *The Wedding Planner* in 2001 that catapulted J. Lo into stardom, after 11 feature films and 4 starring roles in different genres.

Beltrán rightly notes that the rom com is 'a genre through which notions of white American femininity have often been articulated and conversely in which Latinas have seldom been cast' (2009, p. 148). The issue of the representation of different ethnicities in mainstream romantic comedies is, of course, a very significant change in the genre's structure in the last two decades. Nevertheless, the image that Jennifer Lopez has constructed through the assistance of an intricate web of managers, publicists and the media has 'Americanized' what could have been a positive reinforcement of the Latina film star. As Beltrán underlines, 'Lopez's makeover from fleshy Latina to lean and expensively groomed icon arguably assisted in selling her to a broader audience and cemented her Hollywood star status' (2009, p. 147). Although the reasons behind the 'Americanizing of a Latina Star' and the use of J. Lo 'as a woman of a thousand ethnic faces', discussed by Beltrán and Steven Knadler (2005) respectively, deserves further investigation, in addition to the absence of any cinematic reference to the actress's ethnic background, this chapter will not take these questions under consideration and will focus on the issues of pregnancy and motherhood, reserving the representation of different ethnicities for the last chapter.

The Back-Up Plan begins with Zoe lying on a gynaecological chair while the audience listen to her thoughts and the reasons that led her there, having just had some unknown donor's sperm – CRM 1014 to be exact – planted into her uterus. While she hopes the procedure will work even though having a child through *in vitro* was not exactly her first choice, two insert scenes show why she finally decided on buying semen. The first shows her at the house of her best friend Mona (Michaela Watkins), who has four kids. Their discussion on motherhood is not only funny but revealing as Mona rebuffs Zoe's idealized idea of what it means to be a mother. She bluntly says: 'It's awful. They've ruined my life', while she casually removes the intestines of a chicken in preparation for a meal and the kids run around, screaming and shouting, in a house that seems to be mainly decorated by their toys, crayons and painted pictures. The camera moves along with the two actresses as Mona is in constant motion picking up and smelling clothes while shouting instructions the children simply ignore and trying to convince Zoe she does not want that reality. *The Back-Up Plan* includes a more realistic, albeit hilarious, depiction of how hard it is to raise four kids even when you are married. Mona represents most women 'out there', who, unlike celebrity moms, cannot afford nannies, the best schools and/or tutors, nor can they maintain the perfect figure or have their face and hair made up 24/7. Mona's life therefore creates a 'reality' interlude in a usually utopian fictional cosmos and helps the identification process of a larger portion of the audience who may even recognize themselves in this secondary character, who in addition to offering comic relief, as most sidekicks do, also anchors the narrative to real motherhood.

The second insert scene shows Zoe's unsuccessful attempt to persuade her slacker employee/friend Clive (Eric Christian Olsen) to be her donor. Clive vehemently refuses the offer as he believes that fathering a child will deprive him of his sexual escapades, even though Zoe tells him 'he wouldn't have to involved, at all'. Despite Mona's warnings about the difficulties of being a mother and Clive's refusal to become a sperm donor, Zoe still goes on with her back-up plan and the *in vitro* sequence ends with her walking out of the building, happy and exhilarated. She does not even mind the pouring rain and she hails a taxi. Once she is in the car, however, she finds that another man has opened the opposite door. Feeling satisfied and happy, Zoe decides to let this stranger have her taxi and jumps out of it. She meets him again, however, in the farmers market she goes to with Mona, and he introduces himself as Stan (Alex O'Loughlin), a cheese maker.

Although Zoe is obviously interested in this new man who shows his admiration, she thinks she cannot get involved with someone now she is trying to get pregnant on her own. However, Stan pursues her and she finally agrees to have dinner. Before they go out, Zoe takes a pregnancy test but does not manage to read the results because her disabled little dog gets hold of the pregnancy stick. Frustrated but late for her date, Zoe leaves with Stan for a dinner that also ends in disaster when he accidentally pours red wine over her dress and then sets fire to the romantic table he had carefully prepared in a New York community garden. Both Zoe and Stan turn what could have been a catastrophe into an opportunity for playing. Using the hose Stan found to put out the fire, they start pouring water on each other, laughing and acting like teenagers, and as they later walk back home, all drenched but relaxed, they talk and share intimate life anecdotes.

Not only does the film follow the meet-cute rule but also retains the initial, comic yet joyful discovery of the couple's respective stories of the past. Zoe comes home only to discover the broken pregnancy test which confirms she is expecting and decides to tell Stan the truth. She visits his farm the next weekend but due to her hormonal sensitivity, she cannot help but have sex with him before revealing her secret. In a rare instance of a representation of female sexual expression, Zoe has an orgasm while Stan kisses her, before they even have sex. The female sexual climax is rarely represented in romantic comedies and especially by a pregnant woman – and most mainstream American film genres for that matter – with the exception of Sally's classic yet fake orgasm in *When Harry Met Sally* (1989), and the already-discussed Heigl's climax in *The Ugly Truth*. Although, Zoe's orgasm is rendered quite benign, attributed to her changing hormones and also associated with Lopez's Latino background, whose cinematic 'old-age stereotypes' of the Latina woman include the 'harlot or spitfire' representations (Beltrán, 2009, p. 2), its depiction in *The Back-Up Plan* is empowering insofar as it constitutes a taboo breaker.

Interestingly, after Zoe's revelation and Stan's initial disappointment and rejection, the two form a relationship and Stan finds himself becoming a parent. When the first sonogram reveals Zoe is carrying twins, Stan has a panic attack and finds solace in a Central Park playground. There he meets a stay-at-home dad who in a way shares Mona's view on parenthood. The dad basically finds that children deprive him of sleep, free time, and sex with his wife but every once in a while they do something incredible that makes everything worthwhile.

Once again, this scene echoes real life and also shows the man's reaction and feelings towards parenthood. Simultaneously, it gives voice and screen time, albeit uncomplicatedly and briefly to 'Mr Mom', in a specific socio-political time which witnessed fathers becoming 'the primary caregivers for about a quarter of the nation's 11.2 million preschoolers whose mothers work', mainly because of their higher unemployment rate (Russell, 2010). In 2009, stay-at-home dads accounted for 7.4 per cent of primary caregivers 'in married-couple families with children under 18' (Sue Shellenbarger, 2010). This percentage constitutes a two-point increase 'from 2008 and the highest on record', according to Sandra Hofferth, a University of Maryland family-science professor and researcher on family time use (Shellenbarger, 2010). The embrace of this family trend is usually attributed to the 2008 economic recession, which led to a high unemployment rate among men. However, recent studies conducted in the UK add that many husbands choose to stop working and take care of their child/children because their wives are the higher earners (Mark King, 2011). However, both reasons mainly link the Mr Mom 'practice' with financial rewards first, leaving the emotional, psychological and/or personal validation in second place. Thus, stay-at-home dads are either direct products of a global recession which does not leave any alternative than their caring for their offspring or a by-product of a consumer, neoliberal climate which dictates individuals construct their lives according to their earnings. The media representations of Mr Moms, however, only imply the financial side and stress the bond a father can create if he spends more time with his child/children. On the other hand, *The Back-Up Plan* uses Stan's friend in order to imply the prospect of his staying at home, in case his business does not succeed. This possibility makes the hero more anxious and, at the same time, creates the necessary narrative challenges between the couple.

Therefore, Zoe and Stan's relationship is troubled not just by the fact Zoe is gradually changing and undergoing all the traditional stages of pregnancy but because Stan is trying to finish night school so that he could be able to provide the children with a good quality of life and an expensive education. In another narrative twist – and leaving Zoe's ethnicity aside – she is the one with the money. Just like Dianne Keaton in *Baby Boom*, Zoe used to work in the corporate world and decided to abandon everything and buy a pet store. At the same time, Stan used to run an unsuccessful hotel business with his ex-wife and was forced to move in with his parents until he paid off his debts.

However, the fact she is richer and more 'accomplished' than he considers himself to be is not the reason behind their break-up. Zoe is the one who pushes him away when in an angry mood he says that the children 'are not his'. Abandoned by her father at an early age and orphaned by her mother,

Zoe had to learn very early to be on her own and not depend on anyone. Their break-up does not last for long and the couple reunites when Zoe finds and confronts Stan at the farmers market and acknowledges her mistake. Her water breaks at the same time and their reconciliation takes place on the way and in the hospital. The end finds Stan at the *vernissage* of his 'sustainable gourmet shop' where he publicly proposes and Zoe happily accepts.

Both *Baby Mama* and *The Back-Up Plan* along with the other films of the cycle end with the emergence of a nuclear family, whether their heroines began their journey single or not. One could therefore claim that these films offer nothing new but a re-affirmation of the sanctity of family and children and a re-valorization of traditional values, 'represent[ing] new iterations of post-feminism that ultimately restore conservative ideas that valorize pregnancy and motherhood as women's imperative' (Kristen Hoerl, and Casey Ryan Kelly, 2010, p. 360). Nevertheless, I argue that instead of just focusing on the conservative ending, we should pay attention to what the female representations in *Baby Mama* and *The Back-Up Plan* promote. First of all, they make pregnancy visible in the mainstream and do not approach it as a burden or surround it with sombre overtones. Instead, the pregnant women in these romantic comedies become 'unruly women' as they 'disrupt the norms of femininity and the social hierarchy of male over female through excess and outrageousness' (Rowe, 1995, p. 30). The pregnant heroines in both films eat 'like pigs' and they gain weight, changing the shape of their bodies; they have mood swings; they are flatulent; and they develop unique eccentricities. The adoption of characteristics that are usually associated with male images on screen not only disrupts but also challenges traditional gender performance as it likens a series of male-centred films, such as *The Hangover* (2009), *Due Date* (2010), and *The Change-Up* (2011), that emphasize 'the importance of the bodily, and particularly the sexual, elements within romance, the scatological and carnal motif' (Jeffers McDonald, 2007, p. 147).

In addition, these narratives emphasize female initiative and approach motherhood as an autonomous choice that should be made available to women who have not found a partner. Although the main heroines manage to have a child quite easily, despite the comic complications, the films also include secondary characters who present the difficulties both mothers and fathers face: the lack of personal time, the substantial expense and an almost constant state of irritation are a few of the problems these romantic comedies touch upon, offering a representation that is more in touch with what happens in real families and counteracting the images of perfect mothers, dads and children that bombard contemporary celebrity culture and are daily diffused by the mass media.

9 The man-com cluster

In 1995, Rowe (p. 27) observed that 'love is one of the few areas where Hollywood allows women to take charge'. This remark signifies that not only is the romantic comedy genre the par excellence 'shelter' of female protagonists, but that these narratives allow for various and even subversive representations of femininity. Of course, there were always romantic comedies that balanced their emphasis between the female protagonist and the male one, starting with the screwball comedies. William Powell was just as narratively important as Carole Lombard in *My Man Godfrey* (1936), Cary Grant was equally significant in *Bringing Up Baby* (1938), as well as was Rock Hudson in his cinematic encounters with Doris Day in the sex comedies of the late 1950s and early 1960s. The male-centred rom com is certainly not something new. Who could argue, after all, that all of Woody Allen's 'nervous romances' are not imbued by his male personal voice?

The new millennium saw an increasing number of romantic comedies narrated by a male point of view which has already attracted academic attention. Jeffers McDonald (2009, p. 147), for instance, notices this shift of focus from the female to the male hero, and defines the 'homme-com', as a group of male-centred filmic narratives which prioritize 'the importance of the bodily, and particularly the sexual, elements within romance, the scatological and carnal motifs' in films such as *40 Days and 40 Nights* (2002), *Along Came Polly* (2004) and *The 40-Year-Old Virgin* (2005). However, I argue that not all homme-coms emphasize gross-out jokes and/or insist on sex, as Jeffers McDonald suggests. For instance, *What Women Want, Dan in Real Life* and *Made of Honor* do not include any jokes that have to do with bodily functions or place narrative importance on the sexual act, despite the fact that both Nick Marshall (Mel Gibson) and Tom Bailey (Patrick Dempsey) are serial womanizers who enjoy meaningless numerous one-night stands in *What Women Want* and *Made of Honor*.

In addition, the wide variety of different dominant features in male-centred romances – from the rare instance of an interracial relationship in *Hitch*, the supernatural element in the fantasy rom coms *Just Like Heaven* and *Ghost Town*, to the 'nervous' *Whatever Works* – does not permit the inclusion of all the man-centred romantic comedies in a single cycle. Therefore, I will use

Grindon's term 'cluster', defined as a group of films that do not include 'a coherent model or common motifs among productions from the same period' (2011, p. 25) to designate the totality of what I will call the 'man-com' cluster of the new-millennium romantic comedy. Not only is the number of male-centred romantic comedies significant – from the 161 films included in the corpus, 41 or a little over 25 per cent opt for a focus on the male perspective – but their negotiations of masculinity have such diverse focal points that including them in a single cycle would not do them justice. I will, therefore, be using the term 'man-com' as an umbrella term to designate this broad cluster of films composed of different cycles, one of which corresponds with what Jeffers McDonald calls the 'homme-com'. This chapter will examine the various masculinities presented in the man-com, with a view to determining how narratives that are 'told' from a male point-of-view negotiate masculinity in a neoliberal millennial environment.

In 1994, Susan Jeffords provided an insightful connection between politics and the male macho images that had inundated the big screen in the 1980s. She argued that the Reagan administration promoted, once again after the Carter presidency, the ideal of the macho man. Thus, the 'hard bodies' of mainly warrior-type characters, embodied by actors such as Sylvester Stallone in *First Blood* (1982) and *Rocky IV* (1985), Arnold Schwarzenegger in *Commando* (1985) and *Predator* (1987) and Chuck Norris in *Missing in Action* (1984), among others, supported a masculine ideal based on physical strength, patriotism, individuality and independence which likens the incorruptible lonely hero of the western in the 1940s. Nevertheless, as Jeffords adds, this type of masculinity (the exaggeratedly muscular body, the patriotic, decisive and violent man who saves the day) was not the only male representation that was diffused in the media during the Reagan presidency. The late 1980s and early 1990s witnessed 'a rearticulation of masculine strength and power through internal, personal, and family-oriented values' (Jeffords, 1994, p. 13). For instance, in *Dead Poets Society* (1989), Robin Williams plays a teacher who tries not only to imbue love for poetry and literature to the students of a private school but also to teach them the importance of solidarity, love and friendship. Harrison Ford in *Working Girl* is a gentle, however aspiring, man, while in *Regarding Henry* (1991), it takes an accidental shot by a thief during a robbery at a convenience store to turn his character from an adulterer and ruthless lawyer to an emotional and compassionate father and husband as he tries to regain his memory and his bodily functions.

Jeffords (1994, p. 13) maintains that these two distinct masculine models 'the hard body and the "sensitive family man" are overlapping components of the Reagan Revolution', as they comprise both 'a strong militaristic foreign-policy position' and 'a domestic regime of an economy and a set of social values dependent on the centrality of fatherhood'. Jeffords (1994, p. 13) concludes that the diffusion of these two masculinities through popular culture media, and especially film, assisted the articulation of the state itself 'as the unified national body of masculine character'. It is true that in English, there is a tendency to assign gender epithets to ideas, things and even states that are by definition without gender. A boat is a 'she', many countries can also be referred to as 'she', while individuals can masculinize of feminize personal objects with sentimental value. However, the feminization or masculinization of a nation – or even an insignificant object – is not without consequences, as it instantly bestows the now gendered concept and/or thing with more epithetic qualities. Thus, a male nation can be seen as traditionally aggressive and decisive, while a female boat can be seen as beautiful, or as Katharine Hepburn described her in *The Philadelphia Story* (1940), 'yar'. Thus, the masculinization of the USA, as Jeffords suggests, through the use of male cinematic representations, as well as the exploitation of the image of a president who was also associated with the traditional macho man during his career as an actor, corresponded to Reagan's harsh domestic politics, which lacked the feminine qualities of compassion and sensitivity.

The theoretical association of cinematic representations of masculinity with the presidency continues to the present differing from Jeffords's approach in one respect. While Jeffords distinguished two types of masculinities, David Greven (2009, p. 15) observes that '[t]he masculine individualism that Hollywood has represented since the late 1980s has been a fissured one' and that the various and often contrasting male representations lack 'any notion of a structural masculine coherence'. Greven goes on to examine the various masculinities during three presidencies (George H. W. Bush, 1989–93, Bill Clinton, 1993–2001 and George W. Bush, 2001–8), while Peberdy (2011) examines various on-screen masculinities from the 1990s and 2000s, analyzes the performances as well as places them in the specific historical contexts. Recent academic work is indicative, not only of the different representations masculinity can take on screen and their complexities, but their direct link to the US political scene in distinct historical periods.

Greven (2009, p. 4) contends, for instance, that the George H. W. Bush administration marks 'a profound shift in gendered representation' as far as popular culture is concerned. Greven notes (2009, p. 4) that Bush's four-year term (1989–93) witnessed the apogee of queer cinema, and a great number of both mainstream and independent films, such as *The Silence of the Lambs* (1991), *Basic Instinct* (1991), *My Own Private Idaho* (1991) and *The Crying Game* (1992), 'foregrounded non-normative gendered identity and sexualities', which 'transformed Hollywood film's representation of gender and sexuality', and whose influence is still evident in the new millennium. The Clinton years on the other hand, 'constructed male emotional blockage as an extremely dangerous condition' (Greven 2009, p. 171) and, thus, mainly promoted a more effeminized masculinity. In addition, however, as Brenton J. Malin points out (2005, pp. 186–87), masculinity during the Clinton administration 'open[ed] up arguments for increased sensitivity in our communications at the same time that it sanction[ed] brutal violence and bloodshed'.

The presidency of George W. Bush and the post-9/11 climate allowed for 'the re-emergence of *Homo Reaganomicus* – the recharged militarized masculinity', 'that proudly proclaims the United States not only as the world's only true superpower, but the axis of an emerging global empire, beholden and accountable to no one' (Michael Kimmell, 2010, p. 7). Finally, the Barack Obama term (2008–present) has already attracted academic attention,[1] and despite the fact it has yet to be completed so that its analysis and potential influence can be fully examined, it has been associated with positive types of masculinity, assertive yet sensitive and compassionate. Marc E. Shaw and Elwood Watson (2011, p. 145) underline that Obama's 'masculinity can be framed in stark contrast to the shoot-'em-up cowboy masculinity of the Bush administration', while Kimmell (2010, p. 8) notes that 'the happily married egalitarian husbands and involved and expressive fathers that are the current president and vice president may augur a new vision of manhood that may ripple through the culture'.

It therefore becomes apparent that masculinity is not only a concept attached to specific sociopolitical times, but also a notion 'troubled' by its many performances and/or meanings, even during the same period. The majority of popular cinematic representations of masculinity in the millennial male-centred franchises (X-Men, Spider-Man, Batman, Pirates of the Caribbean, the Harry Potter films), and blockbusters, such as *Iron Man* (2008), *Iron Man 2* (2010) and *Inception* (2010), stress 'their the gun-toting hypermasculinity' (Douglas Kellner, 2010, p. 168) in an effort to compensate for the hard realities men had to face in a post-9/11 social climate and a recession 'sometimes referred to as mancession', which saw new highs for the male unemployment rate, culminating in a 2011 Labor Department report that showed 'that unemployment rates were slightly higher for men than for women' (Stanley, 2011).

At the same time, these representations not only 'bid adieu' to the Stallone/Schwarzenegger ultra-macho model of the 1980s but also its 1990s substitute, which Wood characterizes as 'a kinder, less blatant, less parodic, and less downright silly form of it', exemplified by actors such as Harrison Ford, Mel Gibson, Ben Affleck and Matt Damon, who represented 'a more emotional, more vulnerable, more *human* image of maleness' (2003, p. xxxvi). The soft side of masculinity is still evident in the cinematic texts of the last decade, but what is underlined is the multi-layered and often contradictory aspects of it. For instance, the Wolverine may at first represent an ultra-macho male machine but by the fourth instalment (*X-Men Origins: Wolverine*, 2009), the audience realizes he is basically a little boy who never had a steady home, was rejected as a child by his own mother and was consequently an easy prey for the male-dominated army system which turned him into a deadly weapon. Similarly, the millennial Batman representation 'serves as a means to negotiate the binary opposition of good and evil' (Johannes Schlegel, and Frank Habermann, 2010, p. 32), as the Dark Knight not only operates at the margins of the law but has also a dark side which blurs the once clear-cut good-versus-evil dichotomy.[2]

Based on the above, it comes as no surprise that the man-coms of the last decade were widely varied in theme and tone. Some of them were also impressive box-office hits, with two specific films reaching the top-ten of the most commercially successful films in the history of the genre. The $374 million that *What Women Want* grossed worldwide and the $368 million of *Hitch* place the films in the third and sixth place respectively. Their success can also be attributed in part to their stars' appeal despite their association with different genres. Mel Gibson had only starred in an action romantic comedy, *Bird on a Wire* with Goldie Hawn in 1990, but in the late 1990s he was enjoying the success of the *Lethal Weapon* franchise (the fourth instalment was released in 1998) and was already considered an accomplished filmmaker, having won the Oscar for directing and producing the epic *Braveheart* (1995). On the other hand, by 2005, the year of *Hitch*'s release, Will Smith was enjoying global popularity, having starred in *Independence Day* (1997) and the two *Men in Black* films (1997 and 2002). Furthermore, *What Women Want* was directed by Nancy Meyers, who had previously enjoyed considerable success in the genre as the screenwriter of *Private Benjamin* (1980), *Baby Boom, Father of the Bride* and *The Parent Trap* (1998), among others. Her name was, therefore, another factor that contributed to the global appeal and impressive returns of *What Women Want*. Conversely, *Hitch* became one of the first mainstream studio productions that placed a mega star in an interracial relationship and as such attracted an even wider audience, while 'normalizing' the coupling of an African-American with a Latina, as will be discussed in the last chapter.

What Women Want and *Hitch* aside, the cluster of the man-coms can be further divided into the three following cycles:

The 'Peter Pan' cycle, which includes films such as *What Women Want, The Bachelor* (2000), *40 Days and 40 Nights* (2002), *Down with Love* (2003), *Wedding Crashers* (2005), *Hitch, Failure to Launch, A Good Year* (2006), *Knocked Up, Made of Honor* and *Ghosts of Girlfriends Past* and addresses the cliché of the commitment phobic man who just wants to 'party' and does not plan to settle down. The male protagonist is a 'man's man', and irrespective of his age – he may be in his 20s (*40 Days and 40 Nights*), 30s (*Down with Love*) or 40s (*What Women Want*) – he is admired by his male friends, loved by women and successful in his chosen profession. While he begins his narrative journey as a classic Don Juan, he soon learns, influenced by that special someone, that empathy and sensitivity are the path to his personality's completion and the only way to a more fulfilling life.

The 'neurotic' cycle, which comprises the recent Woody Allen films, such as *Hollywood Ending* (2002), *Anything Else* (2003), and *Whatever Works*, but also films such as *Along Came Polly* (2001) and *Sideways* (2004), negotiates male neuroses and places the female protagonist in the role of the male psyche healer.

Finally, the 'high-maintenance' cycle, made up of films such as *Me, Myself & Irene* (2000), *Shallow Hal* (2001), *About a Boy* (2002), *The 40-Year-Old Virgin* (2005), *Dan in Real Life* and *Ghost Town*, which focus on 30- or 40-something men who are not conventionally attractive, such as Jack Black,

Steve Carell and Ricky Gervais, with emotional troubles that vary from split personality disorder (*Me, Myself & Irene*) to depression manifesting as sheer obnoxiousness (*About a Boy, Ghost Town*).

The knowledgeable reader will notice that the 'the slacker–striver romance', defined by Denby in 2007 is missing from my categorization and is actually included in the 'high-maintenance' and 'Peter Pan' cycles. Denby (2007) argues that 'the slacker–striver romance' negotiates a romance between 'the slovenly hipster and the female straight arrow', a man in his 30s or younger, who 'spends a lot of time with friends who are like him [...] anti-corporate, but [...] not bohemian'. However, I believe there are considerable differences in the male heroes of the films Denby includes in his film categorization. For instance, I find that Jack Black in *Shallow Hal* and Vince Vaughn in *The Break-Up* vary significantly in that although they both seem quite superficial and not very career driven, the first is a guy who views women as objects while the second is committed to a long-term relationship despite the eventual outcome, foreseen by the film's title. Finally, Denby's category also includes films that are considered pure comedies, such as *Old School* (2003), *School of Rock* (2003) and *You, Me and Dupree* (2006), and as such are excluded from my corpus. Finally, also excluded from this discussion are the recent 'bromances', such as *Superbad* (2007) and *I Love You, Man* (2009), which emphasize male bonding at the expense of the female characters and cannot, therefore, be considered as romantic comedies.

Made of Honor and *Whatever Works*: Mainstream vs. 'auteuristic' masculinities

The two man-coms that will be discussed in this chapter are *Made of Honor* and *Whatever Works*: two exemplary male-centred romantic comedies, which present two men who begin to question their gender performance and are led to revise their masculinities when faced with unexpected circumstances. In the first film, Patrick Dempsey plays Tom Bailey, the rich inventor of the coffee paper sleeve that allows one to hold a plastic cup full of hot liquid without fear of getting burnt. Tom is a 30-something handsome New Yorker who spends his time sleeping around with women but never getting attached to them. He does not need to invest in a loving relationship with any of these women since his best friend since college, Hannah (Michelle Monaghan), an art conservator, fills this gap; they have coffee together, they lunch together, they share their sex life stories; in short, they know everything there is to know about each other. However, once Hannah finds the man of her dreams on a business trip in Scotland, Tom realizes his feelings go deeper than the friendship they share and decides to act as her 'maid of honor', organizing the bridal shower, helping her choose lingerie for her wedding night, but secretly trying to destroy Hannah's wedding and start a relationship with her. *Made of Honor* presents the inverse scenario of *My Best Friend's Wedding* (1997), since this time it is the male protagonist who tries to ruin his best female friend's wedding. At the same time, it is also a film which draws from the tradition of *When Harry Met Sally* in its insistence of the importance of the male–female friendship and how this bond may very well represent the basis of a long-lasting marriage. Male friendship is also accentuated through various scenes that depict the hero playing basketball and confiding in his four best friends, thus confirming Deleyto's observation about a 'broader tendency in romantic comedy to examine the importance of friendship in contemporary society and to explore the tensions that it creates in its rapport with heterosexual desire' (2003, p. 171).

In *Whatever Works*, 62-year-old Larry David serves as yet another Woody Allen cinematic alter ego, playing Boris Yelnikoff, a genius, suicidal misanthrope who was once considered for a Nobel Prize and is now spending his days teaching chess to children or 'incompetent zombies', as he calls them, having divorced his brilliant and wealthy wife and abandoned his academic career. In a way, Boris represents the mature version of Denby's slacker, a man who dresses comfortably and not to impress, and who works just to get by. One night, Boris meets Melodie (Evan Rachel Wood), a 21-year-old runaway from Mississippi and reluctantly welcomes her into his basement apartment and eventually into his heart. The two films differ significantly as the first is a Hollywood mainstream production and the second an 'auteuristic' narrative. However, it is interesting to observe their similarities vis-à-vis a 'deteriorated' millennial masculinity which struggles to find a new balance in two different age groups.

Made of Honor stars Patrick Dempsey, an actor who was once destined for the A-list with widely popular teen rom coms, such as *Can't Buy Me Love* (1987) and *Loverboy* (1989), but had to wait until his second chance at stardom with the TV dramedy *Grey's Anatomy* (ABC, 2005–present) and his portrayal of the eminent Seattle neurosurgeon Derek Shepherd, aka Dr. McDreamy. The worldwide popularity of the television show and Dempsey's newfound appeal as a sexy, mature man attracted the film's director and/or producers, who wanted to capitalize on the actor's image. Once again, Dempsey had acquired the star 'capital', which 'can be used to create advantage in the market for films and secure profits' (McDonald, 2000, p. 14). In other words, Hollywood executives considered that Dempsey's appeal alone would attract more viewers and secure the success of a film. They were not wrong. Both romantic comedies starring Dempsey in the new millennium (the fantasy rom com *Enchanted*, and *Made of Honor*) grossed more than $340 and $105 million respectively and can therefore be considered box-office successes considering their budgets ($85 and $40 million respectively).

Tom begins his narrative journey as a textbook alpha male: he is handsome, fit, wealthy, smart, well-mannered, well-liked and well-educated. His masculinity seems perfectly secured until we learn about his 'rules'. He never sleeps with the same woman two nights in a row, he only calls a new 'conquest' at least 24 hours after he gets her telephone number and he never takes a lover on family functions or weddings. This phobia of commitment is readily explained, as in one of the first sequences of the film, Tom has to attend yet another of his dad's wedding's, the sixth one. Thomas Sr., played by Sidney Pollack in his last acting performance before his death during the film's release, is a serial groom.[3] Tom is sitting in the church with his dad just before the latter walks down the aisle. At the same time, they both listen to dad's lawyer negotiating the prenuptial contract on the phone with the future Mrs Bailey, who is in the car, circling the block and is determined not to go through with the wedding until she is completely satisfied with the contract conditions. Once the 20-something trophy bride finally agrees to have sex with Thomas Sr. four times a week on the condition he exercises, the wedding ceremony begins, and the viewer understands that the alpha male Tom embodies may not be so alpha after all. Not having a stable relationship to emulate growing up, Tom's fear of emotional solidity could easily be attributed to a father who, although loving and caring, seems to continue to act as a child in his golden years, who collects beautiful 'things' – trophy wives, for instance – that are destined to 'break down'.

However, the hero's real confrontation with his masculinity comes when Hannah introduces him to her fiancé, the Scottish Colin (Kevin McKidd), another star of *Grey's Anatomy*, who was not afraid to ask her to marry him after a one-month courtship. In a funny scene at a trendy New York restaurant, Tom bumps into – not once but twice – the same waiter, breaking platters filled with food. This slapstick moments cause laughter but also serve a narrative function. Although humour is said to constitute 'a momentary break in [the narrative] continuum' (Kristine Brunovska Karnick, 1995, p. 128), I agree with Deleyto's thesis which claims that '[n]arrative and humour, are […] inextricably linked in the comic way chosen to present the vicissitudes of love and desire' (2009, p. 22). In this scene, Tom's two falls not only make him ridiculous in the eyes of Hannah and cause the audience's laughter, they serve as the first two blows to his impeccable masculinity and belittle him in the eyes of his new rival as he will be remembered as a clumsy man who could not even walk straight. In other words, his gradual acknowledgement of the many facets of masculinity has just begun.

Tom hesitantly agrees to become Hannah's maid of honour, convinced by one of his best friends that this is the only way to destroy the wedding. Walking on the street, the two men stop outside a women's clothing store. There, Felix (Kadeem Hardison) pushes Tom to the window, and a shot from behind the two actors actually shows Tom as if he were in the pink dress shown in the window. This momentary, albeit fantastic, instance of cross-dressing is important insofar as it addresses the change Tom has to undergo in order to eventually win Hannah's heart. At the first level, it connotes that he will have to undertake a role traditionally served by a woman, but most importantly, he will have to get in touch with his feminine side and start caring for the little things that are going to make Hannah happy. Finally, this shot serves as homage to the gender-bending classical romantic comedy *Tootsie* (1981), directed by Sidney Pollack, who portrays Tom's father in the film.

The wedding preparations begin and Tom has not only to organize the perfect bridal shower, visit the church, help Hannah with china patterns, but also 'find the dirt' on Colin and prove that he is not the perfect man Hannah thinks he is. However, Colin proves to be an exceptional male specimen. Even though he has never played basketball in his life, he manages to dunk the ball in the basket every time, humiliating Tom and his friends in the 'manhood test' they considered would be a walk in the park. Tom's defeat becomes complete as he and his friends witness Colin take a shower and notice he is not only athletic but also extremely 'well-endowed'. In a society where men are still obsessed with penis size, Colin becomes the embodiment of the masculine man who is also sensitive enough to woo his beloved by sending her the rarest flower bloom for her bridal shower. Tom has no choice but to take his 'maid of honor' duties seriously, and in an effort to beat the new alpha male, he discovers that getting in touch with his femininity proves also to be a way to get to know himself better, not to mention alter the perception Hannah had of him. For instance, his knowledge of Hannah's likes and dislikes, as well as the suggestions he offers during the meeting with the reverend who will perform the ceremony, impress Hannah who seems surprised at how many personal details and events of her life Tom remembers. In addition, his preparation of the bridal shower replaces the 'guys poker nights' which Tom spends with two of his friends – the third leaves them to go to a strip-club because 'he can feel his sperm dying inside of him', watching his friends take pleasure in preparing gift baskets with scented candles and body creams and decorating them with colourful ribbons. Tom learns everything there is to know about weddings and flies to Scotland only to be humiliated again, this time wearing a very short kilt, which puts him in an awkward position and accentuates the fluidity of gender identities. He is once again defeated by Colin in the traditional pine toss, the last of the Highlands games of strength and agility, where each man has to throw the trunk of a tree to determine which 'warrior' will claim the bride.

One could argue that the Colin–Tom antagonism is not just a case of male rivalry over the heart of a woman, but also an indirect allusion to the rivalry between the USA as part of the 'New World' and Europe as part of the 'Old World'. Colin is a bona fide aristocrat. He comes from a very old family with royal affinities and he even holds the title of duke. He is part of an old country, rich with traditions, and he is reliable and strong, both physically and mentally, but also a sensitive man who plays music, sings and knows everything there is to know about courtship, drawing from a rich European literary tradition. Meanwhile, Tom is an upper-class New Yorker who invented the coffee cup paper sleeve and does not need to worry about money for the rest of his life. He embodies the American dream and his millennial masculinity is both characterized by his commitment phobia, his endless affairs and his metrosexuality – he chooses carefully which shirt to wear before his meeting with Hannah after her long trip, validating the fact he pays attention to the way he looks.

However, in the battle between the two worlds, the USA is the winner. Not only does Hannah succumb to the romantic feelings she has always nurtured for Tom and which the narrative underlined through looks and gestures since the beginning of the film, but she dismisses Colin and by extension part of his European identity, as it is shown that he is adamant and not at all inclined to abandon his family's centuries of traditions, regarding, for instance, the name of the children he may have with Hannah or to stop hunting because his fiancée cannot stand him shooting animals. However, Tom triumphs at the end, arriving on horseback at the church like a true medieval European knight only to fall flat on his face as the church doors open. Once again this comic instance serves as a narrative catalyst and not only a source for laughter as it interrupts the wedding ceremony and allows Tom to share his true feelings with Hannah in front of everyone. The wedding is of course cancelled but the cut that follows replaces the Scottish ceremony with a New York one uniting the two friends in the city where they spent their lives. *Made of Honor* underlines the importance of friendship and true partnership in the heterosexual romance while deconstructing the alpha male, substituting him with a more feminized version of a man who finally acknowledges that companionship is nothing he should be afraid of.

Whatever Works is also set in New York City but being a Woody Allen film, it carries the seal of an experienced filmmaker who almost single-handedly defined the cycle of the 'nervous romances' of the 1970s. Even though Woody Allen's films were 'instrumental in bringing about the rebirth of the genre in the late 1970s' and 'even though the New York director continued to make (and still does) one film every year, his movies have virtually disappeared from discussions of 1980s and 1990s romantic comedies' (Deleyto, 2009, p. 51). Deleyto claims that this absence is due to the fact that these films 'cannot be made to fit the formally constraining and ideologically deterministic definitions of the genre that have dominated generic theory and analysis' (ibid.). In other words, since Allen is an awarded writer/director with a vast and appreciated oeuvre that spans five decades, an 'auteur' who has absolute control over his filmic text, his romantic comedies must be something more than the simplistic products Hollywood releases each year. Of course, I would argue that Woody Allen's comic romances are as formulaic and predictable as any mainstream rom com, and as a result scholarly attention has naturally diminished, while it turned to the examination of mainstream romantic comedies, which are considered a rich and until recently an uncharted terrain of gender representations.

In the last decade, Allen wrote and directed 11 feature films, while he abandoned his familiar New York setting and started shooting in Europe. *Match Point* (2005), *Scoop* (2006), *Cassandra's Dream* (2007), and *You Will Meet a Tall Dark Stranger* (2010) were shot in the UK, while *Vicky Christina Barcelona* (2008) was filmed in Spain.[4] Beach (2002, p. 158) underlines that 'Allen's comic persona has remained remarkably consistent. The neurotic, neurasthenic, sexually tormented, angst-ridden, death-obsessed character established in his early films has become a defining postmodern antihero for the late twentieth century', as well as the beginning of the new millennium. The Woody Allen millennial New Yorker romantic hero may assume different names and exist fictionally as a 20-something aspiring writer Jerry (Jason Biggs) or a 60-something retired academic Boris (Larry David), but his pre-occupations remain the same: religion, the meaning of life and the inevitability of death.

Whatever Works is in many ways Allen's return to several aspects of his rich cinematic past. It constitutes a return to the Big Apple after five years since he made the New York–based *Melinda and Melinda* (2004), a return to one of his classic nervous romances since *Anything Else* (2003), a return to a more mature protagonist since the director's last appearance as the lead actor in *Hollywood Ending* (2002) and finally a return to the May–December romance, which has been present in several of his films (*Manhattan*, 1979, *Mighty Aphrodite*, 1995, and *Deconstructing Harry*, 1997, among others). It would therefore be interesting to see how Allen revisits the city, the genre, love and the characters towards the start of the new millennium, but most importantly examine the construction of his male character, Boris. As already noted Boris, a retired academic with an IQ of 200 meets 21-year-old runaway Melodie (Evan Rachel Wood) and lets her stay in his apartment. Despite his constant insults, Melodie begins to feel attracted to the charismatic yet frequently obnoxious Boris and the two get married despite the four decades that separate them. Echoing Allen's real life story – in 1992 he separated from long-time partner Mia Farrow to marry her adopted daughter Soon-Yi, 35 years his junior – Boris and Melodie's affair may be construed as another case of 'fusion of the public and private selves' (Sam B. Girgus, 2002, p. 1). Girgus argues that while Allen may have achieved success during his public and long-term relationship with Mia Farrow, he also had to face the publicity and criticism after his break-up and his subsequent controversial marriage. In addition, the repetitive use of the Pygmalion subtext – the older man who has to teach the young, ignorant woman everything there is to know about life – along with the unavoidable connection to Allen's private life made film reviewers sceptical. *Time*'s Richard Corliss, in an otherwise positive review, wondered if the audience would dismiss the film as '[a]nother Woody Allen movie that propagandizes crabby old guys attracting cute young women' (2009).

Whatever the connection audiences worldwide may or may not be interested in making, it is interesting to observe how Allen constructs the evolution of his male antihero as he covers the seventh decade of his life. With the exception of a few romantic dramas that deal with men in their late 60s or even 70s (*Away from Her*, 2006, *Starting Out in the Evening*, 2007), the romantic comedy genre has always targeted and was fictionally preoccupied with a much younger demographic as if the 40s constituted an arbitrary chronological marker, after which both men and women would have to abandon any ideas about falling in love and/or having sexual relationships.

Fortunately, the new millennium gave way to mature female protagonists and consequently depicted the older man as their object of desire. Allen's Boris is not only a 60-something-year-old object of desire but he is the central protagonist and as such a rarity in the last decade's rom com universe. His masculinity is, of course, imbued by Allen's trademark character and as a consequence, Boris is not only a mature man simply looking for love but 'socially inept and highly self-conscious about his own ethnicity', as well as 'intellectually and culturally sophisticated' (Beach, 2002, p. 158).

Despite his genius, his absolute views on politics and societal issues, he ends up agreeing to marry Melodie after she professes she has 'developed a crush on him', and despite assuring her that 'love [...] does not conquer all, nor does it usually last'. The narrative then flashes forward and Boris and Melodie have already been married for a whole year. However, theirs is not the traditional marriage based on either friendship and/or pathos that completes the narrative of the mainstream rom com. As Boris himself reveals in one of his many direct addresses to the camera and audience, his decision was basically based on a fundamental human need, that of the search for something to give life the illusion of meaning. In addition, Melodie's cheerfulness, her non-possessive character and her willingness to keep him company in the emergency room after his panic attacks help Boris avoid stress and as a result he does not feel he should end this relationship as he did with his first wife, the brilliant and wealthy Jessica (Carolyn McCormick). Boris concludes that although he did not expect it, the year of his wedding to Melodie 'was not the worst year of my life'.

However, what he describes differs significantly from what people think of modern marriage. Boris does not talk about intimacy, sex, mutual respect, understanding and/or trust, the basic pillars of the modern heterosexual union, in his description of his second wedding. On the contrary, the narrative infers that it is Melodie who respects, understands and takes care of her husband while at the same time withstands and/or does not really care about Boris's insults, his constant complaining and his obvious lack of affection – there is not a single scene in the film that shows the two of them kissing or hugging or even suggesting they share something more than a common dwelling. One should not hasten to suggest that Melodie is just a naïve and simplistic young girl transformed in the hands of her more knowledgeable and mature man. Although she progressively learns and indeed accepts some aspects of Boris' theory on life, she still retains her joy for life, her work as a nanny and her new life in the big city. In a way, this marriage is a portrayal of a mutual agreement between two people, who out of fear of loneliness or homelessness decide to spend their life together.

More importantly, it is Melodie who eventually meets a man her own age, falls in love and decides to divorce Boris. Although Boris seems to accept the dissolution of his second marriage when Melodie asks him for a divorce, stating that 'love relationships are invariably transient', the next time we see him on the screen, he attempts suicide for a second time, validating his secret need to be loved despite his palpable misanthropy. Of course, Allen does not kill his protagonist but surprises the audience with one of the weirdest meet-cutes of the genre as Boris lands on a woman who will later be his next companion. After a wealthy and intellectual first wife, a much younger and much less intellectual second one, Boris ends up with Helena (Jessica Hecht), a psychic no less. The film ends with a party Boris is throwing in his apartment to celebrate the New Year. In a final address to the camera, he unexpectedly abandons, probably temporarily, his pessimism and his nagging and encourages everyone watching to seize 'whatever love you can get and give, whatever happiness you can filch or provide, every temporary measure of grace, whatever works'. The congenial party atmosphere, combined with the joy and exhilaration associated with the New Year, and Boris's surprising concluding remarks along with him looking happy when Helena puts her arms around him are a departure from the bitter and frustrated Boris who first addressed the audience in the first sequence of the film and talked about 'the horror, and corruption, and ignorance, and poverty, and genocide, and AIDS, and global warming, and terrorism [...] and the family value morons, and the gun morons that reign in modern American society.

From being 'a social misfit' (Beach, 2002, p. 159), as many Allenesque heroes are, Boris is transformed through love although the audience does not witness how this relationship grew. Instead, the narrative chooses to place its hero in a relationship quasi doomed to begin with, in order to show that even though Boris knew the relationship with Melodie could not endure, he still did not hesitate to give love another chance. Therefore, Boris can be also characterized as an unconventional romantic, whose acute intelligence and apparent misanthropy, do not prevent him from manifesting, admittedly rarely, his feminine traits which enable him to associate with other human beings – and even form romantic relationships. More importantly, however, the narrative implies that love and companionship are not the prerogative of youth and that people who have already gone through the bigger part of their life are still in need of the beloved other, not in the sense that he/she will be necessarily their soul mate who will 'complete them' but because without him/her, life can sometimes look meaningless.

Made of Honor and *Whatever Works* are certainly dissimilar but their focus on their male leads assists the analysis of masculinity. Tom, the young, robust womanizer clashes with Boris, the older and almost insufferable neurotic. Yet they both avoid intimacy with women as their different kinds of masculinity do not let them open up and reveal that they, too, enjoy a loving relationship. Tom embodies the perfect neoliberal subject, untouched by the beginning of the 2008 recession, a resourceful and inventive individual, who produced a single great idea that resolved his financial problems, most probably for the rest of his life, and allowed him the freedom to consume and enjoy both objects (clothes, expensive food, cars, etc.) and beautiful women he sleeps with only once. Tom is initially represented as a 'man's man', an alpha male who enjoys professional success, as well as female and male admiration, having achieved the main goals of the neoliberal agenda: the insertion of a new and useful product in the market by an aspiring entrepreneur and the subsequent consumption of goods with the use of the money earned by this person's 'hard' work. However, during the narrative, Tom's gender performance changes as he is presented with a situation he cannot overcome just by writing a check or delivering a witty line. His best female friend, with whom he is secretly in love, is getting married to someone else. When Tom realizes his 'old tricks' cannot bring Hannah into his open arms, he undergoes a personal change. He recognizes that some feminine traits, mainly openness and sentimental honesty regarding the affairs of the heart, are not superficial and do not pose any threat to masculinity. Therefore, once Tom accepts to be true, first to himself and then to Hannah, does he 'get the girl' in a luxurious and elegant Manhattan ceremony.

On the other hand, Boris presents an alternative version of the 'man's man'. In his case, it is not his appealing appearance, polite manners or wealth that attracts admiration but his intellect. His vast knowledge and his sharply articulated arguments about the state of the world, on the one hand, reveal his contempt for the human species as a totality, and on the other, expose the mechanisms of a political system that strives to keep individuals submissive. In his first address to the camera, Boris's quick-paced monologue is a direct attack on the habits and obsessions of contemporary New Yorkers, who spend their lives mainly discussing 'morality, science, religion, politics, sports, love, children, health, Christ', while they allow some 'idiots' to tell them 'all about life and define for [them] what's appropriate'. Boris draws a parallel between the state of the world today and the word 'horror', uttered by the fictional character Kurtz in Joseph Conrad's novella *The Heart of Darkness*, which was published 1903. Imbuing humour in an otherwise very serious speech, Boris, says:

> Lucky Kurtz didn't have *The Times* delivered in the jungle, then he'd see some horror. But what do you do? You read about some massacre in Darfur, or some school bus gets blown up, and you go, 'Oh, my God, the horror!' And then, you turn the page and finish your eggs from free-range chickens. Because what can you do? It's overwhelming.

Boris does not only vehemently criticize the neoliberal system which perpetually devises ways to subdue its subjects, while it dictates standard behaviours, and promotes new consumer habits. He condemns the collective inactivity of the majority of citizens, who may be shocked by the injustice and the horror that reigns all around the world, but do not take any action. One could only wonder how Boris would react to the sight of hundreds of citizens who have started protesting – starting in Spain in May 2011 and spreading to most European countries before arriving at Manhattan's Zuccotti Park and the Occupy Wall Street movement in September 2011 – against the neoliberal invasion, after its devastating effects on their countries' economies.

However, during the filming and release of *Whatever Works*, Boris's political comments not only cast light on the 'ugly truth', that is, the system's aggressive agenda which further widens the gap between what is known as 'the wealthiest 1 per cent and the 99 per cent', and the inertia of those people who suffer most from the consequences of such a system, but place the hero in the role of the leader who knows best. While Boris never insinuates he would like to possess a position of power – after all he quit his job as a professor at Columbia University to teach chess to children in parks – he remains the male protagonist of the narrative around whom everyone and everything revolves.

And just like Tom in *Made of Honor*, Boris has to acknowledge that the acceptance of some of his feminine traits and a loving relationship is the only way that can bring him a relative peace of mind and prevent him from another suicide attempt. Both these man-coms arrive, therefore, to the same conclusion, albeit using contrasting ways. Despite being filmed during the same period, *Made of Honor* focuses more on the escapist element (wealthy protagonists, luxurious New York settings, sequences that accentuate the natural beauty of the Scottish landscape). On the other hand, *Whatever Works* chooses to portray 'ordinary' people, centres on an older male protagonist and 'constrains' the plot in a specific sociopolitical atmosphere. However, this difference in the 'wrapping' of the story does not lead to a divergence in the essence of the depiction of the male heroes, as the end of both narratives insinuates that their confused protagonists can commit to an intimate relationship mainly through the understanding and the acknowledgement of their feminine traits.

10 The indie rom com

people are debating what independent cinema is (research should start w/ these people)

More often than not, discussion of romantic comedies is limited to films produced and released by the major Hollywood studios. However, the genre of the romantic comedy is not only thriving in the mainstream Hollywood arena, and as Deleyto (2009, p. 150) notes, 'there has also been life for the genre, and a very exciting one, outside the mainstream'. The American independent cinema, and especially the cinema that emerged in the 1980s, has been steadily producing very interesting romantic comedies, whose structural, and sometimes visual, elements have found their way into the mainstream, as will shortly be discussed. On the other hand, it should be noted that recent independent films, regardless of genre, compete with mainstream productions in every aspect (from considerable two- to three-figure budgets, 'big' Hollywood names, wide distribution, to worldwide appeal and commercial success). For instance, the audience would not easily recognize that awarded, popular, star-laden, and/or 'auteuristic' films, such as *Chicago* (2002), *Gangs of New York* (2002), *Lost in Translation* (2003), or *There Will Be Blood* (2007), are independent films if they did not specifically notice their distributors and/or production companies. At the same time, films that cost no more than $20,000, such as *The Blair Witch Project* (1999) and *Paranormal Activity* (2009), managed by word of mouth, and the use of contemporary social networks respectively to accumulate $248 million and more than $193 million, proving that cinema in the digital era need not always be dependent on huge budgets, CGI effects and/or star presence.

American independent cinema designates such an impressive range of films, genres, movements, directors, writers and actors, that its definition is still problematizing film theory and history (see John Berra, 2010, Yannis Tzioumakis, 2006, Chris Holmlund, and Justin Wyatt, 2005, and Geoff King, 2005). Independent films can be approached from different perspectives (production/economics, aesthetics and ideology) and this complicates further a general description and/or delineation. King (2005, p. 2) notes that there are independent films that 'operate at a distance from the mainstream in all three respects [...] [while others] exist in a closed, sometimes symbiotic relationship with the Hollywood behemoth, offering a distinctive touch within more conventional frameworks'. Moreover, many independent film companies are owned by major studios which are, in turn, part of global conglomerates, which further obscures the issue of real autonomy and release of films which have been made without any restrictions and/or compromises to the vision of the filmmaking team. In addition, whereas the independent output is impressive, its box-office power is precarious. Schatz (2009, p. 27) underlines that 'in 2007, the true independents responsible for some 60 percent of all releases suffered their worst year ever due to over-production and intense competition from the conglomerate-owned indie divisions', at exactly the year which proved to be 'the movie industry's best year ever, with the conglomerate-owned companies enjoying record revenues in both the domestic and world-wide theatrical markets ($9.63 billion and $26.7 billion, respectively)' (ibid. p. 26). Despite the ups and downs of the independent sector, however, certain films enjoy significant artistic and commercial success. In the 2010 Academy Awards ceremony, where, for the first time, the number of films nominated for the Best Picture award category was increased from five to ten, six nominations belonged to independent productions (*District 9, An Education, The Hurt Locker, Precious, A Serious Man* and *The Blind Side*), and only four films were produced and/or co-produced by major studios (*Avatar, Inglourious Basterds, Up in the Air* and *Up*).

Although the exact contours of what constitutes the American independent cinema go beyond the scope of this book, this chapter will examine the romantic comedies produced in this film sector, which according to Deleyto (2009, p. 150) can, in part, account for 'the variety of narrative and ideological approaches to intimate matters articulated by the genre in recent years'. Whereas mainstream romantic comedies most usually have to obey a series of conventions (a stellar cast, a predictable plot line, an urban atmosphere, luxurious settings and costumes, and more often than not a happy ending), independent productions are allowed more, if not complete, freedom regarding every aspect of the narrative – from the music, the construction of the characters, to the dénouement of the plot. That, of course, does not mean that the boy-meets-girl, boy-loses-girl, boy-gets-girl at the end formula is absent, but that it can be replaced by either a boy-meets-boy or a girl-meets-girl scenario or by a different organization of the plot, which can offer new insights on romantic relationships and their politics, while simultaneously commenting on socially relevant events.

The output of the independent production in the romantic comedy genre in the 2000s consists of an impressive variety of narratives. Films as diverse as the multi-character *Sidewalks of New York* (2001), *Meet Market* (2008), *Say Goodnight* (2008), and *The Romantics* (2010); the worldwide hit and number three in the top ten of the most successful romantic comedies of all times, *My Big Fat Greek Wedding* (2002); the star-driven *Punch-Drunk Love* (2002), *Side Effects* (2005), *The Oh in Ohio* (2006), *Dedication* (2007), *Jack and Jill vs. the World* (2008), *Management* (2008), *I Hate Valentine's Day* (2009), *The Good Guy* (2009), and *Happythankyoumoreplease* (2010); the visually complex *Eternal Sunshine of the Spotless Mind*; the lesbian *Kissing Jessica Stein*

(2001), *Gray Matters* and *Puccini For Beginners* (2006); the offbeat *Amy's Orgasm* (2002), *Falling for Grace* (2007) and *Waitress* (2007); the teen *Juno* (2007); the narratively challenging *(500) Days of Summer* (2010); the mature rom coms *Never Again* (2002) and *Sideways* (2004); the time-travel fantasy *Happy Accidents* (2001); the gay *Touch of Pink* (2004) and *I Love You Phillip Morris* (2009); the couple-centred *My First Wedding* (2006), *How to Make Love to a Woman* (2009), *Nights and Weekends* (2009), *Barry Munday* (2010) and *The Freebie* (2010); the interracial *Something New* (2006) and *The Locksmith* (2010); and the African-American *Two Can Play That Game* (2001), *Brown Sugar* (2002), *Breakin' All the Rules* (2004) and *Just Wright* (2010) are just some of the romantic comedies that were produced independently in the last decade. Either targeting niche audiences or attempting to attract a wide audience, the notable number of these comic love stories shows that independent American cinema is supporting the genre and is also delivering films that can assist its evolution and/or direction to new paths.

This chapter will examine *(500) Days of Summer* (2009) and *Happythankyoumoreplease* (2010), two independent romantic comedies that premiered at the prestigious Sundance Film Festival. While the first enjoyed a worldwide release after its warm reception by both film festival audiences and the press, the second was mainly featured in international festivals and had a limited domestic and worldwide release. Nevertheless, both films were chosen because they capture the generation of 20-something people who find themselves at a significant life crossroads, where they have to take decisions regarding who they want to be and who they want to be with. In addition, both films were released towards the end of the first millennial decade, and during the economic recession, and can therefore provide interesting insight into the effects of neoliberalism on this younger generation.

(500) Days of Summer

(500) Days of Summer debuted during the 2009 Sundance Film Festival and its positive reception at one of the most important platforms for independent productions worldwide helped secure its global distribution. The film received mostly positive reviews, which is unlikely for the genre of the romantic comedy. Michael Ordoña (2009) wrote that '*(500) Days of Summer* is something seldom seen: an original romantic comedy'; Lumenick (2009) noted that 'it's the oldest bittersweet story in the book, of course, but music-video director Marc Webb approaches his feature debut with great confidence, flair and a minimum of schmaltz', while Peter Travers (2009) pointed out that '*(500) Days of Summer* hits you like a blast of pure romantic oxygen' and concluded by stating that '*(500) Days* is otherwise a different kind of love story: an honest one that takes a piece out of you'. Not only were the reviews favourable, but *(500) Days* won nine awards – among them the Independent Spirit Award for Best Screenplay by Scott Neustadter and Michael Weber – and received 23 nominations in US film festivals: it was nominated for two

Golden Globes (Best Motion Picture – Musical or Comedy and Best Performance by an Actor in a Motion Picture – Musical or Comedy). In addition to
the film's critical acclaim, *(500) Days of Summer* became a commercial success. With a conservative budget of $7.5 million, it grossed almost $61 million
worldwide, that is more than eight times its initial cost, and placed as one of
the most successful productions of 2009 in the USA.

One would expect that with all the artistic success, critical appraisal and
impressive box office, *(500) Days of Summer* must re-invent the genre or at
least provide an exciting alternative to an already exhausted recipe. However,
the film, as the viewers are told by the deep and authoritative voice of the
extra-diegetic and omniscient narrator (Richard McGonagle), 'is a story of
boy meets girl'. In other words, the story will follow decades of cinematic
history and centuries of theatrical and literary origins. However, at the same
time, the audience feels there is something different. The black screen that
precedes the first shots and the narration includes the 'Author's note', which
assures that 'the following is a work of fiction. Any resemblance to persons
living or dead is purely coincidental'. There are two cuts that immediately
follow this note, which very often accompanies stories that have been based
on true events in order to avoid potential lawsuits. The first writes 'Especially
you Jenny Beckman' and the second consists of a single word: 'Bitch'. This
extra-diegetic knowledge not only causes laughter but guarantees that what
will unfold is to an extent based on something that has really happened and
as such attracts and invites the audience to invest in the narrative even before
the opening credits. Indeed, Scott Neustadter (2009), who wrote the script
with Michael Weber, has admitted to Mike Ryan that the script 'is a
little *too* me. It's a little *too* singular', and that he 'went through this kind of
experience', and then decided to write about it.

Just after the revelation of the writer's 'truth', and the title of the film, a few
animated buildings and a tree are sketched in front of our eyes and the
number 488 appears in brackets along with a shot of a park bench where
we find a young man and a young woman looking into each other's eyes
before we listen to the narrator's voice. There is another cut preceded by the
number 1 and with the help of the narrator we are introduced to our hero
Tom (Joseph Gordon-Levitt) and our heroine Summer (Zooey Deschanel).
We learn that Tom has always been fantasizing about meeting the one, influenced by 'sad British pop music' and 'a total misreading of the movie *The
Graduate*', and that Summer, whose parents divorced when she was a child,
loved only two things: 'Her long dark hair and how easily she could cut it off
and feel nothing'. The opening credits start rolling and home videos show
everyday moments of what we assume is little Tom and little Summer with
the use of a split screen. Right from the start the narrative establishes two
things. First, that the audience will watch a story that most probably happened in real life, and second, that the story involves two completely opposite
personalities: a dreamer and a realist. The first sequence preceded by the
number 290 shows someone riding a bike and arriving at Tom's apartment.

At the door, we see a pre-teenage girl, greeted by Tom's two best friends, Paul (Matthew Gray Gubler) and McKenzie (Geoffrey Arend), who tell her that 'they didn't know who else to call'. The girl, who is the hero's little sister, Rachel (Chloë Grace Moretz), is there to comfort her much older brother and help him through another breakup. Tom explains to everyone how Summer broke up with him while an insert scene shows the two at the diner where their relationship ended.

The first sequence ends and the number 1 brings us back to the day Tom and Summer met, in a greeting cards company in Los Angeles, where Tom has been working as a writer and Summer was just hired as the director's, Vance's (Clark Gregg), assistant. By the eighth minute of the film, the audience becomes aware of the third major characteristic of the plot; the fact that it will not unfold in chronological order and that the numbers that precede the sequences will serve as 'time signs' in Tom and Summer's relationship. On the one hand, this back and forth in time emulates the way we look back on past memories, and on the other, it follows a cinematic tradition that may go back to silent films but has recently re-emerged and produced very interesting and diverse-in-style films, such as *Memento* (2000), *Irreversible* (2002) and *5x2* (2004). In addition, this fragmentation of time provokes the audience while at the same time demands more attention from them in order to understand how this love story began and why it ended.

Leaving the narrative inventiveness aside, *(500) Days of Summer* presents a contemporary love story with an authenticity that is sometimes lacking from mainstream, big-budget romantic comedies. First, Tom and Summer are both middle-class people who have to work to make ends meet. Their jobs are not the coveted positions that are usually held by most romantic comedy heroes and heroines; for instance, Cameron Diaz is an executive in *What Happens in Vegas*, 2008; Patrick Dempsey is a successful lawyer as is Cynthia Nixon in *Enchanted*, and the two *Sex and the City* films respectively; Eva Mendes and Jennifer Aniston are accomplished journalists in *Hitch* and *The Bounty Hunter*, and the list could go on. Tom's dream may have been to become an architect but since his efforts were not successful after obtaining his degree, he found a job as a greeting card writer. Although, he is obviously bored and unhappy with his employment, he cannot leave. He is not only afraid of not being able to sustain himself but he is also afraid of failing. At the same time, Summer, who has just moved to the big city from Michigan, has no ambition whatsoever regarding her professional future and is perfectly satisfied with working under Vance. These two characters in their mid-20s present the embodiment of the neoliberal environment, which reached its maturity in the USA in the 2000s. Even though the narrative does not explicitly comment on the 2008 Wall Street crash and the subsequent rise in unemployment, the audience can easily infer that Tom's reluctance to chase his dream can also be caused by uncertainty and his knowledge that job opportunities are scarce. Moreover, when he breaks up with Summer and starts to draw again as a means to externalize his emotions and also find a way to channel his energy, he makes a long list of architectural firms and after each interview, he crosses them out, one by one, showing not only that the path to success is difficult but more importantly that employment has become a rare commodity.

What is more, the main characters are constructed as exemplary neoliberal subjects in that their gender performance expresses their unique individuality but without any connection to neoliberal consumerism. Tom is therefore presented as a softer male, a metrosexual with distinct choice in clothes and music. His reaction to the breakup in the film's first sequence, his anger, his breaking plates and his subsequent depression, as well as his shy efforts to approach Summer when he meets her, not only endow him with qualities the audience is used to expecting from heroines but can also be linked to Barack Obama's model of masculinity, which differs from that of George W. Bush. Watson and Shaw (2011, p. 143) observe that although Obama's masculinity has been characterized as 'mellow' at times, '[w]hen Obama needs to assert himself, he has no problem rising to the occasion'. Most importantly, Watson and Shaw (ibid.) argue that 'Obama's masculinity is rooted in authenticity'. Tom's masculinity is presented as a mixture of sensitivity – he confides to Paul that he listens to 'She's Like the Wind' every time he thinks of her and that he loves to watch her sleep – and assertiveness – he protests when Summer wants to break up and he goes after the job of his dream. However, despite his oscillation between heightened emotions, and passivity – traditional female qualities and determination and decisiveness – traditional male qualities – Tom is represented as an authentic subject who is performing a number of masculinities depending on any given narrative situation and is not constrained by mainly right-wing demands regarding proper male 'etiquette'.

Whereas Tom is presented as a multifaceted male individual, Summer's character conveys a much stronger sense of individuality, combining male and female characteristics. Although her wardrobe in the film, with many knee-length, pastel dresses that accentuate her waist, alludes to the 1950s, the decade of the 'suburban housewife', the perfect housekeeper and mother, Summer provides the complete opposite female model. First of all, she is not looking for a relationship and during her first night out with Tom and his friend McKenzie, she says she doesn't 'feel comfortable being anyone's boyfriend, or anyone's anything' because she believes that love is a fantasy. Not only is a female character denouncing love but Summer is doing it in the context of the genre that by definition celebrates the romantic union of two people. Summer's comment and insistence on the fantasy element of what the western world perceives as love points not only to the social construction of romantic love 'by a group of poets in Southern France in the eleventh century' and the subsequent union of love and marriage and the birth of the romantic comedy in Shakespeare's time (Evans and Deleyto, 1998, pp. 4–5) but also to the self-reflexivity the cinematic genre has started to demonstrate during the 1970s and the emergence of the 'nervous' romantic comedies. Jeffers McDonald (2007, p. 94), however, argues that while the films of the 1970s acknowledged 'their own awareness of themselves as romantic comedies within traditions', while also inventing new ways of negotiating romantic love in contemporary time through self-referentiality, the later romantic comedies use this self-awareness through intertextuality mostly to 'generate a nostalgic sentiment' and not 'to improve upon their inspirations in terms of increased realism, but merely to evoke them to share any left-over romantic charge they may carry'. However, I would argue that in the case of *(500) Days of Summer*, the heroine's thesis on the non-existence of romance, not only helps the construction of the character but can serve as an ironic observation both diegetically and extra-diegetically. Firstly, it points to the artificiality not only of the concept of love but of the film itself as an artefact, and secondly, it can be used as an extra-narrative criticism on love in the new millennium.

Summer's attitude is also significant as it comes from the heroine and not the hero. Her views against romance, which are contradicted by her wardrobe and her otherwise gentle personality, clash with Tom's romanticism and reverse completely the gender roles the audience usually ascribes to the heroes and heroines of the romantic comedy. In the evolution of the story, it is Tom who passively accepts and reciprocates Summer's first kiss, it is Tom who consents to a 'casual' sexual relationship, respecting Summer's wishes and suppressing his own, it is Tom who does the best he can to keep Summer happy and bursts into a song and a whole musical number when they sleep together for the first time and it is Tom who is left heartbroken when Summer ends their sexual relationship, asking to be 'just friends'.

Summer's masculine side is confirmed during their breakup scene, where she parallels their relationship with Sid and Nancy – the notorious relationship between the British bassist of the punk rock group The Sex Pistols and his girlfriend Nancy Spungen that resulted in Nancy's death under mysterious circumstances in 1978 – in order to show she is unhappy. When Tom reminds her that 'Sid stabbed Nancy', Summer instantly interrupts him by admitting: 'No, I'm Sid'. This casual yet firm appropriation of a male identity, and especially a male identity full of obsession, addiction, but also passion, confirms that gender cannot be limited to a strict dichotomy between male/female but is a fluid concept that can be used by every subject according to a given context.

Thus, when Summer marries and later meets Tom, the audience gets a glimpse of a softer, more feminine heroine who never really wanted to hurt the hero but was also never in love with him. Summer enters the narrative as someone who does not believe in love but leaves the story as a happily married woman. This apparent 'contradiction' could be used to argue that the two men who wrote the script and the male director wanted to present the female heroine as a confused subject in order to easily blame her for the hero's torment and/or present her as the villainess. However, I would argue that Summer, being the personification of the third feminist wave in that she enjoys her life by making individual choices independent of social constrains, is the one that helps Tom to become the perfect neoliberal subject, that is 'a self-enterprising citizen-subject who is obligated to become an "entrepreneur of himself or herself'" (Aihwa Ong, 2006, p. 14). Thus, although Tom's heart breaks, he soon recovers, and energized by his experience with Summer, he quits his job and starts studying architecture again while looking for a job in the field he loves. In other words, Summer becomes the force that activates Tom and pushes him to a new life path.

(500) Days of Summer includes many structural and visual elements that distinguish it from a great number of contemporary romantic comedies. However, despite its narrative fragmentation, the cinematography which introduces the audience to another side of downtown Los Angeles that functions as the perfect setting for a romantic relationship the same way New York does and the insertion of brief pseudo-documentary scenes, as well as a black-and-white homage to the French nouvelle vague and Ingmar Bergman, the film does follow a traditional story of a love affair. The main difference is that the boy-meets-girl, boy-loses-girl, boy-gets-girl-in-the-end formula is transformed into boy-meets-girl, boy-loses-girl, boy-meets-another-girl-in-the-end. The alternative 'happy ending' proposed by the film – Tom may have broken up with Summer but in the last scene he meets and is about to have coffee with another young woman, ironically named Autumn – follows a number of paradigmatic romantic comedies of the past, such as *Annie Hall* (1977) and *My Best Friend's Wedding* (1997), which do not complete their narrative circle with the heterosexual union of the main protagonists. What *(500) Days of Summer* proposes is the recognition of the existence of multiple femininities and masculinities in the same individual, regardless of sex, and the acknowledgement of the intricacies and complications of modern erotic relationships in the first decade of the new millennium.

Happythankyoumoreplease

Happythankyoumoreplease, written, directed and starring Josh Radnor, famous for his television role as Ted Mosby in the successful CBS sitcom *How I Met Your Mother* (CBS, 2005–present), premiered at Sundance in January 2010. Although Radnor's writing and directorial debut won the Sundance audience award, it met with quite mediocre reviews during its limited US and worldwide release in 2011 (see, among others, John Anderson, 2010, Holden, 2011, and Nestoras Poulakos, n.d.).

This romantic comedy chronicles the erotic and sentimental entanglements of four friends in their late 20s as they navigate life in New York City. Sam (Josh Radnor) is an aspiring writer who writes beautiful short stories but cannot really commit to a novel, who meets and tries to help an African-American boy on the subway and ends up letting him stay with him. Annie (Malin Akerman) is an optimistic young woman with alopecia who tries in vain not to succumb to her ex-boyfriend's frequent sexual overtures, while Charlie (Pablo Schreiber) and Mary Catherine (Zoe Kazan) are a loving couple faced with a serious dilemma. The characters' lives progress in a linear order and the writer/director/star Radnor chooses to mostly concentrate on close-ups, fragmenting the body, to capture a glance that hides a secret or a small gesture that betrays an emotion.

Just like *(500) Days of Summer, Happythankyoumoreplease* tries to encapsulate the romantic struggles of four young men and women at a specific social climate, without the sparkle and shine provided by mainstream romantic comedies regarding settings and costumes. Sam does not live in a luxurious apartment he cannot afford, and Annie does not hold a glamorous position as an executive, editor or manager but a middle-management position in a nameless company, while Charlie is thinking of relocating to LA with Mary Catherine in order to pursue a partnership that may help them earn more money.

Still, New York remains 'the quintessence of faith in the possibility and attainability of romance' (Jermyn, 2009, p. 13). Despite the lack of shots of the city's skyline – most probably due to budget restrictions – which more than often signal 'entry into rom-com territory' (Jermyn, 2009, p. 11), *Happythankyoumoreplease* pays homage to the city most identified with the romantic comedy genre. From the very first scene that depicts New York awakening and getting ready for another day, the busy streets, the Manhattan parks, and a beautiful woman that makes Sam turn his head and literally stop walking on his way to an important meeting, the city is also starring in the narrative and offers endless possibilities. It is New York that becomes the obstacle between Charlie and Mary Catherine when the former suggests they move to Los Angeles – 'the epicentre of all that is awful' – and the latter vehemently refuses to leave what she considers 'home', for fear that 'her brain is going to melt', in a scene whose dialogue, argumentation and atmosphere can be considered as homage to Woody Allen's fixation with the city. At the same time, New York situates the story in time as in the first sequence Sam passes by a stand which sells souvenirs with Obama's face. Although '[t]he history of corporate and commercial exploitation of the presidential image is long and varied', (Lilly Goren and Justin Vaugh 2010, p. 87) the brief appearance of the President's iconic image places the film in a new era of American history and imbues the characters with the optimism and the possibility of change that accompanied Obama's first year in office.

A CBS poll in February 2009 showed that expectations for President Obama were 'higher than past expectations for both President Bush in 2001 (by 25 points), and for his father, President George H. W. Bush in 1989 (by 30 points)', and that Obama entered 'the White House with the highest favourability ratings of any president in the last 30 years'. Although the President's popularity fell dramatically the next year, the characters of *Happythankyoumoreplease* seem to believe that with great effort, some kind of positive change can happen. Indeed, although Sam has his first novel rejected by a publisher, he does not miss the opportunity to introduce himself to the beautiful woman he saw earlier in the street. Similarly, Annie, whose auto-immune disorder forces her to use fake eyelashes and wear scarves to cover her bald head, is never seen complaining about her 'difference', but is presented as a strong individual who satirizes her condition and even holds a party to celebrate it. Naturally, the narrative does present obstacles for each of the main characters but it also allows for them to deal with them and not abandon the effort, following the social climate of its time. Sam may have to listen to a negative critique about his novel, but he does not stop writing. He also forms an intimate bond with the boy, Rasheen (Michael Algieri), who follows him from the subway even though he knows it is illegal to have him stay at his apartment.

This relationship can also be seen as another tribute the writer/director pays in the film, this time to Charlie Chaplin and the 1921 silent classic, *The Kid*. However, this narrative addition does not simply constitute a simple reference to a landmark film and a master of cinema, but it imbues the text with the essence of Chaplin's *oeuvre*, his humanism. I am not arguing that *Happythankyoumoreplease* and its writer/director are on par with Chaplin or his work but I am suggesting that the relationship Sam forms with little Rasheem is an allusion to the Tramp's constant efforts to battle 'against all accidents in order to affirm in spite of everything the possibility to be human' (Jean-Paul Sartre in Dana Polan, 1991, p. 144). Sam and Rasheen's relationship is authentic and tender in an era where most human contact is governed by a set of complex rules. Contrary to societal pressures and prohibition, Sam and Rasheen freely choose to be with each other, and their interaction is, for the most part of the film, simple, pleasant and effortless, until Sam is arrested for abduction and Rasheen returns to the foster home he ran away from. However, their bond proves that the twenty-first century is not by definition corrupted by an individualist capitalist system and that humanity and optimism are still part of people's lives.

Happythankyoumoreplease is not only an exercise in how optimism can help the individual but also a study in loneliness, fear of romance and uncertainty about the future of an entire generation of young people. When Sam finally forms a kind of relationship with Mississippi (Kate Mara), the woman he met in the bar – they decide not to have a one-night stand, but a three-night stand; that is, they agree to spend three whole days together at Sam's place – they both confess they are not used to trusting people. Mississippi reveals that her 'men were horrible and cruel'. However, their first morning together is accentuated by a shot reminiscent of Harry and Sally's 'morning after', and in particular, Harry's terrified expression after he realizes he has made love to his best friend in the paradigmatic *When Harry Met Sally*. The shot in *Happythankyoumoreplease* shows Sam with the same panicked look in his eyes, as if he is already regretting the decision he had made a few hours earlier. While Sam has no trouble investing emotionally in little Rasheen, spending time with him, helping him develop his talent in drawing, buying him clothes and even attempting to legally have him stay with him, he cannot seem to be willing to enter a romantic relationship. On the same note, when Charlie expresses his preference for Los Angeles to Mary Catherine and then asks her to marry him, she regards his proposal not as a declaration of love or a promise of a deeper commitment but as a clever way of him breaking up.

In one of the most intelligently written scenes of the film, Mary Catherine explains that since she has told Charlie that she never wants to get married as she comes 'from a long line of divorced people', he must have been sure she would decline and would therefore be free to move to the West Coast. Finally, when Annie breaks down, after realizing that sleeping with her ex-boyfriend is not going to bring them back together, she confides to Sam that optimism can be 'fucking exhausting'. However, by the end of the film, all the characters have rediscovered their optimism, through the acknowledgement that love is still a possibility. Although no marriage and no actual relationship, with the exception of Charlie and Mary Catherine, who were already a couple at the beginning of the story, is taking place or is recognized as such, the audience can infer that Sam will eventually get Mississippi back, and that Annie will not be betrayed again by the clumsy yet honest and funny Sam No. 2 (Tony Hale), a colleague she had not noticed despite his persistent attempts.

Even though these two films cannot be said to represent the entire independent production of the romantic comedy genre, a number of conclusions can be drawn from the discussion above. *(500) Days of Summer* and *Happythankyoumoreplease* depart from the romantic comedy recipe in that their protagonists are closer to reality in that they resemble 'real' people in their mid to late 20s who have ordinary jobs and are not the usual glamorous heroes and heroines one encounters in the mainstream genre paradigms. Thus, even though this departure can be attributed to an extent to the by-definition budgetary restrictions an independent production imposes, the characters can be considered more easily identifiable with the audience, and the story can also be regarded as more closely anchored to reality. In addition, both films use a number of intertextual references (from the French nouvelle vague and Ingmar Bergman to *The Graduate* and silent films in *(500) Days of Summer;* to Woody Allen, Charlie Chaplin and *When Harry Met Sally* in *Happythankyoumoreplease*), which are also present in the mainstream, but acquire a special significance in these two independent narratives. While the former film uses them mainly to ironically comment on the contemporary romantic discourse which is greatly influenced by the artefacts of popular culture – mainly films and music – the latter uses them in order to revisit great narratives of the past, rework them and attribute resonance in a contemporary setting.

Through intertextuality, however, both films, self-reflexively question the validity and the viability of the romantic discourse that still permeates most of the mainstream texts. It is interesting to note that there is not a declaration-of-love scene in either of the two films. Tom may confess to his friend that he is in love with Summer but he never summons up the courage or finds the appropriate time to tell her that he loves her. At the same time, after their breakup, Tom breaks down during a meeting at work and accuses popular culture – mainly the cards he himself writes, the movies and pop songs – which are 'to blame for all the lies and the heartache'. At this very moment, he takes Summer's earlier position about love being a fantasy, and attacks the very concept of romance by revealing not only its societal origins and its means of propagation but its use by the capitalist system as merchandise, a valuable product that can be sold to everyone. The same absence of romantic discourse is found in *Happythankyoumoreplease*, where no direct utterance of 'I love you' takes place in the duration of the film. Only Annie uses the word when she realizes that Sam No. 2 can make her happy and calls Tom to tell him, 'Let's be people who deserve to be loved, who are worthy, 'cause we are worthy'. In this case, love is associated with personal value, and lack of love means there must be a personal deficit.

Nevertheless, both *(500) Days of Summer* and *Happythankyoumoreplease* end with a question mark that implies the possibility of an intimate relationship in the new millennium, without necessarily acknowledging the supremacy of romantic love. In the former film, Tom asks a woman out and looks at the camera when she tells him her name is Autumn, wondering if he could take that ironic twist of fate as a sign, whereas in the latter, Sam goes to the club where Mississippi is singing and their eyes meet just as she finishes a song before the end credits. These open endings follow a long cinematic tradition in the romantic comedy genre which showed a preference for this type of more ambiguous closure for specific socio-historical reasons. For instance, in the 1930s, when the institution of marriage was in crisis, sociologists and scientists proposed the replacement of 'the Victorian patriarchal model with a modern egalitarian concept of love companionship' (Glitre, 2006, p. 45). Therefore, a number of screwball comedies of the time, such as *It Happened One Night*, *My Man Godfrey*, *The Philadelphia Story* and *His Girl Friday*, may have ended with the formation of a couple but without the cinematic representation of a wedding ceremony. Similarly, the ending of some nervous romances of the 1970s, such as *Annie Hall*, *Starting Over* (1979) and *Manhattan* (1979), seem to question 'the mutuality of heterosexual coupledom' (Krutnik, 1998, p. 24) in a society 'that has seen the splitting of sex and self from previous guarantees of romantic and emotional fulfillment' (ibid. 18).

Although the Reagan era in the 1980s and the Bush administration in the 2000s, along with a number of social issues that emerged during these two decades (the threat of Aids, the War on Terror, etc.), promoted and succeeded in re-establishing a set of traditional values regarding the family, marriage and the heterosexual union to a great extent, they could not stop the progress and/or changes in the form of the new family and the romantic discourse. Therefore, although these two independent romantic comedies do not treat love with the gusto of the screwball comedy or the distrust of most nervous romances, they adapt it to the end of the first decade of the twenty-first century, an era of individualism, neoliberalism and economic recession; an age of doubt, yet a time of inherent belief and optimism about the future. While they acknowledge the heritage of the past, in terms of narrative structure, they do not simply repeat a well-known myth, but they rework, self-reflect and adjust the generic conventions, allowing for the possibility of love's power while simultaneously admitting heartache is part of the equation.

11 Romantic comedy and the 'other': race, ethnicity and the transcendental star

One of the main criteria for the inclusion of the millennial romantic comedies in the corpus of this book was their worldwide distribution. Commercial success was also another criterion used for the majority of the films that were discussed in the previous chapters. This is because a film's international reach combined with a significant box-office course creates a popular cultural text which seems to resonate with many different cultures, as well as audiences from different sociopolitical, educational and intellectual backgrounds. However, there is an important portion of romantic comedies that deviate from the mainstream texts – and by 'mainstream' I mean both major studio productions and those independent films that manage to attract global attention – in that their protagonists were either African-American or Hispanic.

In 2002, Krutnik (p. 130) noted that since the early 1980s the Hollywood romantic comedy 'has been remodeled for (and reappropriated by) niche audiences defined by ethnicity, sexual orientation or age'. The film industry produced African-American romantic comedies, such as *Boomerang* (1992) and *Breakin' All the Rules*, Hispanic rom coms, such as *I Like It Like That* (1994) and *Tortilla Soup* (2001), and gay romantic narratives, such as *Go Fish* (1994) and *I Think I Do* (1997). Nevertheless, the majority of these romantic comedies did not enjoy a strong distribution mechanism that could allow for these narratives to be enjoyed by an international audience. As will be shown below, most romantic comedies that did not focus on a white, heterosexual couple either had a limited release in the United States and/or a small number of countries overseas, a straight-to-video release or were directly sold to television networks. The African-American romantic comedies *Two Can Play That Game* (2001), *Brown Sugar* (2002), *Breakin' All the Rules* and *I Think I Love My Wife* (2007) were each distributed to a very small number – less than seven – of European countries, aside from their North American release. Only *Brown Sugar* and *Breakin' All the Rules* were released in Australia, whereas none of the films were shown in any Asian theatres. Similar fates awaited the same-sex romantic comedies *Gray Matters* and *Puccini for Beginners* (both 2006), which were featured in several film festivals before finding their way to DVD shelves around the globe rather than international theatres, while the North American-produced Latino romantic comedy *Chasing Papi* (2003) and the interracial romantic comedies *American Fusion* (2005), *Big Dreams Little Tokyo* (2006) and *Something New* faced the same distribution challenges. These data prove that despite the continuous representation of different races, ethnicities and/or LGBT characters in the romantic comedy genre, the mainstream paradigms are still focused on a white heterosexual romantic/sexual partnership.

The dominance of the white race in the genre and the continuing relegation of 'the other' to the periphery of mainstream film raise a number of questions, especially in a decade which witnessed a distribution of the population by race and/or ethnicity in the United States. According to the US Census Bureau statistics for 2010, white people account for 72 per cent, or 223.6 million of the US population, which totals 299.7 people. Hispanics constitute the largest ethnic minority, comprising 16 per cent, or 50.5 million of the total population, whereas the Asian population is the fastest growing major race group, increasing by 43 per cent between 2000 and 2010, accounting for around about 5 per cent, or 14.7 million. Finally, the African-American population represents 13 per cent, or 38.9 million of the total US population. Nevertheless, the apparent racial diversity of the North American population has yet to be represented on the big screen.

On the other hand, it is the small screen that proves more open and attuned to the above social reality. Millennial television has been steadily producing narratives which include people of all races, ethnicities and sexual orientation, thus offering the US audience an opportunity to enjoy an impressive cultural variety. The examples abound: the main cast of ABC's critically acclaimed *Lost* (2004–10) included Asian, African-American and Hispanic characters; *Desperate Housewives* (ABC, 2004–12) features a Latino couple while seasons seven and eight introduced African-American Vanessa Williams as the fifth 'desperate' heroine, while Gregory House's (Hugh Laurie) diagnostic team in *House M.D.* (Fox, 2004–12) included an African-American neurologist, who becomes the dean of the hospital and House's boss in season eight, as well as a young Asian female prodigy. In addition, the fictional Seattle Grace hospital's chief was African-American for the first seven seasons of *Grey's Anatomy* (ABC, 2005–present) whereas the main cast includes an African-American doctor, a Latina orthopaedist who marries her female lover, and a charismatic Asian surgeon – not to mention the whole show was conceived by an African-American woman, Shonda Rimes – while the initial Glee choir in *Glee* (Fox, 2009–present) was made up of four white high school students, an African-American, a disabled teenager, an Asian couple, a Latina lesbian, a homosexual young man and a lesbian cheerleader. And that is not all.

Several millennial sitcoms are also racially diversified. Tracey Jordan is one of the stars in the irreverent *30 Rock* (NBC, 2006–present), while the most wealthy, educated and happily married male character in *Happy Endings* (ABC, 2010–present), the new version of the all-white *Friends* (Warner Bros., 1994–2004) is African-American. What is more, *Modern Family*'s (ABC, 2009–present) patriarch is married to a Colombian woman who proudly insists on following the traditions of her native country, while his homosexual son and his partner have adopted an Asian baby. In *Mike and Molly* (CBS, 2010–present), the hero's best friend is also black, while in *Up All Night* (NBC, 2010–present), one of the three protagonists, Maya Rudolph, is multiracial. Of course, these examples do not imply that television dramas and/or sitcoms with a mostly white cast are few, since the recurring characters in such varied television series as *Damages* (F/X, 2007–present), *Boss* (Starz, 2011–present), *Raising Hope* (Fox, 2010–present) and *Hot in Cleveland* (TV Land, 2010–present), among others, are white; nevertheless, the inclusion of main and/or supporting characters of various races and/or ethnicities in many American television shows proves that the small screen can be considered more progressive, versatile and open to exploring and promoting cultural diversity.

Thus, although American television is spreading multiculturalism in a federal nation, which was after all created by an amalgam of races and/or ethnicities, mainstream cinema is still reluctant in creating opportunities for starring roles for 'the other'. As far as mainstream romantic comedies are concerned, African-American and/or Latino/a characters are rarely included, even in supporting roles; African-American Loretta Devine had a very small role, playing a loud-mouth doorwoman, in *What Women Want*, and *Woman on Top* (2000) included a rare representation of a black transsexual character in few scenes. African-Americans are usually used as funny sidekicks or are even further marginalized in narratives where they portray a single member of an all-white group of friends. That is the case of *Made of Honor*, where one of Patrick Dempsey's friends is African-American, and *Head Over Heels* (2001), where a black woman is one of the four female friends of the heroine. *Failure to Launch* has the white protagonist learn valuable life lessons from a little black boy, a scenario which is repeated in *Happythankyoumoreplease*. This marginalization is evident even in films which feature an ensemble cast of more than eight main characters. For instance, *Couples Retreat* may include an African-American couple, but its cinematic time is significantly limited compared to the sequences which are devoted to the three white couples. *Valentine's Day* (2010) features an evolving interracial relationship between Jamie Foxx and Jessica Biel and also stars Queen Latifah in a small role, while the ensemble of *He's Just Not That into You* (2009) features no black, Latino/a, or Asian characters.

The same racial 'isolation' is faced by Latino/a or Asian characters, even when they are considered bankable commodities. For example, *Over Her Dead Body* avoids the interracial relationship between the Latina star Eva Longoria, one of the highest-paid actresses in television thanks to the success and longevity of *Desperate Housewives,* and the white Paul Rudd by killing the heroine in the first sequence and turning her into an annoying ghost. At the same time, another successful television actress, *Grey's Anatomy*'s Asian Sandra Oh played the sidekick in *Under the Tuscan Sun* and *Sideways*.

However, there are exceptions that may confirm the rule and at the same time provide an interesting terrain for investigation. For instance, the top ten of the most commercially successful romantic comedies of all times, as was already stated in the introduction, includes *Hitch*, an interracial romantic comedy, which explores the relationship between the African-American Will Smith and Eva Mendes, who is of Cuban–American heritage. *Hitch* earned more than $368 million worldwide, surpassing such hits as *As Good as It Gets*, *Runaway Bride* and *My Best Friend's Wedding*. In addition, Jennifer Lopez's romantic comedies (*The Wedding Planner*, *Maid in Manhattan*, and *The Back-Up Plan*) have earned combined more than $326 million worldwide.

However, I would claim that the worldwide appeal and box-office success of the above films is not due to the racial and/or ethnic background of their stars. Rather, I argue that these numbers prove that stardom often transcends any racial, ethnic and/or gender barriers and endows specific stars with the necessary symbolic and cultural capital which allows them not only to command the screen but also to create and maintain the adoration of a faithful international audience. Will Smith, Eddie Murphy, Jamie Foxx, Antonio Banderas, Jennifer Lopez, Halle Berry and Queen Latifah are among those stars for whom their ethnic and/or racial backgrounds do not necessarily signify 'otherness' through their unique, albeit constructed, images. At the same time, however, these images are structured in such a way that the individual cultural characteristics of each thespian are gradually more or less 'neutralized' and/or considered inconsequential to such an extent that the actors' racial and/or ethnic heritage is not taken into consideration in the fictional narratives they appear in, the discussion of their performance or in the general media discussion surrounding their name.

It would, therefore, be interesting to discuss how certain African-American and Latino actors transcend their racial and/or ethnic origins through careful media construction of their image and consequently lead their romantic comedy vehicles to the top of the box office. I maintain that the images of Will Smith and Jennifer Lopez are examples of the neoliberal discourse of colour blindness which is erroneously considered '[t]he path toward the complete elimination of racism' according to Angela Davis (2008). Davis argues that since neoliberalism supports equality through individual obedience to law, then, each citizen, regardless of race, ethnic background and/or gender is responsible for his/her actions and consequently racism is no longer an issue. This deceptive colour blindness applies to an extent to the Hollywood industry which attempts to metamorphose its ethnic stars into profitable commodities by enhancing and taking advantage of their appealing ethnic characteristics and diminishing and/or defusing those traits that may emphasize their 'other' side.

The discussion of Will Smith and Jennifer Lopez will be limited in the context of their work in the romantic comedy universe. As such, the ensuing analysis does not claim to exhaust the issue of racial and ethnic diversity. Not only does such an endeavour go beyond the scope of this book, but the examination of the diverse cultural identities and meanings black and Latino/a stars bring through their onscreen performances and the media texts that surround them deserves a thorough and systematic analysis which will bring out the complexities of racial and ethnic identities in the globalized film world.

Jennifer Lopez: Transcending the stereotype

In May 2011, the actress/musician/dancer/producer/entrepreneur Jennifer Lopez ranked fiftieth in *Forbes*'s 100 List of 'The World's Most Powerful Celebrities', the second Hispanic individual after the athlete Alex Rodriguez who was placed in the forty-ninth place. Lopez was in the company of a total of 22 women and one of the three female representatives of the Latino community, along with the versatile Cameron Diaz, who was ranked number 80, and the 'desperate' Eva Longoria who was placed at 81.[1] Jennifer Lopez started to draw attention in the late 1990s, when she portrayed the tragic story of Tejana singer Selena Quintanilla Perez in the biopic *Selena* (1997). The role of Selena propelled Lopez

> into the limelight as a Latina star who represented a cohort comprising an amalgam of different groups – Latinos born in the United States, primarily English-speaking, whose parents derived from a number of different nationalities, including Mexicano, Cubano, Tejano, Chicano, Hondureno, Chileno, among other, and who were united in their ambitions to improve their economic and social position (Radner 2011, p. 85).

In addition, the release of *Selena* coincided with a specific time period, the 1990s, which 'witnessed a continuation of New Hollywood shifts that amounted to increasing interest in casting and promoting a handful of African American and Latina/o actors as potential stars' as the industry became aware 'of the potential benefits to be earned from the growing Latina/o audience' (Beltrán, 2009, p. 133). *Selena* may have helped Lopez attract the attention of the film industry, but the films that catapulted her to stardom were two romantic comedies, *The Wedding Planner* and *Maid in Manhattan*. Both films remain to date in her top five most commercially successful films in a filmography that counts 18 leading roles and includes a great diversity of genres (from the crime film *Out of Sight* (1998), the animated *Antz* (1998), the thriller *The Cell* (2000) to the dramatic *Enough* (2002) and the biopic *El Cantante* (2007)). According to Beltrán (2009, p. 141), this diversification in Lopez's film choices represents, 'a concerted effort […] to market the actress to non-Latino audiences'.

Beltrán (2009, p. 148) also notes that '*The Wedding Planner* offered Lopez a shot at uncharted territory: the romantic comedy, a genre through which notions of white American femininity have often been articulated and conversely in which Latinas have seldom been cast'. Indeed, not only does the narrative of *The Wedding Planner* avoid any reference to the heroine's ethnic background, it presents Lopez as an American of Italian heritage, and thus, it completely effaces the possibility of any discussion regarding the actress's cultural difference. Instead, Lopez portrays Maria Fiore, an ambitious and thriving wedding planner who unknowingly falls in love with the groom, Steve (Matthew McConaughey) of the next wedding she is organizing. While Maria tries to maintain her professionalism, a whole subplot revolves around her father, Salvatore (Alex Rocco) and his efforts to marry her to Massimo (Justin Chambers), a man of Italian descent as well, with whom Maria used to spend her summers in Italy. The portrayal of Salvatore by veteran actor Rocco, mostly known for playing mafia gangsters, and the Italianate fictional names, divert the attention of the audience away from Lopez's Puerto-Rican origins and direct it to Europe. Although one might argue that there is indeed an affinity not only between the Spanish and the Italian languages but the people of Latin America and those of Italy and most countries of the European part of the Mediterranean basin, the 'removal' of Lopez from her real cultural milieu and her repositioning in a perhaps more approachable and recognizable ethnic background for the globalized audience terrain can be considered as part of a marketing strategy to more easily 'sell' the image of the actress in the international market.

Indeed, this fictional denial of her true identity assisted Lopez's promotion 'to a broader audience and cemented her Hollywood star status' (Beltrán, 2009, p. 147), as is evident by the film's box-office returns mentioned before. In addition, the effort to Americanize the Latina star aims to neutralize not only the possible negative associations connected to those Americans of Hispanic origins, such as shrewdness, petty crimes, and laziness, but also to show that in a neoliberal context, everyone is equal as long as his/her individuality is targeted to perpetuating the ideal of the free market and the reward of the hard-working professional irrespective of racial and/or ethnic boundaries. Thus, *The Wedding Planner* presents an American woman, with origins that are never discussed explicitly and are only hinted at as being European, which begins her narrative journey as an aspiring employee of a wedding agency who asks for a partnership should she manage to land a very important account. Maria's ambition and professionalism are recompensed towards the climax of the romance as, despite her romantic troubles, she never loses her work ethic and she finally signs the partnership papers.

At the same time, *The Wedding Planner* retains and exploits those characteristics that could help the film achieve greater popularity, mainly Lopez's notorious derrière and her dancing abilities. Many shots focus on Maria's figure from behind accentuating her curvaceous body through tight-fitted costumes, while a whole sequence takes place in a dance hall where Maria fights with Steve while dancing an Argentinean tango. The South American dance of passion and lust combined with the actress's dark hair, full figure and dancing abilities point to those Hispanic traits the western community admires and the film industry seeks to capitalize on. Although Beltrán (2009, p. 152) fittingly observes that the discourses surrounding Lopez's body 'demonstrates an unchanging paradigm of racialization' which 'have long been associated with Hollywood Latinidad'. I would add that the performer's refusal to surgically alter her body type, as well as her own promotion of her 'attributes' through gowns and dresses that emphasize specific body parts, have contributed to a wider media acceptance of full-figured women – and simultaneously endorse a healthier feminine image.

In other words, Jennifer Lopez is not just a 'commodity' that is directed by the film or the music industry, as she managed to control her image, and consequently, her career. According to Priscilla Peña Ovalle (2010, p. 98), Lopez 'capitalized on the sexualization of her own body for personal profit' the same way Madonna started doing in the mid-1980s. Peña Ovalle (ibid.) also stresses the parallels that exist between Lopez and another Hollywood icon of Latino descent, Rita Hayworth, and underlines that '[i]n many ways, Hayworth's investment in herself as a business asset of property – something beyond national, political, or ethnic affiliation – was a precursor to Jennifer Lopez's multicultural business savvy'. Just as Hayworth managed to 'occupy a kind of whiteness that afforded a mainstream career (Peña Ovalle, ibid.), Lopez has been constantly playing with a number of cultural identities. However, as Knadler (2005) points out, the star mainly 'remains a Republican friendly and de-Africanized emblem of the new Latina'. Knadler (2005) argues that

> [i]f J. Lo is the representative of the new Latina, it is precisely because she can both 'pass' as 'white' AND because her flavoring blackness is reduced to an 'asset'–a sign that is emptied of any living history, racial trauma, or African diaspora cultural expression that might challenge U.S. nationalism's white self-conceptualization.

This dichotomy between Lopez's whiteness and Latino heritage is evident in her second romantic comedy, *Maid in Manhattan*, where she assumes her real ethnic identity as a Latina single mother, born and raised in the Bronx and working as a maid in a luxurious Manhattan hotel. Unlike *The Wedding Planner*, *Maid in Manhattan* insists on the heroine's ethnic background. The film does not start with the usual shots of landmark Manhattan buildings or recognizable New York spots, but images of the Bronx, which is not only Marisa Ventura's home but the actual borough Jennifer Lopez was born in and grew up in. The merger of the actress's real neighbourhood with the fictional heroine's home, which was the theme of Lopez's hit song 'Jenny From the Block', released a few months before the film, is used by the narrative to underline Marisa's eventual transformation into something more than the average working-class Hispanic woman. In addition, the first sequence, which shows Marisa taking her son, Ty (Tyler Posey) to school, emphasizes her heritage by including Spanish words in her dialogue, such as *'papi'* and '*abuela*', thus attracting the Hispanic audience which can relate to the character who is constructed on the screen.

Marisa Ventura may belong to the working class but she has aspirations to become assistant manager and improve her life and consequently her social standing. She is presented as an intelligent, knowledgeable, alert working woman who takes pride in her work and knows how to handle even the most difficult hotel guests. During a routine cleaning duty, her friend asks her to try on a designer suit for fun that belongs to a British socialite. Hesitantly, Marisa dons the expensive suit. However, before she has a chance to get undressed, she accidentally meets Assemblyman Christopher Marshall (Ralph Fiennes), who is instantly attracted to her and asks both Marisa and her son to join him for a walk. Marisa takes the opportunity to experience what it feels like to be treated as an equal and not 'the help' but she soon realizes the repercussions of her actions. After their walk in Central Park, Christopher sends an invitation for lunch to what he thinks is Marisa's suite, only to have the real resident knock at his door, the British heiress Caroline (Natasha Richardson), who takes this unexpected opportunity to find another boyfriend after the unfortunate ending of her last relationship.

Marisa tries to avoid any complications, but as she works at the same hotel Christopher is using as the headquarters of his political campaign, she runs into him again, this time as she walks to the subway once her shift is over. When Christopher sees her in the street, he immediately gets out of his car and tells her he is on his way to the Bronx to give a speech on the housing projects. His nonchalant attitude about an issue Marisa finds important frustrates her. In a slightly ironic tone, Marisa advises Christopher to spend a little time in the borough before delivering a few well-prepared lines without actually knowing anything about those living conditions. Her obvious irritation at the wealthy, white politician who thinks he can run for the senate with a few strategically executed speeches and appearances but without any real experience of the issues is not only an explicit political comment that is a rare part of the romantic comedy cosmos, but accentuates once again Lopez's Latino background and her humble beginnings before achieving wealth and stardom. In addition, Christopher's reaction to Marisa's aggravation is 'unflappable and cavalier, thus devaluing the meaty issue of urban housing and the related problem of ethnic segregation in U.S. cities' (Diana I. Rios, and Xae Alicia Reyes, 2007, p. 96). However, in the context of the romantic comedy genre, I would claim that even the mention of this serious issue should be considered as progress, since the dominant feature of these films is the protagonists' course towards a sexual relationship. In other words, one cannot expect the romantic comedy genre to fully examine the political and social inequalities that exist in the USA, the same way one cannot expect to laugh while watching a documentary on the consequences of famine in Africa.

In addition, *Maid in Manhattan* does not limit its sociopolitical commentary to a mention of the Bronx housing issue. The narrative also criticizes the 'superiority' of the white race through Christopher, as well as the hotel management which comprises exclusively white managers and executives who are 'surprised' when Marisa expresses an interest in a vacant managerial post. However, it is also implied that it is only through their help that the 'other' can become a member of the neoliberal 'high class'. Although Marisa has aspirations to improve her life and that of her son, the romantic aspect of the narrative hinders her path and places her in the role of a Latina Cinderella.

When Christopher asks her to join him at a campaign dinner, Marisa is transformed, with the assistance of all the hotel staff, a designer gown, expensive jewellery and professional make-up and an elegant hair bun, into a stunningly beautiful woman who exudes confidence but more importantly seems to belong among people who paid thousands of dollars to attend an event just to get a glimpse of the candidate. Christopher is mesmerized by Marisa's beauty, and despite her fear – and the fact that Caroline almost recognizes her – she spends the night in his room making love. However, their night of passion is followed by the unveiling of the truth, as Caroline does remember her when she accidentally runs into her outside Christopher's room and notifies the management of the hotel. Marisa is accused of impersonating a hotel guest, and she is dismissed without being given the slightest chance to explain. Christopher is overwhelmed and follows her outside the hotel. The two try to have a private conversation while being chased by photographers and journalists who capture what seems to be a scandalous story. Nevertheless, even though Marisa reveals that her feelings for Christopher were real and that she kept on pretending to be someone she is not because he would never have pursued her had he known she was just a maid, Christopher turns back and walks away. His reaction momentarily validates the impossibility and/or difficulties faced, not only by interracial couples, but most importantly by couples who belong to different social strata.

Marisa is left unemployed and heart-broken, while Christopher continues his campaign. However, the narrative does unite the two lovers at the end as little Ty assumes the role of Cupid. The romantic 'order' is restored and the kiss that signifies the end of the film is followed by a series of magazine covers that take the opportunity to profit from the unlikely romance. All the covers underline Marisa and Christopher's ethnic and social differences; one headline reads 'Politics and the Working Class'; another shows Marisa and reads 'The Maid Also Rises', implying the heroine finally managed to become a manager, while the last cover features the couple a year later 'still going strong'.

Maid in Manhattan ends not only by uniting a heterosexual couple, obeying genre conventions and audience expectations. The film pushes the genre borders forward by emphasizing the politics at work behind the romance. The shots of the magazine covers, which are the last images the audience is left with, may not underline Marisa and Christopher's different ethnic backgrounds explicitly, but they do focus on their 'unlikely' cross-class romance, reminding the audience of similar couplings in such screwball comedies as *It*

Happened One Night and *The Lady Eve*. However, in the case of *Maid in Manhattan*, the protagonists' ethnicities are also different and this alternative scenario complicates the class issue even further. First, it empowers the Latina heroine and proves that the 'other' can have the same opportunities in the modern world, by showing 'that the Cinderella template (and by extension the neo-feminist paradigm) can accommodate the variations in "race" and ethnicity that characterize a broad spectrum of the American population' (Radner, 2011, p. 83). Second, it presents, albeit quite superficially, that the ruling class holds its position through lineage, connections and wealth. Christopher is presented as a handsome womanizer with the proper upbringing, education and manners but with no real interest in or knowledge of the social issues he has to deal with and/or propose solutions to. His cinematic political dimension is limited to a couple of meetings with his advisors, who seem to know a lot more than he does, and his silent acceptance to be led by them. Christopher's only decisions are the ones that concern Marisa and even then, he asks his assistant to make the arrangements for her to meet him.

The hero is thus portrayed as a charming and polite individual, yet a shallow and socially ignorant white man. His masculinity is open to discussion insofar as he seems, at least professionally, to accept being guided, controlled and questioned by others. At the same time, his passivity regarding his work contrasted with his energy when it comes to matters of the heart connote the bored 'heir' of a political family, who grew up obeying the law of the father. Nevertheless, it is this precise construction of the male character as a blasé, wealthy 'brat' that serves as a comment and/or criticism of the neoliberal agenda which seeks to uphold the power of the economic elite (Harvey, 2007, p. 202). On the other hand, Christopher's 'weaknesses' are also used as a means to call attention not only to Marisa's ethnic background but also her interest in her work, however monotonous, and of lower status, her social concerns, her genuine efforts to be a good mother and her ambition. The casting of Jennifer Lopez as Marisa is crucial insofar as 'the fact of "race" becomes an important element in the narrative, with the "raced" subject being offered her own version of the fairy story' Radner (2011, p. 84).

The worldwide commercial success of *Maid in Manhattan*, which grossed almost $150 million, on a budget of $55 million, not only assisted Lopez's career in the 2000s but proved that a Latina actress can move away from stereotypical supporting roles and effectively become the centre of a romantic narrative. As Radner (2011, p. 85) points out, 'Lopez represented a new world order of femininity in which the ability to "look good" and work hard, and, thus, incarnate the ideals of the female "striver," became available to a broader demographic of women'.

The über-talented Mr Smith

Will Smith features nineth in the top ten 'Most Successful Actors at the Box Office' as his films have earned more than a staggering $5.7 billion worldwide.[2] Not only is Smith the second youngest actor in this small but coveted all-male group of actors – Orlando Bloom is nine years his junior but his placement in the list is mainly due to his role in the *Lord of the Rings* trilogy – but he is the only actor in the history of cinema to have had 'eight consecutive films gross over $100 million' in the North American domestic box office. Tina Gianoulis (2000, p. 1136) notes that 'Smith has become a crossover performer on many levels. Immensely popular with black audiences, Smith has been able to make elements of black identity and black popular culture not only accessible but comfortably appealing to white audiences'. Gianoulis (ibid.) adds that although Smith is African-American and expresses himself both in the vernacular and cultural genres of black culture, he has an everyman kind of humour that disarms white audiences. Similarly, Maggil (2009, p. 127) notes that the star 'presents a fantasy of black identity that ambivalently challenges the color line through a liberally racial vision of black masculinity that calms white cultural fears'. Indeed, most of Smith's roles are portrayals of heroic figures, whether fictional as Captain Steven Hiller, Agent J and military virologist Robert Neville who save the Earth from alien attacks in *Independence Day* (1996), *Men in Black* (1997), *Men in Black II* (2002)[3] and *I Am Legend* (2007) or real as in the biopic *Ali* (2001), where he portrayed the boxer Muhammad Ali, and *The Pursuit of Happyness* (2006), which presents the from-rags-to-riches story of American entrepreneur Chris Gardner.

With a career that counts nineteen films, seventeen of which were starring or co-starring roles, four highly successful solo music CDs and five music collaborations with DJ Jazzy Jeff, Will Smith is unquestionably one of the most recognizable and bankable African-American stars today because he enjoys 'crossover appeal, which attracts both black and white audiences […] in both film and music' (Geoff King in Philippa Gates, 2009, p. 223). Never-theless, despite 'Smith's good looks and playful, low-key style' (Gianoulis, 2000, p. 1136), the actor has only starred in a single romantic comedy, which is among the ten most commercially successful hits in the genre's history.

Hitch is the story of the 'date doctor' Alex Hitchens, aka Hitch (Will Smith), who makes his living by teaching timid and nervous men to approach and win over the girl of their dreams. In other words, Hitch is a modern-day matchmaker, in the cinematic tradition of Dolly (Barbra Streisand) in *Hello, Dolly!* (1969), Yente (Molly Picon) in *Fiddler on the Roof* (1971) and Emma (Gwyneth Paltrow) in *Emma* (1996). The differences between Hitch and the predominantly female matchmakers before him are not only his gender and race, but the fact he has actually turned what is usually conceived as a simple arrangement into a complex and quite lucrative profession. In other words, Hitch has brought matchmaking into the twenty-first century, abiding by all the rules of the neoliberal market. He transformed a practice that has been in existence for centuries into a highly exclusive 'concierge' job, targeting the men who can afford his services. Although no mention of his actual salary or that of his clients is even hinted at in the narrative, one can safely assume

Hitch's income is the least of his worries, based on his spacious and luxurious apartment filled with state-of-the-art appliances and his wardrobe. One of the first sequences of the film shows Hitch in action and validates his operation as a high-flyer who tapped into the insecurities of many modern men, who are concerned enough to seek his help regarding their love life. While it has been a canon in both literature and film for women to ask for or unknowingly be supported by a matchmaker's help, this gender subversion comments on the vulnerability, insecurity and fear masculinity may hide when the male does not conform to the media images of strong, virile and athletic stars he is constantly bombarded with. Thus, both Hitch and his clientele represent a softer side of masculinity, offering on the one hand additional insight in the 'permeation of a discourse of masculinity crisis during the 1990s and 2000s (Peberdy, 2011, p. 7) and on the other, supporting the performative aspect of male identities, especially through the behavioural patterns the clients are asked to follow in order to achieve their goal.

What is important, however, in the discussion of *Hitch*, is how Smith's racial identity is never 'seen', commented on or used by the narrative. The only time the issue of race and/or ethnicity is employed by the film is in the context of courtship. When Hitch meets Sara (Eva Mendes), a strong-minded, career-oriented journalist, he realizes that the conventional flirting rules would not help him achieve the desired result and he decides to surprise her. He organizes their first date on a Sunday morning and he takes her to Ellis Island, the first place millions of immigrants had to pass through to start a new life in the United States as early as the 1890s. Hitch has also planned to offer Sara a 'personalized' tour since he managed to retrieve one of her ancestor's signatures. Indeed, Sara is both impressed by this refreshing date idea and the museum; however, as she silently wanders in the halls and looks at the black-and-white photographs on the walls of suffering, tired, but also hopeful people from all around the world, her cheerful face takes a thoughtful impression. Although Sara's mood swing and her subsequent outburst when she sees her great-great grandfather's signature is used for comic relief as the next Manhattan scene reveals her ancestor was a serial killer and consequently the family's dark secret everybody has been trying to forget, the inclusion of Ellis Island in a romantic comedy cannot be dismissed as the mere preparation for a punch line.

The cultural and historical importance of this specific site directly connotes two things: first, the fact that the USA is an immigrant nation, in the sense it was built, inhabited and developed by people from different ethnicities and races that arrived in this 'new' part of the world, and second, it is an explicit reference to the cultural background of the heroine. However, since the heritage of the majority of white heroes and heroines of the romantic comedy universe is rarely mentioned, one wonders why *Hitch* stresses Sara's Cuban descent, constructing her as the 'other' and, in particular, a person whose country of origin has had a long, turbulent relationship with the USA. The answer lies in the race of the hero. Hitch/Smith is a cool, witty and successful protagonist but these are the characteristics of almost every hero in the romantic comedy genre. His African-American cultural capital is only implicitly managed through his co-star, the Cuban-American Eva Mendes. Not pairing Will Smith with a white actress validates Chito Childs's (2009, p. 12) thesis, which states 'often it is safer to pair a man of color with a Latina woman, who is almost, yet not quite, white'. Chito Childs (ibid.) adds that

> in *Hitch*, the problem of who to cast opposite Will Smith and the solution of pairing him opposite Eva Mendes shows what filmmakers think will alienate viewers and allows the familiar story to be told of a black man who is sexually savvy and slick teaching a white man how to get a girl without the threat of Will Smith wanting a white woman too (thereby also not posing a threat to the white man who he instead is helping.)

The reluctance to match up Smith with a white actress is indicative of the film industry's tendency to avoid interracial romances in mainstream narratives even after Obama became the Commander in Chief in 2008. In addition, Will Smith's star persona as well as his character in *Hitch* is stripped of the main characteristics associated with traditional black masculinity, such as bodily strength and virility, aggressiveness and power over women. On the other hand, it should be stressed that these characteristics are themselves constructions of 'slavery, colonization, racism, white supremacy, social class, and sexual orientation' which have formed, for their purposes of power maintenance, a single model of masculinity for 'men of African descent' (Orelus, 2010, p. 86). Just as a white male can perform a number of masculinities dependent on different communicational contexts, 'different forms of black masculinities can be performed ideologically, politically, and socially to reach certain goals' (ibid. p. 85). Similarly, Bryant Keith Alexander (2006, p. 74) adds that

> [t]he diversity that exists within the character of the Black man is not acknowledged, hence he is relegated to a stereotypically pathologized position, in which any variation might be constructed as inauthentic or not being real, passing for something that he is not.

It, therefore, seems that a theoretical impasse is created. If Will Smith in *Hitch* is considered as a representation of a black man stripped of his cultural heritage for the sake of the film's profits, then it becomes problematic as, on the one hand, it indicates that the African-American tradition still poses a threat to today's society, and, on the other, it superficially incorporates a 'raced' subject into the neoliberal cosmos, conforming to the promotion of colour blindness as the way to eliminate the issue of race. However, if Smith's portrayal of *Hitch* is viewed as the representation of a black man who is part of a significant portion of the US population, a number of questions arise as to the ways he expresses his masculinity, and the extent to which his gender performance follows his cultural heritage. Maggil (2009, p. 128) observes these contradictions in the image of Smith and concludes that his 'persona works to defuse the racial threat so as to claim a safer masculinity that still "keeps it real"'. In other words, Hitch is a black man who is helpful to his white clientele, and is in no way a sexually intimidating subject as his object of desire is of Cuban origin.

The discussion of the romantic comedies which feature Jennifer Lopez and Will Smith raises interesting questions regarding race and ethnicity. Although the focal films of this chapter are 'benign' narratives in that their objective is the quest for love, and not the eradication of racism, it is true that the USA is still troubled by these issues, which historically date back to the establishment of the nation. Even though the White House has been the home of the first African-American President for the last three years, a fact which has initially brought hopes for improvement in every facet of the social sphere, in terms of race, it also had the opposite result. For instance, Joe R. Feagin (2010, p. 266) underlines that 'especially after the 2008 election, [...] white-supremacists and other hate-based organizations, both in the United States and overseas, have grown significantly in number and impact'. Although the alarming rise in white-nationalism in both the USA and Europe is partly attributed to the global economic recession, as well as the power accumulated by a few 'other' individuals, this is only an obvious and easy concealment of an issue which has resulted in wars and genocide.

Although romantic comedies are not the film narratives where controversial issues, such as race, ethnicity, education and/or poverty, can or should be treated in depth, they do touch upon important subjects. One could even argue that the utopian rom com world is the ideal incarnation of a fantasy society where difference is celebrated rather than exorcised, and where every person can truly be equal to the next. On the other hand, the analysis that preceded shows that even these mainstream representations of different ethnicities are complex, even in a carefully constructed utopia. However, the fact remains that despite the worldwide box-office success of *Hitch*, *The Wedding Planner* and *Maid in Manhattan*, and the societal changes that were observed in the US population during the last decade, Hollywood still produces romantic comedies centred around a white, heterosexual couple, abiding to the neoliberal law of releasing products, even in the form of people/stars that could return the maximum profit. With the exception of independent rom coms that target niche audiences based on race and/or ethnicity, much more has to be done for the genre to embrace heroes and heroines from various cultural backgrounds and truly accept difference in whatever colour and shape they may come in.

Epilogue

The first decade of the new millennium has passed. Although one clearly needs a substantial historical distance to fully examine and comprehend the reasons, consequences and impact of the 9/11 attacks, the 2008 economic meltdown, the War on Terror, the immense popularity and power of the Internet through the social media, among many others significant events, it is still possible to draw some conclusions at the beginning of the 2010s. Popular culture, and more specifically Hollywood cinema, kept on releasing film texts in this specific sociopolitical context. In particular, its romantic comedies, the main subject of this study, were imbued with sometimes overt and sometimes more subtle comments on what the US nation faced during the first ten years of the twenty-first century.

What I tried to demonstrate in the ten chapters of this study was that the romantic comedy genre is not a naïve and/or light-hearted body of films, but rather a complicated series of narratives which, if examined closely, reveal the intricacies and/or complexities of issues, such as gender, post-9/11 angst, the political landscape and/or the economy. By this, I do not mean to say that all romantic comedies can serve as paradigms of cinematic excellence – there are indeed superficial films that simply repeat the well-known structural formula, but this is also the case of a number of dramas, melodramas, horror and/or even 'auteur' films. Nevertheless, I support that ideology, whether conservative or liberal, is always present in the millennial rom coms, if one is to look beyond their generic 'glossy' package, i.e. the beautiful apartments and/or houses, even those inhabited by protagonists whose job would not allow them to possess such places, the trendy and/or designer clothes and the mainly urban landscape which is shot with such filters and/or in beautiful, sunny days to enhance the romance that is about to bloom.

I have argued that contemporary romantic comedies should be treated as important ideological artefacts that negotiate significant societal issues and be finally acknowledged as academically salient as their precursors (mainly the screwball comedy of the 1930s and 1940s, the sex comedies of the late 1950s and 1960s and the nervous romances of the 1970s). The genre cycles and clusters discussed in the ten chapters of the book and the films that served as their paradigmatic 'representatives' have shown that the meaning of a given cinematic text is always influenced – whether implicitly or explicitly – by the surrounding societal circumstances. The neoliberal principles, the effects of 9/11 and of the 2008 financial meltdown could not help but infuse the romantic comedy genre between 2000 and 2010. Their impact on the Hollywood rom coms can lead to a few major conclusions regarding the relations between romantic love and neoliberalism, gender roles, and genre evolution, which will serve as the epilogue of this study and perhaps provide some thought for future examinations of these film texts.

First, consumerism and personal achievement in the workplace, basic notions of neoliberalism and their consequences instil the millennial romantic comedies in quite interesting ways. The films in the 'battle of the sexes' cycle and the 'new' career woman cycle directly relate the romantic relationships of the protagonist couples to their financial security and/or accumulated wealth. *Intolerable Cruelty* ends with the successful lawyer and the serial bride celebrating not only their romantic relationship but a newfound professional success as co-producers of a successful TV show that ensures a further increase in their bank accounts. Similarly, *The Proposal* unites the career-driven heroine with her male assistant, after having shown that he comes from one of Alaska's wealthiest families. These two rom coms, along with many others that belong in these cycles or others, such as *Sweet Home Alabama, Two Weeks Notice, View From the Top, The Wedding Planner, Someone Like You, 13 Going on 30, The Break-Up, The Holiday, Failure to Launch, 27 Dresses, Four Christmases, Leap Year* (2010), *Eat, Pray, Love*, and the two *Sex and the City* films, imply that the perfect heterosexual union is not simply based on love, respect, trust and support, but financial security – and even better financial affluence.

Whether it is the male hero (*Two Weeks Notice, Music and Lyrics*, 2007, *Made of Honor*), the female heroine (*Knocked Up, Baby Mama, The Back-Up Plan*) or both (*What Women Want, It's Complicated, Ghosts of Girlfriends Past*) that are financially independent, and/or wealthy, the narrative often promotes the comforts that wealth can bring to the couple; whether this takes the form of a helicopter that suddenly appears to take the heroine to the nearest bathroom (*Two Weeks Notice*) or a $100,000 check to be paid to a surrogate mother (*Baby Mama*), romantic comedies create a need for love to be accompanied by material goods as if possessions can assist the consolidation of a relationship. Thus, even though this 'insistence,' albeit rarely discussed explicitly in the narrative, on the 'prerequisite' of a handsome bank account and/or income before the couple's nuptials and/or the continuation of their married life, is indeed part of the rom com cosmos and a genre convention the audience is aware of, it can nevertheless create unnecessary and even impossible demands to the film viewer.

Taking the fact that the romantic comedy genre is not the cinematic place for a 'realistic' examination of the social status quo, it can be argued that in a post-9/11, post-2008 world, many mainstream romantic comedies serve as contemporary fairy tales which celebrate love in a world that does not resemble the reality faced by the audience. At the same time, however, these seemingly utopian narratives convey and spread several of the neo-conservative traits inherited by the Bush administration and the return to more traditional values after 9/11. The increase in the number of male-focused romantic comedies, the repeated representation of successful career women as insensitive, confused individuals in need of transformation, the almost complete absence of on-screen sex and the frequent insistence on the importance of marital vows between a white, heterosexual couple can be regarded as a neo-conservative effort to retreat to the past. On the other hand, the emergence of representations of female sexuality after the age of 50 and the depiction of several reverse May–December romances constitute simultaneously signs of genre evolution, social progression and acknowledgment of the purchasing power of female baby-boomers, and by extension the importance of the female film viewer to the Hollywood film industry.

Furthermore, the great range of romantic comedies and the subtle variations in the treatment of the same narrative structure make it clear that the strict binary opposition of masculinity versus femininity should be replaced by the broader concepts of masculinities and femininities. In other words, when *The Proposal*'s heroine becomes a softer version of herself in the arms of her male assistant at the end of the film, it could be argued that she decides to express her feminine qualities of sensitivity and acceptance, rather than claim she was 'transformed' by a male desire. Similarly, when the hero of *Made of Honor* chooses to win the heart of his best female friend and stop having insignificant short-lived affairs, the film viewer witnesses how different masculinities are communicated through the same individual according to context and personal choice.

The negotiation of gender roles, the genre's *raison d'être*, cannot lead to a single, general conclusion as each film of the different cycles can focus on a particular aspect of femininity and/or masculinity models. For instance, the 'baby-crazed' cycle examines the need for motherhood and comments on how professional women over 35 choose to embark on this journey alone, at the same time acknowledging, applauding and supporting women's ability to act as free, neoliberal agents in a consumer society that even treats life as a commodity. The heroes of this cycle are usually more sensitive men, who embrace their female partners' reproduction choice. However, it cannot be argued that this 'softer' man represents a generalized masculinity crisis, since the action romantic comedy of the same time period as the baby-focused rom coms insists on the representation of the 'macho' male, who saves the day and gets the girl in the end. One could maintain that these two masculinity models are contradictory. Nevertheless, I would propose to view these representations as complementary, because two or more gender identities can be expressed through the same individual (*Down with Love*, *The Break-Up*). It can, also, be concluded that the 'transformation' of either the male or the female protagonist at the end of a romantic comedy could be considered as the recognition of the individual's unconsciously hidden – or concealed for specific reasons – parts of themselves, which further underlines that the femininity/masculinity dichotomy is not a sufficient means of analyzing gender in the twenty-first century.

It becomes clear that the millennial romantic comedies are filled with contradictions in that there are texts which promote neo-conservative messages regarding marriage, sexual relationships and gender roles, and others, which opt for a more liberal consideration of the above. This richness in approach of the same main subject – the heterosexual romantic relationship – is the driving force behind the durability of one of the oldest genres in film history. The popularity of the romantic comedy genre is still evident in the beginning of the second decade of the new millennium. In 2011, the genre witnessed yet another successful year with the release of *Bad Teacher, Crazy, Stupid, Love, Friends with Benefits, Larry Crowne, Something Borrowed, Just Go with It, How Do You Know, New Year's Eve, I Don't Know How She Does It, No Strings Attached, What's Your Number?* and *Midnight in Paris,* twelve romantic comedies that returned more than a $1.2 billion in admissions worldwide. Although, most of these films belong to the cycles included in this book (*Crazy, Stupid, Love* examines the deterioration of a long-lasting marriage, *I Don't Know How She Does It* offers yet another perspective on the career woman rom com, *Midnight in Paris* revisits the neurotic hero, while *Larry Crowne* unites two 1990s genre icons, Julia Roberts and Tom Hanks, in a 'mature' comic love story), a new tendency emerged. *Friends with Benefits* and *No Strings Attached* opted for the re-introduction of sex scenes and were considered 'raunchy' by the majority of the press (see Erin Brown, 2011, Lorraine Zago Rosenthal, 2011). This emphasis on sexual interaction between the couples of these two films, their respective focus on female–male friendship and their wedding-free endings prove that the genre is still able not only to adapt to its sociopolitical environment but also invent and/or re-invent new ways to talk about the forms romantic relationships can take in the future.

Appendix

Top 50 most commercially successful romantic comedies (2000–2010)

Title	Domestic Gross (in $)	Worldwide Gross	Director(s)	Writer(s)
Mr. & Mrs. Smith	186,336,279	478,207,520	Liman, Doug	Kinberg, Simon
Sex and the City	152,647,258	415,252,786	King, Michael Patrick	King, Michael Patrick
What Women Want	182,811,707	374,111,707	Meyers, Nancy	Goldsmith, Josh and Cathy Yuspa
My Big Fat Greek Wedding	241,438,208	368,744,044	Zwick, Joel	Vardalos, Nia
Hitch	179,495,555	368,100,420	Tennant, Andy	Bisch, Kevin
Enchanted	127,807,262	340,487,652	Lima, Kevin	Kelly, Bill
The Proposal	163,958,031	317,375,031	Fletcher, Anne	Chiarelli, Pete
Runaway Bride	152,257,509	309,457,509	Marshall, Gary	McGibonn, Josann and Sara Parriott
Something's Gotta Give	124,728,738	266,728,738	Meyers, Nancy	Meyers, Nancy
Marley & Me	143,153,751	244,082,376	Frankel, David	Scott, Frank and Don Roos
Knight and Day	76,253,227	228,211,583	Mangold, James	O'Neill, Patrick
What Happens in Vegas	80,277,646	219,375,797	Vaughan, Tom	Fox, Dana
Knocked Up	148,768,917	219,076,518	Apatow, Judd	Apatow, Judd
It's Complicated	112,735,375	216,089,906	Meyers, Nancy	Nancy Meyers
Valentine's Day	110,485,654	213,009,598	Marshall, Garry	Fugate, Katherine
The Ugly Truth	88,915,214	205,298,907	Luketic, Robert	Eastman, Nicole and Karen McCullah Lutz
The Holiday	63,224,849	205,135,324	Meyers, Nancy	Meyers, Nancy

(continued)

Title	Domestic Gross (in $)	Worldwide Gross	Director(s)	Writer(s)
The Break-Up	118,703,275	204,999,686	Reed, Peyton	Garelick, Jeremy and Jay Lavender
Eat, Pray, Love	80,574,010	204,594,016	Murphy, Ryan	Murphy, Ryan
Two Weeks Notice	93,354,851	199,043,242	Lawrence, Marc	Lawrence, Marc
50 First Dates	120,908,074	196,482,882	Segal, Peter	Wing, George
I Now Pronounce You Chuck and Larry	120,059,556	186,072,214	Dugan, Dennis	Fanaro, Barry and Alexander Payne
Sweet Home Alabama	127,223,418	180,622,424	Tennant, Andy	Cox, C. Jay
He's Just Not That into You	93,953,653	178,846,899	Kwapis, Ken	Kohn Abby and Marc Silverstein
The 40 Year-Old Virgin	109,449,237	177,378,645	Apatow, Judd	Apatow, Judd and Steve Carell
How to Lose a Guy in 10 Days	105,813,373	177,371,441	Petrie, Donald	Buckley, Kristen, Brian Regan and Burr Stevens
Along Came Polly	88,097,164	171,963,386	Hamburg, John	Hamburg, John
Couples Retreat	109,204,945	171,844,840	Billingsley, Peter	Vaughn, Vince, Jon Favreau and Dana Fox
Mr. Deeds	126,293,452	171,269,535	Brill, Steven	Herlihy, Tim
Four Christmases	120,146,040	163,733,697	Gordon, Seth	Allen, Matt, Caleb Wilson, Jon Lucas and Scott Moore
27 Dresses	76,808,654	160,259,319	Fletcher, Anne	McKenna, Aline Brosh
Norbit	95,673,607	159,313,561	Robbins, Brian	Murphy, Eddie and Charles Q. Murphy
P.S., I Love You	53,695,808	156,835,339	LaGravenese, Richard	LaGravenese, Richard and Steven Rogers
Maid in Manhattan	94,011,225	154,906,693	Wang, Wayne	Wade, Kevin
Date Night	98,711,404	152,262,628	Levy, Shawn	Klausner, Josh
Me, Myself & Irene	90,570,999	149,270,999	Farrelly brothers	Farrelly brothers

Title	Domestic Gross *(in $)*	Worldwide Gross	Director(s)	Writer(s)
Music & Lyrics	41,252,000	145,896,422	Lawrence, Marc	Lawrence, Marc
Shallow Hal	70,839,203	141,069,860	Farrelly brothers	Moynihan, Sean and the Farrelly brothers
America's Sweethearts	93,607,673	138,191,428	Roth, Joe	Crystal, Billy and Peter Tolan
The Princes Diaries 2: Royal Engagement	95,170,481	134,734,481	Marshall, Garry	Rhimes, Shonda
The Bounty Hunter	65,958,846	134,451,846	Tennant, Andy	Thorp, Sarah
17 Again	64,154,187	134,417,568	Steers, Burr	Filardi, Jason
Bewitched	63,313,159	131,426,169	Ephron, Nora	Ephron, Nora and Delia Ephron
About a Boy	41,385,278	130,549,455	Weitz, Chris and Paul Weitz	Hedges, Peter, Paul and Chris Weitz, based on Nick Hornby's novel
Failure to Launch	88,715,192	128,406,887	Dey, Tom	Astle, Tom J., and Matt Ember
The Heartbreak Kid	36,787,257	127,766,650	Farrelly brothers	Armstrong, Scot, Dixon Lesie, the Farrelly brothers and Barnett Kevin
Intolerable Cruelty	35,327,628	120,217,409	Coen Joel and Ethan	Ramsey, Robert, Matthew Stone and the Coen brothers
Bride Wars	58,715,510	115,049,554	Winick, Gary	DePaul, Greg and Casey Wilson
Fool's Gold	70,231,041	111,231,041	Tennant, Andy	Claflin, John and Daniel Zelman
Sideways	71,503,593	109,706,931	Payne, Alexander	Payne, Alexander

(continued)

Title	Domestic Gross (in $)	Worldwide Gross	Director(s)	Writer(s)
Romantic comedies analyzed in the book				
(500) Days of Summer	32,391,374	58,706,943	Webb, Marc	Scott Neustadter and Michael H. Weber
The Back-up Plan	37,490,007	77,237,270	Poul, Alan	Angelo, Kate
The Wedding Planner	60,400,856	94,728,529	Shankman, Adam	Folk, Pamela and Michael Ellis
Ghost Town	13,367,624	27,044,665	Koepp, David	Koepp, David and John Kamps
New in Town	16,734,283	29,007,747	Elmer, Jonas	Ken Rance, C. Jay Cox
Sydney White	11,892,415	13,620,075	Nussbaum, Joe	Creasey, Chad Gomez
Chasing Liberty	12,195,626	12,313,323	Cadiff, Andy	Guiley, Derek and David Shneiderman
The Rebound	N/A	20,980,735	Freundlich, Bart	Freundlich, Bart
I Could Never Be Your Woman	N/A	N/A	Heckerling, Amy	Heckerling, Amy
Baby Mama	60,494,212	64,091,028	McCullers, Michael	McCullers, Michael
Whatever Works	5,306,706	35,097,815	Allen, Woody	Allen, Woody
Happy thankyoum oreplease	216,110	N/A	Radnor, Josh	Radnor, Josh
Made of Honor	46,012,734	105,962,760	Weiland, Paul	Sztykiel, Adam and Deborah Kaplan

Notes

1 Introduction

1   See the respective reviews of Ella Taylor (2008), A. O. Scott (2005), A. O. Scott (2010) and Stephen Holden (2010).
2   All the box-office data in the book are drawn from www.boxofficemojo.com unless otherwise noted.
3   The MPAA theatrical market statistics for 2010 can be found at: http://www. mpaa.org/Resources/93bbeb16–0e4d-4b7e-b085–3f41c459f9ac.pdf.
4   Frank Krutnik (2002, p. 130) argues that since the early 1980s, the Hollywood romantic comedy 'has been remodeled for (and reappropriated by) niche audiences defined by ethnicity, sexual orientation or age'. Therefore, several rom coms centered on African-American protagonists such as in *Boomerang* (1992) and *Brown Sugar* (2002), Hispanic couples as in *I Like It Like That* (1994) and *Tortilla Soup* (2001) and same-sex couples as in *Go Fish* (1994) and *I Think I Do* (1997).
5   The films were gathered in this ten-year period. The additional information regarding the cast, the characters, the filmmaking team and the production process is taken from www.imdb.com while box-office information throughout the book is taken from www.the-numbers.com and www.boxofficemojo.com, unless otherwise stated.

3 The 'new' career woman rom com

1   Rosin does not differentiate between single and married women but the statistics she refers to are most interesting as women have started 'to dominate middle management, and a surprising number of professional careers as well. According to the Bureau of Labor Statistics, women now hold 51.4 percent of managerial and professional jobs – up from 26.1 percent in 1980. They make up 54 percent of all accountants and hold about half of all banking and insurance jobs. About a third of America's physicians are now women, as are 45 percent of associates in law firms – and both those percentages are rising fast'. Rosin (2010) also adds that '[t]he working class […] is slowly turning into a matriarchy, with men increasingly absent from the home and women making all the decisions.'
2   Should the info regarding *New in Town*'s budget from www.listal.com prove accurate, it cannot be considered a failure, since for a film to 'break even', it needs to bring at least the money invested in the production by one and half times. Therefore, *New in Town* can be considered a success since it returned its initial budget by more than three times.
3   I should note that I do not consider the films Barker mentions as belonging to the new-millennium career women cycle, except *Sweet Home Alabama*, based on

Jakobson's theory of the 'dominant', outlined in the introduction. Setting aside the British productions, which are also excluded from this study, I argue that *How to Lose a Guy in 10 Days* belongs to the 'battle of the sexes' cycle while *13 Going on 30* is part of the 'fantasy' cycle.

5 The action rom com

1   However, it should be added that according to research, women also enjoy action films (see Barna William Donovan, 2010), whereas both male and female viewers have been discovered to experience similar physiological responses watching romance and action scenes (see Kayla Meagher, 2003).

6 The teen rom com

1   Between 1984 and 1987 Hughes directed and/or wrote six teen films, which treated teenagers with great sensitivity and emotional depth and contributed to a significant change in their depiction in the teen film genre in later films of the 1990s and 2000s (Timothy Shary, 2006, pp. 211–13).
2   It is important to note that the Riot Grrrl bands are not simply a part of music history. According to Kevin Dunn and May Summer Farnsworth (2012, p. 136), 'The Riot Grrrl punk bands were only one aspect of Riot Grrrl's overall purpose and goal'. Dunn and Farnsworth trace the birth of the movement and its important contribution to not just the music scene but its multifaceted efforts, through zines, DIY self-publishing, meetings and conventions to challenge the patriarchal status quo and empower girls and young women in their twenties.

7 The 'mature' rom com: heroines and heroes 'of a certain age'

1   See Jessica Wakeman 2010.
2   The categorization of the two *Sex and the City* films is quite problematic because even though Carrie Bradshaw (Sarah Jessica Parker) is considered the main heroine, the sub-plots her three friends construct around their lives examine different relationship issues and offer interesting perspectives. Thus, in the first film, Miranda (Cynthia Nixon) and Steve's (David Eigenberg) marriage has to overcome the latter's infidelity, and Samantha (Kim Cattrall) turns 50 and decides to break up with her long-time and much younger lover. In *Sex and the City 2*, Carrie is facing a kind of marital stagnation, while Charlotte (Kristin Davis) is overwhelmed with the upbringing of her two daughters and Samantha faces menopause.
3   Although *Something's Gotta Give* can also be part of the cougar cycle, I include it in the mature woman cycle, since its dominant feature is not Dianne Keaton's affair with the much-younger Keanu Reeves but her relationship with Jack Nicholson and the rediscovery of her sexuality.
4   *Just Married* (2003) is also a romantic comedy that explores the tensions that occur in a marriage but because the protagonist couple is in their twenties, it was excluded from this chapter, which focuses on mature male and female representations in a genre mostly known for its young and attractive stars.
5   See all the reviews for *Couples Retreat* at: http://www.metacritic.com/movie/couples-retreat.

9 The man-com cluster

1   The book was written and edited before the November 2012 presidential election.
2   As a final point, it should be noted that leaving aside the link between masculinity and US politics which leads to a great variety of on-screen masculine representations,

the confusion male identities have been facing for several decades can be, in part, corroborated through science. According to Oxford University professor of genetics, Bryan Sykes, the species of men itself is on the road to virtual extinction since '[t]he Y chromosome is deteriorating and will [...] disappear' because it 'can't repair itself'. Sykes contends that '[m]en are genetically modified women' since 'the human template is a female: the Y chromosome kicks in a few weeks after conception and makes a boy'(Watt, 2008). Syke's conclusions may represent a sci-fi scenario but since the eventual disappearance of the Y chromosome is not to take place in the next 125,000 years, men will have plenty of time to restore their masculine side (Watt, 2008). Although I do not wish to resort to biological determinism in order to explain and/or verify the cinematic representations discussed throughout the book, I believe that this scientific evidence can offer an additional perspective on gender issues. Interestingly enough, while this chapter was being written, an entire episode of the eighth season of the popular medical drama *House M.D.* centred on the biological side of masculinity. In episode 13, entitled 'Man of the House', the central patient is a male marriage counsellor who collapses while he advises men to get in touch with their feminine side in order to save their relationships. After numerous medical exams, it is concluded that the patient's feminine traits are directly linked with his low testosterone levels, which resulted from being violently hit in his genitalia a few years ago. Although this explanation is absolute and erroneous in its generalized insistence that the sexes and therefore gender behaviours are biologically pre-determined and cannot be altered, it is interesting to observe how science enters popular representations of gender performances.

3   It should be noted that the film is dedicated to Sidney Pollack's memory.
4   According to Allen, '[H]e could no longer afford to shoot in New York, even though European shoots require him to adjust his stories to fit the location' (Steve Pond, 2010).

11 Romantic comedy and the 'other': Race, ethnicity and the transcendental star

1   This chapter will use the terms Latina/o and Hispanic as interchangeable terms to 'to reflect the new terminology in the standards issued by the Office of Management and Budget in 1997 that are to be implemented by January 1, 2003' (Roberto R. Ramirez and G. Patricia de la Cruz, 2003). For a more detailed discussion on the debate that still exists regarding the two terms, their similarities, discrepancies and the theoretical and/or social context in which the terms have been used and continue to be used see Linda Martin Alcoff (2000), Ofelia Schutte (2000), Jorge J. E. Gracia (2000), Arlene Davilia (2001), and Claudio Iván Remeseira (2010).
2   Available at: <http://www.toptenz.net/top-10-most-successful-actors-at-the-box-office.php>.
3   At the time of the writing, *Men in Black III* was scheduled for a May 2012 release.

Bibliography

*Annology bc editor (not authors)
+ place*

Abbott, S. and D. Jermyn, eds., 2009. *Falling in Love Again: Romantic Comedy in Contemporary Cinema.* London: I. B. Tauris.

Alcoff, L. M., 2000. Latino Identity, Ethnicity and Race: Is Latina/o Identity a Racial Identity? In: J. E. Gracia and P. Greiff, eds. *Hispanics/Latinos in the United States: Ethnicity, Race and Rights.* New York: Routledge, pp. 25–36.

Alexander, B. K., 2006. *Black Masculinity: Race, Culture and Queer Identity.* Lanham, Md.: AltaMira Press. *(monograph bc place of publication)*

Allen, W. R., ed., 2006. *The Coen Brothers: Interviews.* Jackson: University Press of Mississippi.

Altman, R., 2006. *Film/Genre.* London: BFI.

Anderson, J., 2011. Rev. of *Happythankyoumoreplease. Variety,* [online] 23 January. Available at: <http://www.variety.com/review/VE1117941948/> [Accessed 12 December 2011].

Anon., 2001. Alcohol Sentence for Bush Daughter. *BBC News,* [online] 8 June. Available at: <http://news.bbc.co.uk/2/hi/americas/1379000.stm> [Accessed 10 November 2012].

——, 2008. Surrogacy a Booming Business in India. *Igovernment,* [online] 26 August. Available at: <http://www.igovernment.in/site/surrogacy-a-booming-business-in-india> [Accessed 22 September 2012].

——, 2009. CBS Poll: Americans Optimistic About Obama. *cbsnews.com,* [online] 11 February. Available at: <http://www.cbsnews.com/stories/2009/01/17/opinion/polls/main4729887.shtml> [Accessed 12 December 2011].

——, 2011. 2010 News Release. Demand for Plastic Surgery Rebounds by Almost 9%. *cosmeticplasticsurgerystatistics.com,* [online] 4 June. Available at: <www.cosmetic-plasticsurgerystatistics.com/statistics.html#2010-NEWS> [Accessed 13 February 2012].

Aristotle, 2008. *Poitiki.* Translated from ancient Greek by D. Lypourlis. Athens: Zitros.

Arroyo, J., 2000. *Action/Spectacle Cinema: A Sight and Sound Reader.* London: BFI.

Babington, B. and Evans, P. W., 1989. *Affairs to Remember: The Hollywood Comedy of the Sexes.* Manchester: Manchester University Press.

Balio, T., 1998. A Major Presence in All of the World's Important Markets: The Globalization of Hollywood in the 1990s. In S. Neale and M. Smith, eds. *Contemporary Hollywood Cinema.* London: Routledge, pp. 58–73.

Barker, D., 2008. The Southern-Fried Chick Flick: Postfeminism Goes to the Movies. In S. Ferriss and M. Young, eds. *Chick Flicks: Contemporary Women At the Movies.* New York: Routledge, pp. 92–118.

Basinger, J., 1993. *A Woman's View: How Hollywood Spoke to Women, 1930–1960.* London: Wesleyan University Press.

Beach, C., 2002. *Class, Language and American Film Comedy.* Cambridge: Cambridge University Press.

Bellin, J. D., 2005. *Framing Monsters: Fantasy Film and Social Alienation.* Carbondale: Southern Illinois University Press.

Beltrán, M. C., 2009. *Latina/o Stars in U.S. Eyes: The Making and Meanings of Film and TV Stardom.* Urbana: University of Illinois Press.

——, 2004. Más Macha: The New Latina Action Hero. In Y. Tasker, ed. *Action and Adventure Cinema.* London: Routledge, pp. 186–200.

Berra, J., 2010. *Directory of World Cinema: American Independent.* Bristol: Intellect Books.

Blyth, M., 2008. One Ring to Bind Them All: American Power and Neoliberal Capitalism. In J. Kopstein and S. Steinmo, eds. *Growing Apart?America and Europe in the Twenty-First Century.* Cambridge: Cambridge University Press, pp. 109–35.

Bouchez, C., 2007. *Dating Older Women: Does Age Matter?* [pdf]. Available at: <http://www.womenspeak.com/pdf/datingolder.pdf> [Accessed 10 November 2009].

Brode, D., 2005. *Multiculturalism and the Mouse: Race and Sex in Disney Entertainment.* Austin: University of Texas Press.

Brodesser-Akner, C. and Stembergh, A., 2010. The Star Market: The Definitive Vulture Analysis of Divisive Rom-Com Queen Katherine Heigl. *New York Magazine,* [online] 4 June. Available at: <http://nymag.com/daily/entertainment/2010/06/katherine_heigl_career.html> [Accessed 20 December 2011].

Brook, H., 2007. *Conjugal Rites: Marriage and Marriage-like Relationships Before the Law.* New York: Palgrave MacMillan.

Brown, E., 2011. Hollywood's Current 'Romantic Comedies' Heavy on Hook Ups, Light on Romance. *Culture and Media Institute,* [online] 30 March. Available at: <http://www.mrc.org/articles/hollywoods-current-romantic-comedies-heavy-hook-ups-light-romance> [Accessed 21 April 2012].

Brunovska Karnick, K., 1995. Commitment and Reaffirmation in Hollywood Romantic Comedy. In K. Brunovska Karnick and H. Jenkins, eds. *Classical Hollywood Comedy.* New York: Routledge, pp. 123–46.

Burns, D., 2011. Baby Boomers are STILL the Largest Consumer Group in America Even in a Recession. *BabyBoomer-Magazine.com,* [online] 3 October. Available at: <www.babyboomer-magazine.com/news/165/ARTICLE/1217/2011-10-03.html.> [Accessed 13 February 2012].

Bushby, H., 2002. Older Actresses Hit Back at Hollywood. *The BBC News,* [online] 17 May. Available at: <http://www.globalaging.org/elderrights/us/olderactors.htm> [Accessed 17 October 2011].

Campbell, N. and Kean A., 2000. *American Cultural Studies: An Introduction to American Culture.* New York: Routledge.

Cavell, S., 1981. *Pursuits of Happiness.* Cambridge: Harvard University Press.

Cele/bitchy, 2010. Gwyneth Paltrow Sanctimoniously Goops About Motherhood. *celebitchy.com,* [blog] 22 December. Available at: <http://www.celebitchy.com/132198/gwyneth_paltrow_sanctimoniously_goops_about_motherhood/> [Accessed 22 December 2011].

Chito Childs, E., 2009. *Fade to Black and White: Interracial Images in Popular Culture.* Lanham, Md.: Rowman & Littlefield Publishers.

Cohen-Tanugi, L., 2008. The Atlantic Divide in Historical Perspective: A View from Europe. In S. Steinmo and J. Kopstein, eds. *Growing Apart? America and Europe in the Twenty-First Century*. Cambridge: Cambridge University Press, pp. 211–24.

Cohn, D'V. Fry R., 2010. Women, Men and the New Economics of Marriage. www.pewsocialtrends.org, [online] 19 January. Available at: <http://www.pewsocial trends.org/2010/01/19/women-men-and-the-new-economics-of-marriage/> [Accessed 20 December 2011].

Connell, R. W., 2005. *Masculinities*. Berkeley: University of California Press.

Cook, P. and Bernink, M., 1999. *The Cinema Book*. 2nd ed. London: BFI.

Coontz, S., 2005. *Marriage, a History: How Love Conquered Marriage*. New York: Penguin.

Corliss, R., 2009. Woody Allen's Latest: *Works* Like a Charm. *Time*, [online] 29 June. Available at: <http://www.time.com/time/magazine/article/0,9171,1905522,00.html> [Accessed 23 October 2011].

Currie, D., Kelly, D. M. and Pomerantz, S., 2009. *'Girl Power': Girls Reinventing Girlhood*. New York: Peter Lang Publishing.

Dargis, M., 2007. Someday My Prince Will […] Uh, Make That a Manhattan Lawyer. *The New York Times*, [online] 21 November. Available at: <http://movies. nytimes.com/2007/11/21/movies/21ench.html> [Accessed 27 December 2011].

——, 2009. A September-September Romance. *The New York Times*, [online] 24 December. Available at: <http://movies.nytimes.com/2009/12/25/movies/25compli-cated.html?ref=movies> [Accessed 20 December 2011].

——, 2009. From the Corporate Jungle to Wild Alaska: Taming the Savage Boss. *The New York Times*, [online] 18 June. Available from: <http://movies.nytimes.com/2009/ 06/19/movies/19proposal.html> [Accessed 20 January 2012].

——, 2009. Girl Meets Ape, and Complications Ensue. *The New York Times*, [online] 23 July. Available at: <http://movies.nytimes.com/2009/07/24/movies/24ugly.html> [Accessed 19 December 2011].

Davilia, A., 2001. *Latinos Inc.: The Marketing and Making of a People*. Berkeley: University of California Press.

Davis, A., 2008. Locked Up: Racism in the Era of Neoliberalism. *The Drum*, [online] 19 March. Available at: <http://www.abc.net.au/news/2008-03-19/locked-up-racism-in-the-era-of-neoliberalism/1077518> [Accessed 7 February 2012].

DeAngelis, M., 2010. Tom Cruise, the 'Couch Incident' and the Limits of Public Elation. *The Velvet Light Trap*, 65: 42–3.

Deleyto, C., 2003. Between Friends: Love and Friendship in Contemporary Romantic Comedy. <u>*Screen*, 44 (2): 167–82.</u>

——, 2009. *The Secret Life of Romantic Comedy*. Manchester: Manchester University Press.

DeMartino, G., 2000. *Global Economy, Global Justice. Theoretical Objections and Policy Alternatives to Neoliberalism*. London: Routledge.

Denby, D., 2007. A Fine Romance: The New Comedy of the Sexes. *The New Yorker*, [online] 23 July. Available at: <http://www.udel.edu/anthro/ackerman/A%20Fine% 20Romance.pdf> [Accessed 24 October 2011].

Department of Professional Employees Fact Sheet, 2010. [pdf]. Available at: <http:// www.pay-equity.org/PDFs/ProfWomen.pdf> [Accessed 12 December 2011].

Doll, J., 2011. New Yorkers Are Migrating Away from New York. *The Village Voice*, [online] 2 August. Available at: <http://blogs.villagevoice.com/runninscared/2011/08/ new_yorkers_are_leaving.php> [Accessed 15 November 2011].

(handwritten margin note:) journal name → no place of publication / weird #s

Dominus, S., 2011. If Cinderella Had a BlackBerry ... *The New York Times*, [online] 25 August. Available at: <http://www.nytimes.com/2011/08/28/magazine/if-cinderella-had-a-blackberry.html?_r=1&pagewanted=all> [Accessed 15 September 2011].

Donovan, B. W., 2010. *Blood, Guns, and Testosterone: Action Films, Audiences, and a Thirst for Violence.* Lanham, Md.: Scarecrow Press.

Doom, R. P., 2009. *The Brothers Coen: Unique Characters of Violence.* Santa Barbara: Praeger.

Dougherty, E., 2011. Amanda in Wonderland. *Elle*, [online] 7 March. Available at: <http://www.elle.com/Pop-Culture/Cover-Shoots/Amanda-In-Wonderland#mode=base;slide=0;> [Accessed 21 October 21].

Douglas, S. J. and Michaels, M. W., 2004. *The Mommy Myth: The Idealization of Motherhood and How It Has Undermined All Women.* New York: Free Press.

Driscoll, C., 2011. *Teen Film: A Critical Introduction.* Oxford: Berg Publishers.

Dunn, K. and Farnsworth, M. S., 2012. We ARE the Revolution: Riot Grrrl Press, Girl Empowerment, and DIY Self-Publishing. *Women's Studies*, 41 (2): 136-57.

Ebert, R., 1987. Rev. of *Wall Street*. *Chicago Sun Times*, [online] 11 December. Available at: <http://rogerebert.suntimes.com/apps/pbcs.dll/article?AID=/19871211/REVIEWS/712110302/1023> [Accessed 28 December 2011].

——, 2007. Rev. of *Enchanted*. *Chicago Sun Times*, [online] 21 November. Available at: <http://rogerebert.suntimes.com/apps/pbcs.dll/article?AID=/20071120/REVIEWS/711200302> [Accessed 28 December 2011].

Elisberg, R. J., 2011. Audiences Won't Go to See an Action Movie That Stars Women. *The Huffington Post*, [online] 10 May. Available at: <http://www.huffingtonpost.com/robert-j-elisberg/audiences-wont-go-to-see_b_859971.html> [Accessed 12 February 2012].

Erickson, T. M., 2010. *Surrogacy and Embryo, Sperm, and Egg Donation: What Were You Thinking?* Bloomington, Ind.: iUniverse.

Evans, P. W. Deleyto, C., eds. 1998. *Terms of Endearment: Hollywood Romantic Comedy of the 1980s and 1990s.* Edinburgh: Edinburgh University Press.

Fanning, E., 2008. All Heigl the New Queen of Rom Com. *The Independent*, [online] 16 March. Available at: <http://www.independent.ie/entertainment/film-cinema/all-heigl-the-new-queen-of-rom-com-1318849.html> [Accessed 20 December 2011].

Feagin, J. R., 2010. *Racist America: Roots, Current Realities, and Future Reparations.* 2nd ed. New York: Routledge.

Fielding, M. and Moss, P., 2011. *Radical Education and the Common School: A Democratic Alternative.* Oxon: Routledge.

Fisher, L., 2009. Black Babies: Hollywood's Hottest Accessory? *ABC News*, [online] 31 March. Available at: <http://abcnews.go.com/Entertainment/story?id=7218470&page=1> [Accessed 12 February 2012].

Ford, R., 2012. Fewer Female Directors Worked on Top Films in 2011. *The Hollywood Reporter*, [online] 24 January. Available at: <http://www.hollywoodreporter.com/news/women-directors-film-study-284321> [Accessed 27 January 2012].

Fowkes, K. A., 1998. *Giving Up the Ghost: Spirits, Ghosts, and Angels in Mainstream Comedy Films.* Detroit: Wayne State University.

——, 2010. *The Fantasy Film.* Malden: Wiley-Blackwell.

Franklin, D. P., 2006. *Politics and Film.* Lanham, Md.: Rowman & Littlefield Publishers.

Garrett, R., 2007. *Postmodern Chick Flicks: The Return of the Woman's Film.* New York: Palgrave MacMillan.

Gates, P., 2009. *Detecting Men: Masculinity and the Hollywood Detective Film.* Albany: State University of New York Press.

Geertsma, A., 2011. Redefining Trauma Post 9/11: Freud's Talking Cure and Foer's Extremely Loud and Incredibly Close. *As/peers*, 4: 91–108.

Gehring, W. D., 2002. *Romantic vs. Screwball Comedy: Charting the Difference.* Lanham, Md.: Scarecrow Press, Inc.

Genette, G., 1982. *Palimsestes: La littérature au second degré.* Paris: Seuil.

Gentleman, A., 2008. India Nurtures Business of Surrogate Motherhood. *The New York Times*, [online] 10 March. Available at: <http://www.nytimes.com/2008/03/10/world/asia/10surrogate.html?pagewanted=all> [Accessed 12 November 2011].

Geraghty, L. Hollywood: A history? Extract from *Directory of World Cinema: American Hollywood.* Bristol: Intellect, pp. 8–9. In *Film Comment*, May/June 2011.

Germain, D., 2009. Hollywood Counters Reality with Decade of Escapism. *Boston.com*, [online] 8 December. Available at: <http://www.boston.com/ae/movies/articles/2009/12/08/hollywood_counters_reality_with_decade_of_escapism/> [Accessed 9 December 2011].

Giannetti, L. and Eyman, S., 2001. *Flash-Back: A Brief History of Film.* 4th ed. Upper Saddle River, N.J.: Prentice Hall.

Gianoulis, T., 2000. Will Smith. In T. Pendergast and S. Pendergast, eds. *Filmmakers 3, Actors and Actresses.* 4th ed. Farmington Hills, Mich.: St. James Press, pp. 1135–6.

Gibson, V., 2001. *Cougar: A Guide for Older Women Dating Younger Men.* Toronto: Key Porter Books.

Gill, R. and Scharff, C., 2011. Introduction. In R. Gill and C. Scharff, eds. *New Femininities: Postfeminism, Neoliberalism and Subjectivity.* Houndmills: Palgrave-MacMillan, pp. 1–17.

Girgus, S. B., 2002. *The Films of Woody Allen.* 2nd ed. Cambridge: Cambridge University Press.

Gleiberman, O., 2009. Rev. of *Couples Retreat. EW*, [online] 9 October. Available at: <http://www.ew.com/ew/article/0,20310596,00.html> [Accessed 10 November 2011].

Glitre, K., 2006. *Hollywood Romantic Comedy.* Manchester: Manchester University Press.

Goren, L. and Vaugh, J., 2010. Profits and Protest: The Cultural Commodification of the Presidential Image. In L. A. Murray, ed. *Politics and Popular Culture.* Newcastle upon Tyne: Cambridge Scholars Publishing, pp. 85–99.

Gracia, J. E., 2000. *Hispanic/Latino Identity: A Philosophical Perspective.* Malden: Blackwell.

Grant, B. K., 2007. *Film Genre: From Iconography to Ideology.* London: Wallflower.

Gray, B., 2009. Weekend Report: 'Couples Retreat' Advances, 'Paranormal Activity' Spikes. *boxofficemojo.com*, [online] 12 October. Available at: <http://boxofficemojo.com/news/?id=2619&p=.htm> [Accessed 14 January 2012].

——, 2010. Weekend Report: 'Toy Story 3' Charms Again, Sandler Doesn't Grow, Cruise Capsizes. *boxofficemojo.com*, [online] 28 June. Available at: http://box-officemojo.com/news/?id=2838&p=.htm [Accessed 21 February 2012].

Greven, D., 2009. *Manhood in Hollywood from Bush to Bush.* Austin: University of Texas Press.

Grindon, L., 2011. *The Hollywood Romantic Comedy.* Malden: Wiley-Blackwell.

Hamilton, B. E., Martin, J. A. and Ventura, S. J., 2010. *Births: Preliminary Data for 2009.* [pdf]. Available at: <http://www.cdc.gov/nchs/data/nvsr/nvsr59/nvsr59_03.pdf> [Accessed 18 September 2011].

Harvey, D., 2007. *A Brief History of Neoliberalism*. Oxford: Oxford University Press.

Harvey, J., 1998. *Romantic Comedy in Hollywood: From Lubitsch to Sturges*. New York: Da Capo Press.

Hawkins, H., 1990. *Classics and Trash*. Toronto: University of Toronto Press.

Haywood, C. and an Ghaill, M. M., 2003. *Men and Masculinities: Theory, Research, and Social Practice*. Buckingham: Open University Press.

Heckerling, A., 2008. Interview on *AV Club*. Interviewed by Noel Murray, [online] 20 March. Available at: <http://www.avclub.com/articles/amy-heckerling,14217/> [Accessed 15 January 2012].

Henry, A., 2004. *Not My Mother's Sister: Generational Conflict and Third-Wave Feminism*. Bloomington: Indiana University Press.

Highmore, B. 2002. *Everyday Life and Cultural Theory. An Introduction*. London: Routledge.

Hoerl, K. and Kelly, C. R., 2010. The Post-Nuclear Family and the Depoliticization of Unplanned Pregnancy in *Juno, Knocked Up*, and *Waitress. Communication and Critical/Cultural Studies*, 7(4): 360–80.

Holden, S., 2009. Tales of a Spike-Heeled Dialoguer in a Land of Okey-Dokeys. *The New York Times*, [online] 30 January. Available at: <http://movies.nytimes.com/2009/01/30/movies/30town.html> [Accessed 22 October 2011].

——, 2010. In a Baste and Switch, a New Father Is Born. *The New York Times*, [online] 18 August. Available at: <http://movies.nytimes.com/2010/08/20/movies/20switch.html> [Accessed 14 November 2011].

——, 2011. Singles, City and Child. *The New York Times*, [online] 3 March. Available at: <http://movies.nytimes.com/2011/03/04/movies/04happy.html> [Accessed 12 December 2011].

Hollinger, K., 1998. *In the Company of Women: Contemporary Female Friendship Films*. Minneapolis: University of Minnesota Press.

Holmlund, C. and Wyatt, J. eds., 2005, *Contemporary American Independent Film: From the Margins to the Mainstream*. London: Routledge.

Jakobson, R., 1981. *Selected Writings III: Poetry of Grammar and Grammar of Poetry*. The Hague: Mouton.

Jeffers McDonald, T., 2007. *Romantic Comedy: Boy Meets Girl Meets Genre*. London: Wallflower.

——, 2009. Homme-com: Engendering Change in Contemporary Romantic Comedy. In S. Abbott and D. Jermyn, eds. *Falling in Love Again: Romantic Comedy in Contemporary Cinema*. London: I. B. Tauris, pp. 146–59.

Jeffords, S., 1993. *Hard Bodies: Hollywood Masculinity in the Reagan Era*. Piscataway, NJ: Rutgers University Press.

Jenson, J. and de Castell, S., 2008. Theorizing Gender and Digital Gameplay: Oversights, Accidents and Surprises. *Eludamos. Journal for Computer Game Culture*, 2 (1): 15–25.

Jermyn, D., 2009. I ♥ NY: The Rom-Com's Love Affair with New York City. In S. Abbott and D. Jermyn, eds. *Falling in Love Again: Romantic Comedy in Contemporary Cinema*. London: I. B. Tauris, pp. 9–24.

——, 2011. Unlikely Heroines? Women of a Certain Age and Romantic Comedy, *CineAction*, 85: 26–33.

Johnson, B., 2009. Top 10 Most Successful Actors at the Box Office. [online]. 15 July: Available at: <http://www.toptenz.net/top-10-most-successful-actors-at-the-box-office.php> [Accessed 23 January 2012].

Kaklamanidou, B., 2010. The Mythos of Patriarchy in the X-Men Films. In R. J. Gray II and B. Kaklamanidou. *The 21st Century Superhero: Essays on Gender, Genre and Globalization*. Jefferson, NC: McFarland, pp. 61–74.

——, 2012. Pride and Prejudice: Celebrity Versus Fictional Cougars. *Celebrity Studies*, 3 (1): 78–89.

Kaling, M., 2011. Flick Chicks: A Guide to Women in the Movies. *The New Yorker*, [online] 3 October. Available at: <http://www.newyorker.com/humor/2011/10/03/111003sh_shouts_kaling?currentPage=all> [Accessed 15 October 2011].

Kaplan, E. A., 2000. The Case of the Missing Mother: Maternal Issues in Vidor's *Stella Dallas*. In E. A. Kaplan, ed. *Feminism and Film*. Oxford: Oxford University Press, pp. 466–78.

Karlyn, K. R., 2006. Feminism in the Classroom: Teaching Towards the Third Wave. In J. Hollows and R. Moseley, eds. *Feminism in Popular Culture*. Oxford: Berg Publishers, pp. 57–78.

——, 2011. *Unruly Girls, Unrepentant Mothers: Redefining Feminism on Screen*. Austin: Texas University Press.

Kaveney, R., 2006. *Teen Dreams: Reading Teen Film from* Heathers *to* Veronica Mars. London: I. B. Tauris.

Keegan, R., 2010. Older Actresses Back in the Hollywood Spotlight. *Los Angeles Times*, [online] 12 December. Available at: <http://articles.latimes.com/2010/dec/12/entertainment/la-et-older-actresses-20101212> [Accessed 16 October 2011].

Kellner, D., 2010. *Cinema Wars, Hollywood Film and Politics in the Bush–Cheney Era*. Malden: Blackwell.

Kimmell, M., 2010. *Misframing Men: The Politics of Contemporary Masculinities*. Piscataway, NJ: Rutgers University Press.

King, M., 2011. Stay-at-home Dads on the Up: One in Seven Fathers are Main Childcarers. *The Guardian*, [online] 25 October. Available at: <http://www.guardian.co.uk/money/2011/oct/25/stay-at-home-dads-fathers-childcarers> [Accessed 15 February 2012].

King, G., 2000. *Spectacular Narratives: Hollywood in the Age of the Blockbuster*. London: I. B. Tauris.

——, 2002. *Film Comedy*. London: Wallflower.

——, 2005. *American Independent Cinema*. London: I. B. Tauris.

Knadler, S., 2005. Blanca from the Block: Whiteness and the Transnational Latina Body. *Genders Online Journal*, 41. Available at: <http://www.genders.org/g41/g41_knadler.html> [Accessed 2 January 2012].

Kord, S. and Krimmer, E., 2005. *Hollywood Divas, Indie Queens, and TV Heroines: Contemporary Screen Images of Women*. Lanham, Md.: Rowman & Littlefield Publishers.

Kotsopoulos, A., 2010. Gendering Expectations: Genre and Allegory in Readings of *Thelma and Louise*. In S. Mintz and R. Roberts, eds. *Hollywood's America: Twentieth-Century America Through Film*, 4th ed. Malden: Blackwell, pp. 309–28.

Kovacs, L., 2006. *The Haunted Screen: Ghosts in Literature and Film*. Jefferson, NC: McFarland.

Kozloff, S., 2000. *Overhearing Film Dialogue*. Berkeley: University of California Press.

Krutnik, F., 1998. Love Lies. In P. Williams Evans and C. Deleyto, eds. *Terms of Endearment. Hollywood Romantic Comedy of the 1980s and 1990s*. Edinburgh: Edinburgh University Press, pp. 15–36.

——, 2002. Conforming Passions? Contemporary Hollywood Comedy. In S. Neale, ed. *Genre and Contemporary Hollywood*. London: BFI, pp. 130–47.

Landay, L., 2002. The Flapper Film: Comedy, Dance, and Jazz Age Kinaesthetics. In J. M. Bean and D. Negra, eds. *A Feminist Reader of Early Cinema*. Durham, NC: Duke University Press, pp. 221–50.

Lawton, Z. and Callister, P., 2010. *Older Women–Younger Men Relationships: The Social Phenomenon of 'Cougars': A Research Note*. [pdf]. Available at: <http://ips.ac.nz/publications/files/be0acfcb7d0.pdf> [Accessed 20 February 2011].

Leitch, T., 1992. The World According to Teenpix. *Literature Film Quarterly*, 20: 43–7.

Leonard, S., 2009. *Fatal Attraction*. Malden: Blackwell.

Lévi-Strauss, C., 1963. *Structural Anthropology*. New York: Basic Books.

Lewis, J. 2002. The Coen Brothers. In Y. Tasker, ed. *Fifty Contemporary Filmmakers*. London: Routledge.

——, 1992. *The Road to Romance and Ruin: Teen Films and Youth Culture*. New York: Routledge.

Lichtenfel, E., 2007. *Action Speaks Louder: Violence, Spectacle, and the American Action Movie*. Middletown, Conn.: Wesleyan University Press.

Livingston, G. and Cohn D'V., 2010. The New Demography of American Motherhood. *Pew Research Center*, 6 May. Available at: <http://pewresearch.org/pubs/1586/changing-demographic-characteristics-american-mothers> [Accessed 15 February 2012].

Lumenick, L., 2009. Bittersweet Symphony. *The New York Post*, [online] 17 July. Available at: <http://www.nypost.com/p/entertainment/movies/item_dHYmAYL3jBkPmlug2EqmIP;jsessionid=B38D361CE2DD3061537DC61220F34199> [Accessed 6 December 2011].

——, 2009. Status Update: It's Cheesy. *The New York Post*, [online] 24 December. Available at: <http://www.nypost.com/p/entertainment/movies/status_update_it_chesy_u41a3VXCXmU0crHG34IO7L > [Accessed 16 January 2012].

Maggil, D., 2009. Celebrity Culture and Racial Masculinities: The Case of Will Smith. In E. Watson, ed. *Pimps, Wimps, Studs, Thugs and Gentlemen: Essays on Media Images of Masculinity*. Jefferson, NC: McFarland, pp. 126–41.

Malin, B. J., 2005. *American Masculinity Under Clinton: Popular Media and the Nineties*. New York: Peter Lang Publishing.

Mallory, J. D., 1996. *Battle of the Sexes: How Both Sides Can Win with Honor*. Wheaton, Ill.: Crossway Books.

Massey, D. and Kreinin Souccar, M., 2009. Stress and the City. *Crainsnewyork*, [online] 4 January. Available at: <http://www.crainsnewyork.com/article/20090104/FREE/901039995> [Accessed 15 November 2011].

McCabe, J., 2009. Lost in Translation. In S. Abbott and D. Jermyn, eds. *Falling in Love Again: Romantic Comedy in Contemporary Cinema*. London: I. B. Tauris, pp. 160–75.

McCarthy, T., 2007. Rev. of *Enchanted. Variety*, [online] 18 November. <http://www.variety.com/review/VE1117935452?refcatid=31> [Accessed 27 December 2011].

McDonald, P., 2000. *The Star System: Hollywood's Production of Popular Identities*. London: Wallflower.

Mdelar, 2009. Director Anne Fletcher Interview "The Proposal." [video online] Available at: <http://www.youtube.com/watch?v=hQw3GbqqMxk> [Accessed 14 September 2011].

Meagher, K., 2003. The Emotional and Physiological Effects of Action and Romance: Scenes on Men and Women. Hanover College, PSY 220: Research Design and Statistics.

Media Report to Women, 2005. *Statistics on Women and Media*. Available at: <http://www.ywtf.org/YWTF/getdoc/75087a18-dc8b-4654-a89d-83fa57b95d98/General_Stat itsics.aspx> [Accessed 29 October 2011].

Mernit, B., 2000. *Writing the Romantic Comedy*. New York: HarperCollins.

Morag, R., 2009. *Defeated Masculinity, Post-Traumatic Cinema in the Aftermath of War*. Brussels: P.I.E. Peter Lang.

Mortimer, C., 2010. *Romantic Comedy*, London: Routledge.

MPAA, 2011. *Theatrical Market Statistics for 2010*. [pdf]. Available at: <http://www.mpaa.org/Resources/93bbeb16-0e4d-4b7e-b085-3f41c459f9ac.pdf> [Accessed 24 September 2011].

Mulvey, L. 1975. Visual Pleasure and Narrative Cinema. *Screen*, 16(3): 6–18.

Neale, S., 1990. Questions of Genre. In B. K. Grant, ed. 2003. *Film Genre Reader III*. Austin: University of Texas Press, pp. 160–84.

——, 2000. *Genre and Hollywood*. London: Routledge.

——, 2002. Action-Adventure as Hollywood Genre. In Y. Tasker, ed. *Action and Adventure Cinema*. Oxon: Routledge, pp. 71–83.

Negra, D., 2008. Structural Integrity, Historical Reversion, and the Post-9/11 Chick Flick, *Feminist Media Studies*, 8 (1): 51–68.

——, 2009. *What a Girl Wants? Fantasizing the Reclamation of Self in Postfeminism*. Oxon: Routledge.

Neustadter, S., and Weber, M. 2009. '500 Days of Summer' Writers Discuss Their Offbeat and Charming Film. Interviewed by Mike Ryan, [online] 15 July. Available at: <http://www.starpulse.com/news/index.php/2009/07/15/500_days_of_summer_wri ters_discuss_their> [Accessed December 6 2011].

Nicolson, P. 2002. *Having It All? Choices for Today's Superwoman*. Chichester: John Wiley & Sons, Ltd.

Obst, L., 2011. Early Signs of a "Bridesmaids" Bump. Interview by Rebecca Traister, *Salon*, [online] 27 September. Available at: <http://www.salon.com/2011/09/27/lyn da_obst_interview/> [Accessed 20 February 2012].

O' Day, M., 2004. Beauty in Motion: Gender, Spectacle and Action Babe Cinema. In Y. Tasker, ed. *Action and Adventure Cinema*. London: Routledge, pp. 201–18.

O'Sullivan, M., 2009. 'It's Complicated,' with Meryl Streep, Is Funny Food for Thought. *The Washington Post*, [online] 25 December. Available at: <http://www.washingtonpost.com/gog/movies/its-complicated,1158864/critic-review.html#review Num1> [Accessed 15 January 2012].

Ong, A., 2006. *Neoliberalism as Exception: Mutations in Citizenship and Sovereignty*. Durham, NC: Duke University Press.

Ordoña, M., 2009. Rev. of *(500) Days of Summer*. *The Los Angeles Times*, [online] 17 July. Available at: <http://articles.latimes.com/2009/jul/17/entertainment/et-500days17> [Accessed 6 December 2011].

Orelus, P. W. 2010. *The Agony of Masculinity: Race, Gender and Education in the Age of "New" Racism and Patriarchy*. New York: Peter Lang Publishing.

Palmer, W. J., 1993. *The Films of the Eighties*. Carbondale: Southern Illinois University.

Parker-Pope, T., 2008. Reinventing Date Night for Long-Married Couples. *The New York Times*, [online] 12 February. Available at: <http://www.nytimes.com/2008/02/12/health/12well.html> [Accessed 20 February 2012].

Peberdy, D., 2011. *Masculinity and Film Performance: Male Angst in Contemporary American Cinema*. Houndmills: Palgrave-McMillan.

Peña Ovalle, P., 2010. *Dance and the Hollywood Latina: Race, Sex and Stardom.* Piscataway, NJ: Rutgers University Press.

Pipher, M., 1995. *Reviving Ophelia: Saving the Selves of Adolescent Girls.* New York: Ballantine Books.

Polan, D., 1991. The Light Side of Genius: Hitchcock's *Mr. and Mrs. Smith* in the Screwball Tradition. In A. Horton, ed. *Comedy/Cinema/Theory.* Berkeley: University of California Press, pp. 131–52.

Pomerantz, D. 2011. The World's Most Powerful Celebrities. Forbes, [online] 16 May. Available at: http://www.forbes.com/wealth/celebrities/list [Accessed 28 January 2012].

Pond, S., 2010. Woody Allen Doesn't Heart New York Anymore. *The Wrap,* [online] 24 August. Available at: <http://www.thewrap.com/movies/column-post/woody-allen-says-new-yorks-too-expensive-20351> [Accessed 13 February 2012].

Potter, C., 2002. *I Love you but …* London: Methuen.

Poulakos, N., n.d. Rev. of *Happythankyoumoreplease. Sevenart.gr* [online]. Available at: <http://www.sevenart.gr/movie-kritiki.php?id=1906> [Accessed 12 December 2011].

Radner, H., 2011. *Neo-Feminist Cinema, Girly Films, Chick Flicks and Consumer Culture.* New York: Routledge.

——, 2011. Film as Popular Culture. In W. Guynn, ed. *The Routledge Companion to Film History.* Oxon: Routledge, pp. 16–26.

Ramirez, R. and de la Cruz, G. P., 2003. *The Hispanic Population in the United States: March 2002.* [pdf]. Available at: <http://www.census.gov/prod/2003pubs/p20-545.pdf> [Accessed 13 January 2012].

Reid, J., 2011. Are We Living in the Golden Age of Male Objectification? *New York Magazine–Vulture,* [online] 12 September. Available at: <http://nymag.com/daily/entertainment/2011/09/are_we_living_in_the_golden_ag.html> [Accessed 13 November 2011].

Remeseira, C. I., ed. 2010. *Hispanic New York: A Sourcebook.* New York: Columbia University Press.

Rios, D. I. and Reyes, X. A., 2007. Jennifer Lopez and a Hollywood Latina Romance Film: Mythic Motifs in *Maid in Manhattan.* In M. L. Galician and D. L. Merskin, eds. *Critical Thinking About Sex, Love, and Romance in the Mass Media.* Mahwah, NJ: Erlbaum Associates, pp. 94–105.

Roberts, S. M., 2004. Gendered Globalization. In L. A. Staeheli, E. Kofman and L. Peake, eds. *Mapping Women, Making Politics: Feminist Perspectives on Political Geography.* New York: Routledge, pp. 127–40.

Roberts, S., 2010. More Men Marrying Wealthier Women. *The New York Times,* [online] 19 January. Available at: <http://www.nytimes.com/2010/01/19/us/19marriage.html> [Accessed 23 December 2011].

Robertson Wojcik, P., 2010. *The Apartment Plot: Urban Living in American Film and Popular Culture, 1945 to 1975.* Durham, NC: Duke University Press.

Rosin, H., 2010. The End of Men. *The Atlantic,* [online] July/August. Available at: <http://www.theatlantic.com/magazine/archive/2010/07/the-end-of-men/8135/#.Tn0GJ6cAcrk.email> [Accessed 14 September 2011].

Rowe, K., 1995. *The Unruly Woman.* Austin: University of Texas Press.

Ruffles, T., 2004. *Ghost Images: Cinema of the Afterlife.* Jefferson, NC: McFarland.

Russell, L., 2010. Mr. Moms Become More Common. *CNN,* [online] 20 June. Available from: <http://articles.cnn.com/2010-06-18/living/mr.moms_1_census-bureau-mr-mom-fathers?_s=PM:LIVING> [12 February 2012].

Schatz, T., 2009. New Hollywood, New Millennium. In W. Buckland, ed. *Film Theory and Contemporary Hollywood Movies.* New York: Routledge, pp. 19–46.

Schlegel, J. and Habermann, F., 2010. 'You Took My Advice About Theatricality a Bit ... Literally:' Theatricality and Cybernetics of Good and Evil in *Batman Begins, The Dark Knight,* and *X-Men.* In R. J. Gray II and B. Kaklamanidou, eds. *The 21st Century Superhero: Essays on Gender, Genre and Globalization.* Jefferson, NC: McFarland, pp. 29–46.

Schneider, S. J., 2006. Movies and the March to War. In W.W. Dixon, ed. *American Cinema of the 1940s: Themes and Variations.* Oxford: Berg Publishers, pp. 74–93.

Schui, H., 2005. Neo-Liberalism and the Attack on the Humanities: The New Social Science of Cultural Imperialism. In B. Hamm and R. Smandych, eds. *Cultural Imperialism: Essays on The Political Economy of Cultural Domination.* Peterborough, ON: Broadview Press Ltd., pp. 149–66.

Schutte, O., 2000. Negotiating Latina Identities. In J. E. Graciaand and P. De Grieff, eds. *Hispanics/Latinos in the United States: Ethnicity, Race and Rights.* New York: Routledge, pp. 61–76.

Scott, A.O., 2005. Love Doctor Discovers He's Not Immune Either. *The New York Times,* [online] 11 February. Available at: < http://movies.nytimes.com/2005/02/11/movies/11hitc.html?_r=1> [4 September 2011].

——, 2010. Bickering in Paradise: Honeymoon Is Definitely Over. *The New York Times,* [online] 8 October. Available at: <http://movies.nytimes.com/2009/10/09/movies/09couples.html> [Accessed 6 November 2011].

Setoodeh, R., 2009. Year of the Cougar: Why Older Women Pursuing Younger Men Are All Over TV and Movie Screens this Year. *Newsweek,* [online] 17 June. Available at: <http://www.newsweek.com/id/202538> [Accessed 15 August 2009].

Shary, T., 2002. Teen Films: The Cinematic Image of Youth. In B. K. Grant, ed. 2003. *Genre Film Reader III.* Austin: University of Texas Press, pp. 490–515.

——, 2006. Teen Films. In B. K. Grant, ed. *Schirmer Encyclopedia of Film,* Vol. 4. New York: Schirmer Books, pp. 207–15.

——, 2011. *Teen Movies: American Youth On Screen.* London: Wallflower.

Shellenbarger, S., 2010. Daunting Task for Mr. Mom: Get a Job. *The Wall Street Journal,* [online] 19 May. Available at: <http://online.wsj.com/article/SB10001424052748703957904575252270698575294.html> [Accessed 15 February 2012].

Shira, D., 2011. Julianne Moore Feels Sexiest When She's Away From Her Kids. *People,* [online] 8 February. Available at: <http://www.people.com/people/article/0,20464467,00.html> [Accessed 22 October 2012].

Shumway, D. R. 2003. *Modern Love, Romance, Intimacy, and the Marriage Crisis,* New York: New York University Press,

Sikov, E., 1989. *Screwball: Hollywood's Madcap Romantic Comedies.* New York: Crown Publishers.

Silverstein, M., 2011. 2011 Hollywood Writers Report – Women Make Up 24% of All Writers. *Indiewire,* [online] 19 May. Available at: <http://blogs.indiewire.com/womenandhollywood/2011_Hollywood_writers_report_women_make_up_24_of_all_writers#> [Accessed 27 January 27 2012].

——, 2011. Who Goes to the Movies? Moviegoers Stats from 2010. *Indiewire,* [online] 25 February. Available at: <http://blogs.indiewire.com/womenandhollywood/archives/who_goes_to_the_movies_moviegoers_stats_from_2010/#> [Accessed 20 October 2011].

Smith, P. 2004. Action Movie Hysteria, or Eastwood Bound. In L. Fischer and M. Landy, eds. *Stars: The Film Reader.* Routledge, pp. 43–56.

Stam, R., 1989. *Subversive Pleasures: Bakhtin, Cultural Criticism, and Film.* Baltimore: John Hopkins University Press.

Stanley, A., 2011. Downsized and Downtrodden, Men Are the New Women on TV. *The New York Times,* 11 October, pp. C1–C3.

Steinmo, S. and Kopstein, J., 2008. Introduction. In S. Steinmo and J. Kopstein, eds. *Growing Apart? America and Europe in the Twenty-First Century.* Cambridge: Cambridge University Press, pp. 1–23.

Stevens, K., 2009. What a Difference a Gay Makes: Marriage in the 1990s Romantic Comedy. In S. Abbott and D. Jermyn, eds. *Falling in Love Again, Romantic Comedy in Contemporary Cinema.* London: I. B. Tauris, pp. 132–45.

Stevenson, B. and Wolfers, J. 2007. Marriage and Divorce: Changes and Their Driving Forces. *Journal of Economic Perspectives,* 21(2): 27–52.

Storey, J., 2008. *Cultural Theory and Popular Culture: An Introduction.* 5th ed. Harlow: Pearson-Longman.

Survey of Buying Power, 2009, www.surveyofbuyingpower.com/sbponline/regional/totals-of-population-by-age.jsp [accessed February 13 2012].

Sutton, P. D. and Hamilton, B. E., 2010. *Recent Trends in Births and Fertility Rates Through 2010.* [pdf]. Available at: <http://www.cdc.gov/nchs/data/hestat/births2010/births2010.pdf> [Accessed 13 February 2012].

Tally, M., 2008. Hollywood and the "Older Bird" Chick Flick. In S. Ferriss and M. Young, eds. *Chick Flicks: Contemporary Women at the Movies.* New York: Routledge, pp. 120–31.

Tasker, Y., 1998. *Working Girls: Gender and Sexuality in Popular Cinema.* London: Routledge.

——, 2002. *Spectacular Bodies.* London: Routledge.

——, 2004, ed. *Action and Adventure Cinema.* London: Routledge.

Taylor, E., 2008. Sex and the City: Plotless and Pointless. *The Village Voice,* [online] 27 May. Available at: <http://www.villagevoice.com/2008-05-27/film/sex-and-the-city-plotless-and-pointless/> [Accessed 4 September 2011].

Taylor, K., 2003. *The Battle of the Sexes.* Watford: Exley Publications Ltd.

Thompson, G., 2007. *American Culture in the 1980s.* Edinburgh: Edinburgh University Press.

Tichnell, E., 2011. Scourging the Abject Body: Ten Years Younger and Fragmented Femininity under Neoliberalism. In R. Gill and C. Scharff, eds. *New Femininities: Postfeminism, Neoliberalism and Subjectivity.* Houndmills: Palgrave-MacMillan, pp. 83–95.

Topel, F., 2010. Jennifer Lopez on *The Back-Up Plan. CanMag,* [online] April. Available at: <http://www.canmag.com/nw/15676-jennifer-lopez-the-backup-plan> [Accessed 20 February 2012].

Travers, P., 2009. Rev. of *(500) Days of Summer. Rolling Stone,* [online] 16 July. Available at: <http://www.rollingstone.com/movies/reviews/500-days-of-summer-20090716> [Accessed 6 December 2011].

Tyler, I., 2011. Pregnant Beauty: Maternal Femininities Under Neoliberalism. In R. Gill and C. Scharff, eds. *New Femininities: Postfeminism, Neoliberalism and Subjectivity.* Houndmills: Palgrave-MacMillan, pp. 21–36.

Tzioumakis, Y., 2006. *American Independent Cinema: An Introduction.* Edinburgh: Edinburgh University Press.

US Census Bureau, 2010. *2010 Census Shows America's Diversity. 2010.census.gov*, [online] 24 March. Available at: <http://2010.census.gov/news/releases/operations/cb11-cn125.html> [Accessed 28 September 2011].

Wakeman, J., 2010. Helen Mirren Does Not Worship at the altar of the 18-Year-Old Male Penis. *The Frisky*, [online] 9 December. Available at: <http://www.thefrisky.com/2010-12-09/helen-mirren-does-not-worship-at-the-altar-of-the-18-year-old-male-peni/> [Accessed 20 November 2011].

Walker, M., 2005. *Hitchcock's Motifs*. Amsterdam: Amsterdam University Press.

Wall, G. and Arnold, S. 2007. How Involved Is Involved Fathering? An Exploration of the Contemporary Culture of Fatherhood. *Gender and Society*, 21(4): 508–27.

Walters, J., 2011. *Fantasy Film: A Critical Introduction*. New York: Berg Publishers.

Watson, E. and Shaw, M. E., 2011. Obama's Masculinities: A Landscape of Essential Contradictions. In W. Elwood and M. E. Shaw, eds. *Performing American Masculinities: The 21st-century Man in Popular Culture*. Bloomington: Indiana University Press, pp. 134–52.

Watt, N., 2008. Envisioning a World Without Men. *ABC News*, [online] 28 April. Available at: <http://abcnews.go.com/Health/story?id=4725121&page=1> [Accessed 13 January 2012].

Weber, C. 2006. *Imagining America at War: Morality, Politics, and Film*. Oxon: Routledge.

Wenegrat, B., 1996. *Illness and Power: Women's Mental Disorders and the Battle Between the Sexes*. New York: New York University Press.

Wheldon, W., 2006. *The Battle of the Sexes: Men V. Women – The Truth Once and for All*. Hauppauge, NY: Barrons Educational Books.

Willis, J., 2010. *100 Media Moments That Changed America*. Santa Barbara: Greenwood Press.

Wilson, M. C., 2007. *Closing the Leadership Gap: Why Women Can and Must Help Run the World*. New York: Penguin.

Wood, R., 2003. *Hollywood from Vietnam to Reagan ... and Beyond*. 2nd ed. New York: Columbia University Press.

Wright, D., 2008. Record Births Create Population Milestone. *ABC News*, [online] 17 July. Available at: <http://abcnews.go.com/WN/story?id=5399077&page=1> [Accessed 11 October 11 2011].

York, A. E., 2010. From Chick Flicks to Millennial Blockbusters: Spinning Female-Driven Narratives into Franchises. *The Journal of Popular Culture*, 43(1): 3–25.

Zago Rosenthal, L., 2011. 'No Strings Attached': From Raunchy to Romantic. *www.popmatters.com* [online] 9 May. Available at: <http://www.popmatters.com/pm/review/140197-no-strings-attached> [Accessed 21 April 2012].

Zaslow, E., 2009. *Feminism, Inc: Coming of Age in Girl Power Media Culture*. New York: Palgrave MacMillan.

Index